U.S. ARMY SERIAL NUMBER 37531447

By

Kenneth L. Lenke

ISBN: 1-4033-2529-4 (e-book)
ISBN: 1-4033-2530-8 (Paperback)
ISBN: 1-4033-5243-7 (Dustjacket)

Library of Congress Control Number: 2002092850

This book is printed on acid free paper.

Printed in the United States of America
Bloomington, IN

1stBooks – rev. 12/03/02

Book Review:

…The importance of the forward observer as a vital member of an artillery gunnery team can not be over emphasized. The observer is the only member of the gunnery team who can actually see the enemy forces, the friendly forces and the fire delivered on enemy forces by other friendly forces.

…Sergeant Kenneth Lenke lived this life and performed the duties of the forward observer with diligence and professionalism. Without a doubt, **37531447** saved the lives of many U.S. combat soldiers with his artillery expertise as well as aiding our infantry units succeed in accomplishing their assigned battlefield missions.

…Russell A. "Bud" Pitts
Combat Infantryman, 103rd Division (ETO)
Command Sergeant Major of the Wyoming
National Guard (artillery), retired
Casper, Wyoming

…it is an unpretentious allegory of men at arms…I believe it will become one of the classic stories of WW II and it is fifty years after the fact. I totally understand the story line, and the psychology. The human aspect of the story will be understood by all.

William D. "Bill" Howard
103rd Division Infantryman
North Fort Meyers, Florida

…I have never been drawn to nor enjoyed any book written about World War II as most of them do not appeal to a woman's sensitivity. However, Mr. Lenke's book was different. I found it thoroughly enjoyable, easy to read, and written with a wonderful human and humorous perspective. I envisioned a screenplay all the while reading the same. It certainly comes from a different perspective. I highly recommend it.

…Meria Heller
Founder of "The Universal Wheel" ™
Scottsdale, Arizona

Kenneth L. Lenke, Army Serial Number 37531447 (1944)

This book is dedicated to the memory of those whose names appear on the latest bronze plate attached to the old salt-and-pepper granite monument located nearby the Japanese cannon in front of the Chase County, Kansas Courthouse.

F. Richard Bell	David A. Goodell
Howard E. Blender	Earl W. Howard
Victor Brecht	Robert C. Howard
Rolla R. Bucher	John Garrett Jackson
Victor L. Cole	Ernest I. James Jr.
Hubert R. Denny	Melvin E. Lind
Merlin A. Eason	Neale M. Narramore
Merle G. Fear	Diego Ramos
Robert J. Fillmore	Ivan V. Strange
William E. Foxworthy	Albert L. Swift
T.C. Galbraith	Allen B. Underwood
Edward A. Gardner	Woodrow Waddell
Kenneth George	Charles White

Contents

Acknowledgments xi
Foreword...xiii
Epigraph...xv

Chapters

1. The Path to Fort Leavenworth 1
2. Departing for Basic Training 11
3. Primary Basic Training... 19
4. Intermediate Basic Training 31
5. Advanced Basic Training 47
6. A Change in Military Assignment.................................... 69
7. Camp Howze, Texas... 77
8. Texas to Camp Shanks, New York.................................... 90
9. Ocean Convoy to Europe.. 103
10. Bivouacking on the Mediterranean Sea........................... 122
11. Welcome to Combat 130
12. The Vosges Mountain Campaign 138
13. Over the Vosges Mountains... 154
14. Alsace-Lorraine 165
15. The Ardennes Offensive 179
16. Attacking the Siegfried Line.. 199
17. The Siegfried Line Crumbles... 220
18. The Rhine River Occupation 231
19. The Fighting in Europe Ends... 242
20. Alpine Occupational Duties... 259
21. Final Army Days for 37531447 285
    Epilogue.. 301
    Bibliography 311

Acknowledgments

Marlo Badgett, information of Heart Mountain Japanese-American Relocation Center, Cheyenne, Wyoming; Mary Ruth Blackburn, quotes and assistance with the Heart Mountain Japanese-American Relocation Centers, Ralston, Wyoming; Peggy Boone, Manager, El Paso Tourist and Sales Bureau, motivational cheerleader and for information on El Paso and Fort Bliss, Texas; Bernard F. Cavalcante, head, Operational Archives Branch, Department of the Navy, Navy Historical Center, Washington, D.C., Naval documents; Johnny "Joe" Chavez, CEO, Vietnam War forward observer and adviser, Phoenix, Arizona; Bob Dole, U.S. Senator from Kansas, for graciously penning the *Foreword* pages; Dr. Tom Flack, manuscript reader and for encouragement, Scottsdale, Arizona; Meria Heller, author and founder of the "Universal Wheel" (Tm) for her profound guidance, Scottsdale, Arizona; William "Bill" Howard, 103rd Division Infantryman, suggesting this story be written, Fort Myers, Florida; Betty Campbell Johnson, manuscript reader and for information on Chase County, Cottonwood Falls, Kansas; Joseph A. Kush, manuscript reader, Scottsdale, Arizona; James C. Lenhardt, for helping the author through countless computer glitches, Scottsdale, Arizona; Art Lowenstein, linguist for German translation for letters from Alsace, France, Scottsdale, Arizona; John McCain, United States Senator from Arizona, for obtaining archives material; Leon C. Metz, historical author and Texas historian, for history of El Paso, Texas; Roy Pickering, San Diego Railroad Museum, wartime railroad movements, San Diego, California; Joan Grove Pitts, Japanese-American Relocations, Casper, Wyoming; Russell A. Pitts, 103rd Infantry Division rifleman in Company G, 409th Infantry Regiment, Casper, Wyoming; Mme Jeanne Pomaroli, French World War II Remembrances in Alsace-Lorraine, Ingwiller, France; Fred Rozum, Rails West, Ltd., McCormick Railroad Park, for Missouri Pacific Railroad information, Scottsdale, Arizona; Sammie Smith, writer and master teacher, for typing the handwritten manuscript, Ahwatukee, Arizona.

also

Cindy and Kenja Lenke, wife and daughter, who gave me precious time to work on the manuscript.

Kenneth L. Lenke

Scottsdale, Arizona
March 18, 1998

Foreword...

Ken Lenke and I have a lot in common. We both grew up in small Kansas towns. We both delivered newspapers – he the *Emporia Gazette*, and I the *Salina Journal*. We both enlisted in the Army, we both were shipped off to Europe, and we both were fortunate enough to return home.

Like many world War II veterans, we did not know one another then, and more than 50 years later, we still do not. But we know the kinds of experiences the other endured in the military – leaving home, basic training, bonding with fellow soldiers, going off to war, and the intense emotional peaks and valleys forever etched in our memories. Similar experiences, but no doubt, experienced differently.

The political spotlight has previously illuminated the background of a certain Second Lieutenant from Russell, Kansas. All too often overlooked are the personal stories like that of Ken Lenke and countless others who sacrificed in so many and noble ways during World War II – from mundane to heroic, from the home front to the enemy lines. Hearing these voices now, and in the future, can help us clearly see and better understand the most profound event of the 20th Century.

World War II has been called "The Good War." But there is nothing good about a war for those who have known the horror of battle. Only causes can be good. And in World War II, millions of servicemen – including Ken Lenke – found a cause to justify the greatest losses.

At 20 years old, I had never traveled much beyond my parent's home in Russell, Kansas. I marched off to a war knowing we were fighting against aggression in Europe and Asia. In time, I came to learn we were fighting against evil. Brave young Americans fought until the last town was liberated. Our nation's soldiers fought until the last prison camp was emptied of its gaunt survivors and the last death camp was opened to reveal unimaginable crimes.

Although I did not fully understand it, we were fighting for another cause, as well – to establish a new place for America in the world. On remote, foreign battlefields, our nation renewed its confidence and found its mission. It was a mission unique in human history, and uniquely American in idealism – to influence without conquest and to hold democratic ideals in sacred trust while many people waited in captivity. Today, the freedom America championed is the standard of civilization. At the close of history's most brutal century, America's values have triumphed – not through force, but through example.

That American idealism and abundance inspired a generation of survivors and their children. It transcended old hatreds and divisions and helped explain the universal aspirations of people regardless of nationality. At home in Russell, we marveled at what Americans from so many different backgrounds can accomplish when we stand together in a just and common cause.

Of all the opportunities offered to me after the 1996 presidential campaign, the one I was proudest to accept was as the volunteer chairman of the World War II Memorial campaign. Until then I did not realize that the United States did not yet have a national memorial to honor the sacrifice of the millions of Americans who served in World War II. As time passes, for our nation and for the generation of men and women that served it more than a half century ago, it is more important than ever before that we remember, and learn from, their stories of patriotism, sacrifice, valor, and all-American commitment to the principle of freedom.

We owe these Americans a debt. We repay it with a pledge to preserve their memory against the tide of time. We can remember through Memorials, like the one to be built on the Mall in Washington DC. We can also remember through the individual accounts of those who served. This book is one of those accounts – in many ways unique, in some ways akin to the experiences of others…but always deeply personal…and forever worthy of our remembrance.

…U.S. Senator from Kansas, Bob Dole

Epigraph...

I was born at home on January 7, 1924, at Strong City, (Chase County) Kansas. I was the youngest in a family of six boys. I did not have any sisters. My mother was of Scotch-Irish ancestry, and my father was of German lineage.

My first year of public school was at the age of five. It was the year 1929, mostly remembered for the stock market crash and the beginning of the Great Depression. Chase County is perhaps best remembered by another crash occurring on March 31, 1931 of a tri-motor Ford *Tin Goose* aircraft – ending the life of Knute Kenneth Rockne, the Norwegian-born legendary football coach of Notre Dame University. The crash taking the lives of all aboard the aircraft occurred in the Seward H. Baker pasture ten miles from our family residence.

Other excitement of the time included observing frequent road chases by law enforcement agencies in an effort to catch prohibition-day bootleggers unlawfully running booze to or through the "dry" county and state. Occasionally we would see speeding "silk trains", usually consisting of one baggage railroad car, being pulled behind a hard-working steam engine. The bolts of precious silk coming from Japan were being shipped to garment factories on the east coast to be made into expensive clothing for the stylish of the world. An occasional springtime prairie fire in the Flint Hills would spice the seasonal interest.

Strong City (historically first called Podunk) was mostly a railroad community taking its formal name from the then President of the Santa Fe Railroad, Mr. William Barstow Strong. "Death Valley" Scottie's private train sped through the small town on its journey to Chicago, establishing a railroad speed record from Los Angeles to Chicago until broken by the coming of the diesel engine. Another train passed through the municipality carrying President Franklin D. Roosevelt. It would be the first time and only time I ever saw a president of the United States in person.

Graduation from high school took place in May of 1941. Two months later, the entire country was buzzing over an incident between a man wearing shorts playing golf at the Memphis Country Club, and a group of exuberant soldiers returning from a month of maneuvers in Tennessee. The man on the golf course was United States Army's Lieutenant General Ben Lear. He also happened to be the top commanding officer for the returning convoy. The general issued group punishment for the entire group of soldiers bound for Camp Joseph T. Robinson (Arkansas).

It was the beginning of the our country's involvement in World War II. It was a time of much confusion, doubt, fear, and hate among people. The next years would forever change the lives of multitudes of human beings.

The period was a continuing era of segregation between black and white people living in the United States. This setting apart of the two races carried over into the United States armed forces, creating separate military units for blacks and whites. The segregation policy would end in 1948 when United States President, Harry S. Truman, issued an executive order calling for equal opportunity and equal treatment for all members of the armed forces.

There was often unwarranted suspicion among groups of differing nationality origins. United States citizens of German, Italian and Japanese ancestry were often viewed as possessing un-American allegiances. A larger conflict of opinion erupted among the people of our country when many citizens held the belief *isolation* was the direction our country should pursue. Others held the notion we should go to war against Nazi Germany. This conflicting thorny issue was resolved when Japan's military might struck a devastating blow at the military bases of Pearl Harbor, Hawaii. A short time later, both Germany and Italy declared war on the United States. Our country swiftly became mobilized for World War II.

It was the time in history that would dramatically alter the rest of my life in countless ways.

Prior to my induction into the military, I was employed at the Kansas Ordinance Plant located near Parsons, Kansas. I was an electric forklift operator. My job was moving both seventy-five and 105 millimeter artillery projectiles and explosives to and from the assembly lines.

I was willingly inducted into the United States Army on June 26, 1943 at Fort Leavenworth, Kansas and, assigned the United States Army serial number – 37531447.

Chapter One

The Path to Fort Leavenworth

During my youthful period of growing up in rural Chase County, Kansas, I would often walk or ride my well-used second-hand bicycle from the family home in Strong City to the county seat town of Cottonwood Falls.

The two towns were positioned approximately a mile from each other. The only geographical feature separating the two entities was the usually slow moving muddy algae-laden Cottonwood River.

While crossing over the narrow river bridge connecting the "twin cities", I would observe the aging foundation stone works at the site of the once all-important grist mill. It had been constructed about the time of the Civil War by a Mr. J.B. Smith and L.W. Hinchley.

Pausing briefly to gaze at the serene water flowing over the spillway portion of the concrete and limestone mill dam, I would ponder why the river's murky water always appeared so deceptively clear as it curtained over the structure when rays of sunshine brilliantly danced across the cascading opaque liquid.

Once across the old bridge near Mill Street, the well-worn red paving brick road made a gentle uphill left bend onto Broadway Street. This area was the location for much of the small town's business community.

Glimpsing due south along Broadway Street, I would catch sight of the historical and stately-appearing Renaissance Louis XIII architectural style courthouse building. It was located at the very end of the red brick roadway. This remarkable sturdy edifice had been fabricated by pioneer stone masons using assorted sizes and shapes of fossiliferous Permian Period magnesium limestone obtained from a nearby stone quarry. The front entrance to the courthouse building and the two adjacent sides were protected by limestone retaining walls. During rainy seasons the walls were often coated with a veneer of verdant-colored lichens.

For some unknown reason, my eyes always shifted from the picturesque Mansard-roofed courthouse with its tall cupola. They would now focus on a World War One vintage cannon. The old French seventy-five millimeter weapon had its barrel slightly elevated. It appeared to be faithfully standing guard searching

1

Ken Lenke Photo (1996)
Looking up Broadway Street toward the Chase County (Kansas) Courthouse

Ken Lenke Photo (1996)
Cottonwood River mill dam at Cottonwood Falls, Kansas

for any unwelcome intruders who might be stealthily infiltrating up Broadway Street. The historical French-made artillery piece always seemed to hold some alien type of mystical fascination for me.

While viewing a nighttime fire consume a wood frame house, not too distant from the old cannon, I was subtly introduced to the whooshing whirring sound of shrapnel passing uncomfortably close over my head. The owner of the doomed structure had been imprudent by utilizing a still explosively charged World War One, French seventy-five millimeter souvenir projectile for a doorstop. The heat from the blazing inferno had detonated the projectile, sending multitudinous lethal splinters of jagged steel in all directions. The Superintendent of the Strong City Water Department, who was standing close by, was struck in the throat by the shrapnel, causing his almost instant death. He could well have been the last fatality of World War One. Another lad, slightly taller than I, was also hit by the flying steel and received a non-life-threatening injury. The sound made by the fast moving invisible shrapnel became permanently galvanized on my mind.

More than one Independence Day celebration would find me prankishly tossing lighted "two-incher" firecrackers into the cannon's stubby barrel. The resulting thunderous explosion would propel a beautifully formed smoke ring, shimmering ghostlike, all the way down Broadway Street. It would drift in the general direction of Mill Street and the ruins of the old grist mill before fading away.

French 75mm cannon located on the Chase County (Kansas) Courthouse lawn

3

Almost unnoticed was the salt-and-pepper colored granite marker located slightly west of the French seventy-five millimeter artillery piece. Firmly anchored on the front of the rock slab was a bronze plate listing the names of soldiers who had lost their lives during the "War to End All Wars" (World War One).

I did not devote any significant attention to the names appearing on the bronze tablet. Most had been deceased a "long time" – some seven years preceding the date of my birth. Five years later I would be a soldier with the United States Army's 103rd Infantry Division liberating Nazi concentration work/death camps (satellite camps of Dachau) at Landsberg, Germany.

Before long, I would discover the reason for my seemingly unquenchable attraction to the old war relic standing guard on the courthouse lawn. It was not a coincidence being assigned to a coast artillery unit while beginning my period of army basic training. Neither was it an additional congruity when later, I would be serving in the capacity of a forward observer for a United States Army field artillery battalion. I would be confronting the amoral Nazi forces of Adolph Hitler on the battlefields of France, Germany, and Austria.

Two young males from the Selective Service Board of Emporia, Kansas would soon become members of the military service, One would be myself and the other individual, a Mexican. Both inductees were taken to Fort Leavenworth, Kansas.

Fort Leavenworth is one of many early-day military posts constructed west of the Mississippi River. It was founded by Henry Leavenworth in the year 1827. Henry Leavenworth had served in the war of 1812 and assigned frontier duty in 1818.

Adjacent to the old military post, the town of Leavenworth, named in honor of the soldier who established the frontier post, was founded by settlers from Missouri who favored extension of slavery into Kansas Territory.

In 1858 the Democratic Party of Kansas was formed in the city. In the year 1859, Abraham Lincoln gave a major speech attacking doctrines of Stephen Arnold Douglas ("The Little Giant") over the State Sovereignty System. On December 24th of 1863, J. Wilkes Booth, the infamous actor, was performing at Leavenworth.

Two famous residents of Leavenworth had been: James B. Hickok (Wild Bill) and William F. Cody (Buffalo Bill).

The original purpose of Fort Leavenworth was to provide protection against marauding Indians prowling along the Santa Fe Trail. Leavenworth's Command and General Staff College later provided military training for commissioned army officers. The huge federal penitentiary was located nearby. The land area of Fort Leavenworth was slightly over thirteen square miles.

Upon arriving at Fort Leavenworth one of the first orders of business was the physical examination. This was to be my first complete medical "audit". I had taken some minor physicals when I played high school football, but they were mostly to determine if I had any heart problems or a hernia.

The army physical was an adventure as well as an unexpected education. I had played football in high school and somewhat conditioned to seeing other naked players as we dressed or took showers following practice or games.

It was my first time standing in the proverbial "army line". The entire group of men forming the domino-like formation was absent of all body clothing.

Blood was drawn, feet tickled, knees hit with a rubber hammer, peed in a bottle and given many other tests. I became somewhat apprehensive when the medical doctor ordered me to bend over and spread my "cheeks". This was a new experience for me and I began to have great misgivings about the intent of military doctors.

Slightly later, this feeling was reinforced when the doctor ordered, "Son, milk your penis for me." As a farm boy, this instruction puzzled me for a moment. I had a rather difficult time making the association between milking a penis and milking a cow. The military physician, noting my lengthy hesitation and questioning eyes, informed me, "This test is performed to determine if you have a social disease." It was the first time I ever heard about such a thing as social diseases. Sex or sex education was a taboo subject of conversation in most households of my generation. I was woefully lacking in factual knowledge about the subject.

The doctor further added to my impromptu session of "sex counseling" by relating, "This test is referred to in military terminology as the 'short arm' examination." I received small satisfaction from this additional crumb of "insider" information. Successfully completing the physical, I was ready to be issued basic army clothing. The quartermaster in charge of giving out uniforms briefly looked at our bare physiques and would swiftly determine the "correct sizes" most likely conforming to the body figuration. It was doubtful if this system of issuing clothing was too upsetting to any of the recruits. All of us had just come through the depression and were just happy to have some new clothing. I was surprised most of the clothing issued was near the correct size. The army haberdasher did ask each of us, "What size shoes do you wear?"

All dressed up in army clothing, we were taken to another room where two metal "dogtags" became a significant addition to the uniform. The number on my tag was 37531447. These personal identification tags were to be worn around the neck at all times. The real importance of the dogtags was not explained to us. No one gave mention the tags would aid in body identification as well as listing the blood type of the wearer along with one's next-of-kin and your religious preference.

The "Oath of Allegiance" to the United States of America was administered and we became official soldiers In the United States Army.

The following day we would be returning to our hometowns for the purpose of completing any "loose ends" during the transitional period from civilian life to a strict military regimen.

With nothing else scheduled, free time was available to visit the army post. The only individual I knew was the Mexican lad who came from Emporia with me. Private Torres suggested, "Let's go to the Post Exchange (store and beer garden) and drink a couple of beers." I accepted his invitation. This proved to be the first mistake of my very adolescent military career. Buoyed by the knowledge I was now a "soldier", presented me with a deceptive illusion of being a seasoned guzzler of malt liquor. Much later, my Mexican friend shepherded me back to the correct barracks where I vomited the night hours away.

The following morning all new inductees were issued train tickets for the return home and bus tickets for the return trip back to Fort Leavenworth. Included with my tickets was a set of "pin-on" (acting or provisional) Private First Class rank stripes. I was told by the noncommissioned officer in charge, "This is just a temporary promotion and you are to make certain the 'spic' (Private Torres) returns back to Fort Leavenworth with you."

Once home, I would spend a large share of the time with my girlfriend. I presented her with a diamond engagement ring. I had considerable concerns about the seriousness of the war and spurned my fiance's wishes for marriage before returning to Fort Leavenworth. In return, she wisely spurned my motive for doing anything more serious.

Following the short leave home, I went to the local bus station on the scheduled hour of departure and discovered Private Torres patiently waiting for me. We returned to the Fort Leavenworth Induction Center and Private Torres was "delivered" to the NCO (noncommissioned officer) in charge. I also gave back the temporary PFC chevrons. My Mexican friend was assigned to the Army Air Force. I bade him farewell and wished him well. After his departure, I never saw or heard of him again.

So far I had not been assigned to any specific unit. My desire was for active duty with the air force. The next several days found me practicing close-order marching drills. The extremely new and exciting word "hut", was added to my military vocabulary. In addition to learning how to march, 37531447 was taught how, who and when to salute. We were informed the salute was used to show mutual respect between commissioned officers and enlisted soldiers.

During my entire high school years I had never seen a motion picture film at school and I naturally was quite elated to learn we were going to view a movie. The topic of the movie was not exactly what I expected to see. The educational and graphic presentation was on the subject of "social diseases". After viewing the movie, we were emphatically informed these hostile diseases could not be obtained from a toilet seat or utilizing a public urinal. I was somewhat disappointed that the audio visual did not make mention of the obligatory monthly "short-arm" examination.

Following the film viewing we were given information on the available recreational facilities at Fort Leavenworth. I inquired about the location of the horseshoe pitching area. Perhaps tossing a few of the iron objects might temporarily remove some the uncertainties presently harassing my mind.

A noncommissioned officer informed me, "The horseshoe pitching area is located close to a place called 'Gonorrhea Gulch' near the vicinity where 'darkies' are being processed for military service."

His use of the word "darkies" was slightly more polite than the term "niggers" – an expression commonly used by Anglos to characterize black people during this time in history. The tone of the corporal's voice suggested a possible relationship between the location of Gonorrhea Gulch, where medical facilities to treat social diseases were to be found, and – the location site for Negro inductees. I temporarily dismissed his suggestive remark.

Arriving at the horseshoe pitching area, I was rather disappointed to observe all of the pits were taken by young Negroes waiting to be processed at the induction center. My disappointment was soon changed to astonishment at the amazing scene appearing in front of my eyes. All of the black men were dressed in what appeared to be a contradiction of any clothing fashions that I could ever recall. They were wearing flashy "Zoot" suits.

This unusual style of dress gave me the impression I was observing a minor rebellion against the mainstream establishment of the time, or perhaps it was a last chance effort to wear colorful clothing before being issued olive-drab uniforms.

Zoot suits consisted of glistening patent leather pointed shoes and a pleated high-waisted pair of trousers. Each leg on the trousers could possibly provide me with enough fabric to make a pair of britches. The leg area tapered to what appeared to be a normal cuff size. The long two-button coat, often made of striped material, draped to just above the knees. It was heavily padded in the shoulder region and had extra large lapels. Each side of the coat had large loose deep pockets.

Partially complementing this colorful apparel was a broad brimmed felt hat, an extra length brightly patterned bow tie, and a long metal chain. The chain most likely fastened to a belt or belt loop on the trousers. The chain draped downward from under the left side of the coat, crossing over the front of the trousers just above the right leg cuff and disappearing upward on the right inside of the coat.

I wondered if the chain might have other purposes besides being cosmetic for the zoot suit.

It appeared to me to be impossible how anyone so handicapped by such an outrageous and ill-fitting apparel, featuring the long metal chain in the frontal region, could pitch horseshoes. I was wrong. I had never before witnessed better skill in the art of pitching horseshoes. It was an unexpected and memorable experience in my young life.

8

For a brief moment I reflected about being the only white soldier in the area among this group of Negro inductees. Was this experience meant to be some kind of meaningful message for me?

The following morning I would leave Fort Leavenworth for an unknown destination to begin my basic military training. It would not be with the United States Army Air Force.

Postscript

My thoughts concerning the relationship between "gonorrhea gulch" and the African-Americans being processed into the military at the Fort Leavenworth Induction Center may well have had some validity.

As early as 1932 the United States Public Health Service had already begun the so-called "Tuskegee Syphilis Experiment" enrolling infected black men from Macon County, Alabama. The long-running "experiment" was a modern classic of race (black/white) and medicine which came to the forefront in post World War II.

Black men participating in the Tuskegee Experiment already had the disease of "bad blood". They were mostly poor illiterates whom the Public Health Service had offered incentives to participate in the "program". The men received free physical examinations, free rides to and from the clinics, hot meals on examination days, free treatment for minor ailments, and a guarantee that burial stipends (fifty dollars in 1932) would be paid to their survivors. The men were denied promised benefits and dropped from the program if they received any treatments for syphilis even though successful treatment with penicillin was available in 1940.

The need of combat soldiers (all races) during World War II, led to the usage of penicillin as the medicine of treatment for the disease.

James H. Jones documented the Tuskegee Experiment's legacy in his book – *Bad Blood*.

****

The Mexican-American, Private Torres, should have been given the honor of making certain that I returned back to Fort Leavenworth with him. He was certainly as responsible as I, perhaps more so. He was extremely proud to be wearing the uniform of the United States Army.

The word "spic" is offensive slang used by some Anglos when referring to Spanish speaking Americans. The word may have been derived from the broken English utterance "spigotty" meaning "*No speaka de English*" a phrase often used by Spanish-Americans, or the term possibly was a shortened form of the word, "Hispanic".

****

I graduated from Strong City Rural High School located in Chase County; however, my parents moved shortly afterward to nearby Emporia (Lyon County), Kansas. I registered with the Selective Service Draft Board of Lyon County. This period of time would find me employed at the Kansas Ordnance Plant located near Parsons, Kansas.

Chapter Two

Departing for Basic Training

The following morning a rather sizeable contingent of fresh inductees were boarding a troop train soon to be pulled by a large railroad steam engine. 37531447 would be one of these neophyte soldiers. He was beginning to learn the "military powers to be" seldom, if ever, informs soldiers of their travel routes or the final destination.

A steam engine clearly marked with the logo of the Rock Island Railroad Line, was soon chugging away from Fort Leavenworth and would chart a definite westerly course. I was confident our journey's end would be California.

Reality of leaving home, not knowing were I was going, or if I would ever return, began to furnish me with considerable fear of the unknown. My thoughts were turning into a kaleidoscope of past events reflecting memories of my fiance, parents, friends, and old haunts of my youthful days in the beautiful Flint Hills of Kansas. This form of behavior provided very little comfort for the uneasy feeling that was ferociously churning inside my thought processing machinery.

To make matters worse for an already apprehensive mind, I was beginning to have some serious doubts if the correct decision had been made with my refusal to become married to my fiance before returning to Fort Leavenworth. I was encountering pangs of guilt and began to wonder if I really had been practical-minded with my sweetheart in refusing to become married.

Travelling with unfamiliar persons and being informed what to do and how promptly it should be done was bothersome. I was harboring a realistic perception that control over my life was rapidly becoming fragmented. I also was commencing to learn supplementary vocabulary phrases, including a large group of expressive military "gems" such as: "government issue", "goldbricking", "If it doesn't salute, pick it up.", "general fuck-up, "snafu" (situation normally all fucked up) and "Get your ass in gear."

The list of military idioms would become rather lengthy and more crude in the long months ahead. I had a gnawing feeling this kind of behavioral language was an intentionally designed stratagem used to reduce an individual from a "human being" to that of a machine having a serial number. It most likely meant this soldier would be repeating, in robot manner, the number "37531447" numerous times in the uncertain future.

Along with these legions of jargons came profanity. Most of the profanation I had heard before; however, I was now clumsily uttering these crass words all too freely. In due time, I would be issued cigarettes. Since they were government issue (GI), I rationalized it must be quite appropriate for me to smoke. I certainly wanted to be a good soldier, so unabashed, my lengthy nicotine "trip" was launched.

Many older soldiers aboard the train had uniforms covered with numerous stripes and other military decorations. It made me wonder if I would ever earn the rank of at least a PFC while in the army. This important promotion in rank would enable me to impress my fiance in a couple of months when granted my first furlough home.

Settling back in the railroad coach seat, blankly gazing through the open window, I began witnessing the landscape make its subtle geographic change in topography as the train continued its steady westward journey.

The troop train exited Kansas and was puffing along in Oklahoma. This sudden southerly swing in direction of travel appeared to be ominous. Perhaps Texas would be the destination site for my basic military training. My spirits rose considerably when the troop train entered New Mexico.

It was fairly simple during daylight hours to know which of the forty-eight states we were in. Glancing at front license plates of vehicles stopping at railroad crossings, awaiting the passing of our speeding troop train, provided this information. I was certain New Mexico was west of Texas, and I now felt a sense of relief knowing California could likely be the final destination.

My euphoric period was quickly truncated when I once again began to notice Texas license plates on automobiles stopped at railroad crossings. The smoking steam engine, pulling our troop coaches, had traversed the southeastern quadrant of New Mexico and was re-entering West Texas. I blamed myself for not paying closer attention to my school-days geography class lectures of "Prof" Johnson at Strong City's North Side School. Not too many hours would pass before reaching the previously unknown journey's end. It would be El Paso, Texas, located on the border of Old Mexico.

Close to the hour of 2300 hours (11:00 p.m.), we detrained. The disappointment of not going to California darkened my misery. This was my second major frustration in the past several days. The first nonsuccess was not being assigned military duty with the United States Air Force. Again, thoughts returned to the old home town where I had resided. The cruel pain of homesickness was beginning to manifest itself. It was disquieting.

We climbed into the back of waiting military trucks that would be transporting us the relatively short distance from El Paso to the part of old Fort Bliss commonly know as "Logan Heights". Despite the classy-sounding name, one more appropriate for an up-scale housing development, Logan Heights could best be described as the "slums of Fort Bliss" or "The Dust Bowl".

During the unloading of our bodies and gear from the trucks, a half-naked form resembling a silhouette of a human being, slithered out of one of the small numerous tar-papered buildings. In the late night-time darkness the individual commenced an oratory event expressing his immense displeasure with the current noise level to the sergeant in charge of our late arriving group. The sergeant didn't waste the duration of a single heartbeat in telling the shadowy form, "Go to Hell". The irritated sleeper, now fully awakened, came a step or two closer to the sergeant and introduced himself as lieutenant "somebody" and began the military process generally known as "pulling rank".

I became greatly surprised and delightfully amused when the now piqued sergeant tersely informed the annoyed self-announced officer, "Get your ass back inside your hut you god-damn ninety-day wonder before I knock the shit out of you!" At this point, army life became slightly more interesting for me. The officer grudgingly retreated inside the protective shelter of his billet. As far as I could ever determine, no disciplinary action was ever taken against the surly noncom. The sergeant in charge was "old army" and he realized the young lieutenant was "out of uniform" (improperly dressed). New soldiers quickly ascertained "old army" soldiers had numerous unwritten privileges as well as a thorough knowledge of army rules, regulations and protocol.

Several days later I discovered the peppery old "sarge" was one hell of a skillful boxer. I witnessed him knock out another soldier over a slight difference of opinion.

Moving into our drab tar-paper covered huts, without running water or toilet facilities, left me with an even further devastated frame of mind. At least the dismal shelters were equipped with a vented natural gas heater in the middle area and electric lights. The inside perimeter of the small shack could accommodate up to six single steel cots, each having a straw-filled blue and white striped tick and a matching pillow. The steel cots did have a few cosmetic springs built into them.

The first several days in camp were utilized getting almost endless paper work completed, receiving an additional medical checkup – including the "short-arm" examination. Orientation and cleaning the heavy messy coating of cosmoline (hard petroleum grease) from our newly issued M-1 .30-caliber Garand semi-automatic rifles kept us busy. The size of the military rifle appeared to be colossal when compared to the small .22-caliber gun that I had used to hunt rabbits and squirrels during civilian life. I quickly blotted from my mind the thought of what the intended quarry would be for the weighty army rifle.

Considerable attention was given to learning how to lace the canvas gaiters (leggings) covering the upper shoe and fastening under the shoe with a strap. If the lace hooks were erroneously placed to the inside of the leg, the hooks would come into contact with each other and trip the wearer. In the darkness, I could never lace the awkward items of apparel without usually missing one or more of the metal lace hooks.

Much time and energy was devoted in the toilet and shower facility located in a building some fifty yards away from the living quarters. This seemingly long distance did not bother me since we never had indoor plumbing in the house where I grew up. Our purposeful objective in the shower area was to wash and scrub the newly issued olive-colored fatigue (work clothes) uniforms with gargantuan-size bars of brown-colored GI soap. This puissant body soap had a tendency, when used on the cloth fatigues, to fade the newly issued olive-drab duty uniform. The procedure was designed to create the illusion to other newly arriving inductees, all dressed in their spanking new fatigue uniforms, we were "old hands" at Fort Bliss. My official military address would be:

Army Serial Number 37531447
839th Antiaircraft Automatic Weapons Battalion
United States Coast Artillery Battery D
United States Army

The battalion used .50-caliber machine guns and the Swedish built – forty millimeter Bofors rapid-fire eight-shell clip anti-aircraft towed weapons. The Bofors single barrel automatic antiaircraft weapon was operated by a six-man crew (including the truck driver). It could fire a two-pound shell at the rate of sixty rounds per minute at an effective distance of 12,000 feet.

The cadre (training nucleus) for our newly formed military unit consisted mainly of "old army" servicemen whose previous mission had been protecting the strategically important Panama Canal. The cadre was skilled and experienced with antiaircraft weapons; however, most of these men were also bordering on the crazy and seemingly undomesticated side of life. Perhaps their lengthy tour of duty in jungles of Panama contributed partially to their often erratic behavior.

Eventually the day arrived when the personnel field strength of the battalion was operational and the start of our basic training at Fort Bliss would take on more importance.

Our first unit formation for "Dog" battery was called. It was quite a memorable occasion for many of us, especially for those in the front ranks. We were officially greeted by the first sergeant (top noncommissioned officer, usually referred to as the "top kick"). We were ordered to stand at attention. The tall, lean and leathery-appearing top kick, wearing extremely honestly faded olive drab fatigues, appeared in front of the formation. He slowly turned to face us, paused for a moment, and then gave the order, "Stand at ease, men".

He introduced himself to the formation of mostly new soldiers in a very unorthodox manner. Slowly turning his head while eyeing us, quite similar to that of a rancher assessing livestock at a cattle auction, he commenced to unbutton the fly on his shopworn uniform. Removing from his trousers, for full display, was his male "organ". He then proceeded to rotate the "object" in an orbital motion with his hand.

Informing us, using his slow Louisiana Cajun drawl, he factually stated, "I am the first sergeant." At this point his previous order, "Stand at ease, men." Appeared to be missing much importance in my mind. He continued his short speech by stating, "The commissioned officer's command, but I am the one who runs this outfit." As he concluded, he nonchalantly placed his genitalia back inside his fatigue trousers and securely buttoned the fly. Using the sergeant's suggestive criteria for what it takes to run our new military unit, he would win my vote for the position of Superintendent of West Point. I now had an even lower plateau of thought concerning the process of dehumanization I was presently passing through.

In the months ahead, I would discover the sergeant to be the best top kick I would ever have while in the military. The soldier was knowledgeable about his duties, dedicated and was a man of his word. What he said was exactly what he meant.

Notwithstanding his unconventional introduction at the first formation, this Louisiana man would be genuinely respected by the entire contingent of Dog Battery for his ability to do an exemplary job of running this newly created United States Army military unit – Battery D of the 839th Antiaircraft Automatic Weapons Battalion.

Postscript

The Rock Island Railroad Line used to start our travel from Fort Leavenworth, most likely switched our troop train over to the Southern Pacific Line at Tucumcari, New Mexico, for the completion of the southerly transit into El Paso, Texas. The Rock Island Line did not access El Paso, Texas.

****

I certainly did not have anything against Texas. For me, a young soldier from the Kansas prairies, California appeared in my mind to be a far more exciting place to be stationed for my basic training. I most likely knew California appeared to be some type of sanctuary for the migratory legions of jobless persons during the recent "Great Depression".

****

Although shocking to me to observe the first sergeant display his genitalia in front of the battery formation, I have since been informed this event was somewhat the norm for some males wishing to show evidence of their so-called "manhood" during the Great Depression and World War II.

****

Assignments or situations confronted by service men added to around-the-clock usage of expletives and vulgar utterances. During periods of training and continuing into combat, most of these terms were just part of the "soldierly territory" and not much peer focus was given to such linguistic articulation. The four letter "sh___" word was put to steady usage. It was only exceeded by the quartet of letters, "f___" a noun, along with its "ing" grammar form. The "g" was often dropped from the "ing", shortening the adjective by a one letter. At times, both words appeared to be appropriately coequal for given situations.

****

The term "ninety-day wonder" referred to an individual who had attended Officer Candidate School (OCS) for three months. He was then given a commission of Second Lieutenant.

The mixing of newly commissioned second lieutenants with old army noncommissioned officers – men who had been in the military service for a lengthy period of time – sometimes created ego problems. The scenario required some good common sense arbitration

17

between both groups for achieving the required smooth operational combat readiness of any military unit.

****

The term "old army" was applied to any soldier enlisting in the United States Army before the country had a Selective Service Commission for drafting men for military duty.

It was not too unusual at the time, to give young male civilian trouble makers in a community the choice of enlisting in the military service or serve jail time. The majority of "old army" was made up of men looking for a job, a place to stay and something to eat.

Chapter Three

Primary Basic Training

The land area located within the boundaries of the Fort Bliss Military Reservation contained 618,343 acres or about 966 square miles. The largest portion of this acreage extends into New Mexico. Fort Bliss, Biggs Army Airfield and Logan Heights were clustered rather closely together in the southern portion of the military post near the West Texas city of El Paso.

Similar to Fort Leavenworth, Fort Bliss is also overflowing in early history. Leon Metz, noted modern-day Texas historian, wrote the following events of history. "In the year of 1827, Ponce de Leon (not the Spanish explorer who founded Florida and was seeking the "Fountain of Youth") a resident of *El Paso del Norte* (Juarez, Mexico) acquired 211 acres on the north bank of the Rio Grande River. The original name of El Paso, Texas was "Ponce's Rancho". In 1849, nearly 300 soldiers marching in from San Antonio, took up quarters around Ponce's Rancho. The military reservation became known as the "Post Opposite El Paso, New Mexico." "The El Paso" referred to *El Paso del Norte* (Juarez), the largest town. The "New Mexico" referred to today's West Texas in the later 1840's as attached to the Territory of New Mexico." Historian Metz continues, "The post was entirely infantry. The soldiers met incoming wagon trains at the Pecos River and escorted them to Mesilla, New Mexico."

The situation was rather similar to Fort Leavenworth since one of its missions also was to escort wagon trains along the Santa Fe Trail. The "Post Opposite El Paso, New Mexico" was eventually named Fort Bliss after Brevit Colonel William Wallace Smith Bliss (1815-1853). The title "brevit" (also "brevet") was a commission, often granted as an honor, promoting a military officer in rank without having additional authority or an increase in pay. Bliss was the son-in-law of the United States President, Zachary Taylor.

Fort Bliss soon became the largest cavalry training site in the United States. It was the operational base of the black "Buffalo Soldiers" of the 9th and 10th Cavalry. In the 1870's they were chasing Apache Chief Victorio and his band of "renegades". Fort Bliss had to deal with numerous Mexican revolutions, Francisco Pancho Villa, Indians and countless other problems – including floods, the Civil War and five relocation changes. In 1900, Tony Lama, Sr. was a cobbler with the U.S. Cavalry at Fort Bliss. Eventually he opened up his own business of making boots, not only for the military but also for cowboys and ranchers in the vicinity. It was the beginning of the world famous "Tony Lama" cowboy boots.

General John "Blackjack" Pershing was the commanding officer at Fort Bliss in 1914. He led the unsuccessful mission to capture Pancho Villa. He successfully commanded the United States troops battling German forces during World War One.

From 1919 to 1925, Major General Robert L. Howze was in command of Fort Bliss. Howze was the recipient of the Medal of Honor presented for gallantry in fighting Indians of the Sioux Nation. Howze was instrumental in organizing the First Cavalry Division of the United States Army.

Following our initial arrival at Logan Heights, everyone was automatically quarantined for a two week period of time. This restriction was a health precautionary measure to make certain we had not been exposed to any contagious communicable diseases previous to our arrival at Fort Bliss. The fortnight of mandatory isolation seemed almost endless for 37531447. I was anxious to obtain a pass to visit neighboring El Paso. Perchance a quiet corner of the earth could be discovered where I would not have such a feeling of confinement. The first days of my military ordeal had taken an extremely heavy toll on mental and emotional reserves.

The order "confined" meant just what the term implies. We were required to remain in a relatively small area, unable to go the base movie theater or walk over to a nearby PX (Post Exchange). The PX had civilian employees for the most part. It also was a place to purchase snacks, obtain haircuts, procure extra uniform parts, provide tailoring assistance for sewing patches on shirts and dress coats as well as sewing services for uniform alterations. In addition, the post exchange operated a "beer garden" where one could buy and consume beer. Recalling my disastrous drinking fiasco at Fort Leavenworth, the "garden" did not provide me with any great urge to go there to drink the alcoholic beverage.

On the final day of mandatory confinement, the battery was called to stand an unscheduled formation. On this occasion we were given the hapless tidings, "A soldier from another battery from the battalion has contacted – scarlet fever." This information also increased our period of quarantine for an additional twenty-one days. I greeted this displeasing bit of contemporary information with enormous distress and intense personal frustration.

We were given two new military idioms to help express this recent unwanted proclamation. One was: "Tough Kashitzky". This was a tongue-in-cheek expression suggesting such words would be uttered by a Russian soldier if in a similar situation. The other, "The chaplain will punch your ticket". This latter phrase sarcastically implies if an individual had trouble coping with the circumstances at hand, they should visit with the chaplain of their choice for comfort and guidance through the ongoing crisis.

The following three weeks passed agonizingly unhurried for me. My spirit was given a giant boost when our first mail arrived. There were several letters from my fiance and one from my mother. I opened and read the letters from my fiance first. Then opened and viewed the contents of my mother's letter. Perhaps I felt certain that my mother would always be there for me. The letters contained the normal run-of-the-mill contents which meant the communication from my mother was "motherly". The perfume-scented messages from my fiance suggested she missed me very much and would always be waiting for me until I came back. I was given an additional positive boost in temperament when paired with a Casper, Wyoming soldier for radio training. His name was Russell A. Pitts. He preferred to be called "R.A". or just "Bud". The affiliation with my new sidekick (and often accomplice) placed the brakes on the lengthy downward spiral of 37531447's sagging resolve.

It was during this additional period of continuing "house arrest", the cadre communications staff sergeant began to teach a small number of us about army telephone and radio communications. The sergeant instructor was one of the old army soldiers who had served with an antiaircraft artillery unit in the Panama Canal Zone during the early period of warfare. The sergeant performed an instrumental role in the installation of a large communication cable line across the Isthmus of Panama soon after the war became a reality. The man was highly knowledgeable about all aspects of military communication installations. In addition to his technical skills, he usually was a personable individual.

Eventually our compulsory confinement came to its welcomed conclusion on a Saturday morning and my hopes went soaring over the likely possibility of obtaining a pass to visit the city of El Paso.

On the same morning a formal troop formation was called. We were to be inspected by the commissioned officers of the battery. I had prepared quite well for this inspection. My dress uniform was spotless, my necktie straight, shoes sparkled, buttons correctly fastened, and my brand-new M-1 Garand semi-automatic was meticulously clean inside and out. I was ready for the first official inspection of my military basic training.

At last, the moment of truth finally presented itself when the top kick and a second lieutenant stopped directly in front of me. I held my rifle in inspection position just in case the lieutenant wished to examine the weapon.

The officer snatched the rifle from me for his inspection and after finding it to be in perfect condition, slapped it sharply back into my awaiting hands. I was certain that I had passed my first military inspection as a member of "Dog" Battery and the moment bequeathed me a tremendous surge of great pride. I was not mentally prepared for what happened next. The inspecting officer turned toward the first sergeant and contemptuously remarked, "Sergeant, take down this soldier's name and restrict him to his barracks for the weekend."

The top kick immediately asked the lieutenant, "Sir, what is your reason for confining this soldier to the barracks?"

Displaying a enormous degree of annoyance over the sergeant's unsolicited and unwanted inquiry, the young lieutenant abruptly snapped, "The soldier's hair is too long!"

I was completely stunned by the lieutenant's unwelcome words. It had been over seven weeks since my last haircut at Fort Leavenworth and my hair always was fast growing. I felt certain other soldiers had hair as long or even longer than mine. Ever since my arrival at Logan Heights we had been grounded and unable to go to the PX for the purpose of obtaining a haircut.

Pressed between the almost uncontrollable urge to shed tears or make make my first enemy kill, guaranteeing me rapid return to Fort

Leavenworth, where I could serve the certain lifetime military sentence in the large silver-domed federal penitentiary – seemed to be my only options. Neither choice appeared to be very prudent at this particular moment. Instead I picked a third alternative – "To dislike the bastard".

The commissioned officers soon took their leave from the formation. The first sergeant would dismiss the group. Before dismissing the men he ordered me to remain. Recalling the top kick's unusual introduction of himself at the first formation, I was seriously debating with myself if I should remain or make a sprint for the not-to-distant Mexican Border.

After the other soldiers dispersed, the top sergeant ambled over to where I stood and using his slow Cajun-accented drawl exclaimed, "Son, you all get yourself over to the post exchange and get your hair cut and then report to me at the CP (Command Post)."

I was becoming reluctantly resigned to the way my luck was running. I was certain, beyond any reasonable doubt, I would either be pulling guard duty or KP (kitchen detail) over the weekend. Any hopes for a pass into El Paso had vanished.

Following the cutting of my hair, I reported to the CP as directed. The lanky first sergeant looked at me, then reached into a file box marked "PASSES" and presented me with a weekend pass to visit both El Paso and Cuidad Juarez, Mexico. While handing me the passes he was softly mumbling something about some "fuckin' ninety-day wonder". I recalled the second quote the top kick made at the initial battery gathering, "The commissioned officers command but I am the one that runs this outfit." His words appeared to have a solid ring of truth.

My Wyoming friend, Bud, had the same type of pass. We were overjoyed to know we would temporarily be leaving the dismal tar-papered huts of Logan Heights behind while visiting both border cities of Juarez and El Paso.

Our weekend passes enabled us to become familiar with army transportation from and to Logan Heights. Busses returning to the drop off point for Logan Heights were usually full as the curfew time neared for the return trip. Even standing room was at a premium. My beer drinking bout at Fort Leavenworth did provide a positive lesson for me. I was keenly aware of symptoms of queasiness from over-indulgence. More than once I deftly moved out of the way of a standing soldier attempting to make his passage through the masses in effort to reach an open bus window. Other soldiers often failed to notice the impending problem or would fail to yield the right-of-way and became victims of the unfortunate circumstances often leading to a horrendous chain reaction. I would always prefer to stand on the bus during the return trip from El Paso to Logan Heights if the bus was crowded with returning soldiers.

The passes also gave us a chance to explore both the city of El Paso and Juarez. The experience would provide me experiences to write about when answering letters to my fiance and my parents. I found it to be rather perplexing to know that on one hand, I could write to my parents as well as to my fiance about actually leaving the United States and visiting the foreign country of Mexico; however, it appeared to be rather impossible to tell them about the reality of life in Ciudad Jaurez. I certainly could not describe the action of pimps on nearly every street corner informing us, "I have a sister who desires to sleep (for a price) with you." Neither could I tell them about the lewd performances featuring donkeys and soft drink bottles and senoritas.

Bud and 37531477 were never taken in by either situation. Perhaps this is why we opted to go to a bar to consume whiskey sours, have a thick T-bone steak, and get to know each other.

The following Monday we were scheduled to learn about the operation of the 40 millimeter Bofers antiaircraft gun. I grimaced when I noticed the second lieutenant who restricted me to the barracks because of my long hair. He would be the officer in charge of the gunnery instruction.

The Bofors gun platform is mounted on four rubber tire wheels. It was known in military lingo as a "towed type" (pulled by a motor vehicle) weapon. It also was a rather heavy gun having a couple round steel "shoes" (somewhat comparable to the plates on a modern-day back-hoe) used for stabilizing purposes when the weapon was lowered to the ground. Basically it was similar to a farm hay wagon having a huge heavy gun in the middle which could be suddenly lowered to the ground while the four wheels remained as they were.

When the releasing latch on the Bofors was activated, the big weapon would quickly almost free-fall to the ground and most of its entire mass would rest on the metal support plates. In

**40mm Bofors and Crew with 7th Army in France, 1944
(Photograph courtesy of the Air Defense Artillery Museum of Fort Bliss, Texas)**

**Ken Lenke Photo
Parade Grounds at Fort Bliss, Texas**

an emergency situation the weapon could also be fired as it was being towed without ever lowering the weapon on the stabilizing plates. It was in this latter position when the cocky little second lieutenant strutted in front of us like some damned rooster. He stopped, looked towards us and then his eyes locked on mine as he fondled the release latch mechanism and confidently related, "This is the mechanism that drops the Bofers gun to the ground position."

Woebegone for the lieutenant! In his enthusiasm to impress the group of new soldiers with his military dictionary of knowledge about the heavy gun, he prematurely inadvertently pulled on the release latch – causing most of the Bofors' 4,234 pounds of weight to unexpectedly smash into the west Texas ground. Perhaps he pulled the latch when his gaze noticed the riveted hatred in my eyes directed his way. It may have been the catalyst causing him to lose his "train of thought" if indeed he ever possessed one. In the rapid lowering process, one of the circular weight bearing steel plates completely severed the extreme end from one of the ninety-day wonder's spanking new highly-polished officer's boot. The budding commissioned officer was too visibly shaken over his close call of having some toes amputated that he didn't observe the gratifying smile spreading across my countenance.

Our antiaircraft training covered numerous military objectives as well as providing additional opportunities to further radio skills with classroom education in the permanent structures in old Fort Bliss.

Some of us from "Dog" battery did not participate very often in activities with the battery gun crews. Our time was utilized learning radio and field telephone techniques, under the tutelage of our cadre communications instructor. He taught us how to use different types of military radios and how to construct field wire networks connecting the CP switchboard with each of the Bofors gun placements.

In addition, he also demonstrated how to alter one type of military radio enabling us to listen to the "clear channel" radio station XELO, a station that was about eighty percent commercials and about twenty percent country-western music. The station's "clear channel" transmitter was distantly located in Old Mexico across the border from Del Rio, Texas.

We had a terrific group of men who worked the communication assignments for "Dog" battery. While learning military communication skills, our cadre leader told us about several of the men from his group in Panama who had acquired syphilis (one of those social diseases) from their promiscuous sexual activities while serving in the Panama Canal Zone. The staff sergeant further related, "These unfortunate men would go into the Panamanian jungle and prayerfully invite a malaria-carrying mosquito to sting them." He explained, "The extremely high fever, caused by the sting of and infected mosquito, would destroy the syphilis spirochete." I had no reason to check out the validity of his testimony for this highly unusual "cure" for syphilis.

One member of our group came from Wellington, Kansas. His last name was Boss. His first and middle names were John and Henry – in that order. On one occasion, Private Boss was asked by the payroll clerk to sign his "John Henry" on the monthly payroll sheet. The payroll clerk became momentarily upset with Private Boss when he noticed the sheet had actually been signed "John Henry Boss".

Another member of our crew had the last name of Cobb. In civilian life he was a watch repairman. He had his watch repair kit sent to him from his home. Cobb could earn extra money fixing malfunctioning time pieces for the soldiers. The sandy environment at Fort Bliss caused most watches to fail quickly and often. Bud would always wait until Cobb had the watch out of the case and then the Wyoming soldier would make a couple of wild passes with a broom pretending to tidy the wooden floor. Sweeping would fill the atmosphere with the very fine particles of West Texas desert sand. Cobb, noticing the broom's wild gyrations would become more than slightly agitated. Bud's delicate sense of timing was flawless in determining the exact moment to halt the half-hearted sweeping just seconds before the watch repairman turned into a live hand grenade.

My Wyoming friend appeared to posses some type of gifted apparition informing him whenever Cobb was about to receive a large box of fancy cheeses from the watch repairman's wife in Wisconsin. During Bud's visions of incoming cheese, he stopped his ornery harassment of the watch repairman and became a perfect "Mr. nice guy". Bud always was rewarded by the repairman's generosity with some of the delicious cheese.

Keane, another member of our team, was somewhat older than the rest of us. He was soft spoken, gentle, tall and a hardworking soldier.

He was a father type role model for some of us "youngsters". He added much stability to our communication unit.

Keane did, however, have a rather unpleasant confrontation with a young female clerk working in an El Paso drug store. He was looking to purchase a couple of cans of "Sterno" (Tm), a type of fuel that can be used to warm hands while on maneuvers in the cold New Mexico winter desert, or it could be utilized to heat water for coffee or shaving. Most servicemen asked for the product by its most common name "canned heat".

Keane innocently asked the young lady, "Do you have any canned heat?" She promptly placed a pretty hefty hand slap to the face of our "father image".

The store manager, upon hearing the commotion, rushed over and demanded what happened from the emotional clerk. She tearfully related to the manager, "This soldier made a lewd remark to me!"

When the manager fully understood the issue he quickly explained to the distraught young clerk, "The store does have the product for sale and 'canned heat' was the 'generic' name for Sterno." Apologies all around concluded the incident.

Garfield, another member of the communications section, was the assigned driver of the Dodge weapons carrier. He could have passed as the lead singer of a Mexican mariachi band. Unfortunately he did not possess any proximate ability for crooning on key. The dark handsome soldier adapted right in with the senoritas of both El Paso and Juarez. Bud was a pretty fair guitar player and Garfield would often ask Bud to play the old Roy Acuff tune, *Great Speckled Bird* on the instrument. The soldier from Wyoming usually obliged while he and 37531447 vocalized the lyrics in fulfilling Garfield's odd request. Garfield had a great liking for Mexican music and Bud and I thought it rather peculiar for the soldier to ask for the Acuff tune. The sing-a-long session would usually abruptly desist when Garfield joined in on the "singing" of the lyrics.

A large-framed man rounded out the motley crew, who the sergeant instructor referred to as "his boys". Al Gempler, "Big Al", was also somewhat older than most of us. He too, was a very gentle soft-spoken individual who never let trivial problems bother him. The large-sized soldier was always a great booster of morale.

Even though Bud and I were younger than most of the others, it was a great comfort to both of us to have the wisdom of these older soldiers, patiently guiding us through many of our youthful trials of military life along the Mexican Border.

Postscript

The experience in the border city of Juarez with the "openness" of sexual promiscuity was never written about in letters home. This self-censorship would serve me well when writing home during difficult combat experiences. My letters always ignored the real life I was living and would only mention trivial experiences. Communications home would usually consist of seeing the great cathedrals, geographic features, and other small talk. I would never inform my parents about military duties I was performing.

****

The Bofors antiaircraft weapon was named for the Swedish city of Bofors, where the gun was manufactured. I have been informed that it was first used by navy vessels and was secured to the ships' decking. Later, it was placed on four wheels and utilized by ground forces.

****

Roy Acuff was perhaps the most popular country singer during World War II. Although I never witnessed any of his military service performances, the fiddle playing Acuff was always a hit with the soldiers as he played Tennessee country mountain music, performed yo-yo tricks and balanced the violin bow on his chin.

****

Fort Bliss turned out some of the army's best trained units. It also has been referred to as the "training ground of generals". Four U.S. Chiefs of Staff originated from Fort Bliss.

Kenneth L. Lenke

****

"Biggs Field" was relocated in 1926 and blossomed into Biggs Air Force Base. It was named after James "Buster" Biggs, a local World War One aviator who lost his life in France.

Chapter Four

Intermediate Basic Training

Following several months of intensive primary basic training, many of us received our first military rank promotion and became Privates First Class (PFC). Differing from the Private First Class temporary stripes given to me at the Fort Leavenworth induction center to "...make certain the 'spic' returns back to Fort Leavenworth with you." this stripe could be permanently affixed to my uniform. I had worked diligently to learn the necessary skills required for handling my military responsibilities and felt extremely proud to achieve this first advancement in rank. Other men in the communication section also received promotional stripes, including my friend from Casper, Wyoming.

The antiaircraft artillery battery was performing many more close-order marching drills which often included all battalion units. I came to the conclusion the two deep-voiced grunts "hut" and "harch" shouted by the drill sergeants were in actuality, ancient indigenous sounds and when translated meant, "one of your two feet should immediately be moved in some direction". This battalion strength marching practice would enable us to look sharp when "Passing in Review" for high ranking army officers observing us at the Fort Bliss parade ground. Commissioned military army officials were continuously scrutinizing our training progress at Fort Bliss.

Bud usually kept me laughing much of the time with his creative antics, and even though my fiance was not writing as often, I was beginning to enjoy, to some degree, the brotherhood of military life. The swagger-stick carrying lieutenant who had me grounded because of my long hair, had been judiciously transferred elsewhere. That delightful reality by itself was a colossal boost to my morale.

I usually managed to obtain weekend passes. When Bud was unable to "con" a pass because of weekend detail duty, I would sojourn into El Paso by myself. I had little desire to cross the border for any sightseeing in old Juarez, Mexico.

Strolling the streets surrounding San Jacinto Plaza was a favorite pastime. The plaza had a large grassy area, trees, and a walled

31

alligator pit (Plaza de Logartos) full of the huge drowsy appearing reptiles. It was also a locale where the effects from over-indulgence of tequila, by soldiers as well as Mexican Nationals, could be slept off. I would ponder the close similarity between the sleep-appearing motionless 'gators on one side of the wall and the immobile drunks sobering up on the opposite side of the concrete barrier. Both species of animal life appeared to have a common thread of biological relationship.

Often I would be found visiting the large museum at the El Paso School of Mines. The exhibits displayed in the museum stirred my interest in the history of the Southwest. These visits always made an impression on this small-town lad from rural Kansas.

Seldom would I ever miss the opportunity to stop in at one of El Paso's large downtown classy hotels – the El Paso del Norte (The Pass of/to the North). From the tall hotel one could view two nations, the United States and Mexico, as well as three different states – Texas, New Mexico and Chihuahua, Mexico. While gazing at the marvelous Tiffany stained glass dome of the lobby I would treasure a secluded area to write my personal letters. Military personnel had "franking privileges" (no postage stamps required on letters). By utilizing hotel stationery, generously placed in the lobby, my meagre military pay could be stretched slightly farther.

When the monthly payroll rolled around, we were always paid our stipend with two-dollar bills. The reason given for this rather unusual payment method was to help ensure no large denomination bills from the Fort Bliss military reservation would make their way into Old Mexico. Apparently the enemy had espionage agents in Juarez who were interested in purchasing information about U.S. military activities. It would be more difficult to hide a large stash of two-dollar bills during a cash payoff for espionage information.

While spending the two-dollar bills in the vicinity of El Paso, the new recipients of the money would often tear off a small corner of the paper money. Sometimes more than one corner would be removed. The only explanation given for this unusual custom was that such action was believed to bring the new owner "good luck" or conversely, the paper money would not provide the recipient any "bad luck".

At Logan Heights, Bud and I began to pull additional duties at the battery command post. We both took turns operating the telephone switchboard or serving as radio operators for the captain's vehicle whenever this service was required. After several more months of training we both were highly surprised to receive T-5 rank promotions. We were now called "corporals". I was visualizing how the stripes would appear on my dress uniform when being granted my first furlough to visit my home town. By this time, I had been in the army for over eight months. I was certain my fiance would be quite impressed with the advancement in rank and extremely proud of me. 37531447 had been extremely naïve earlier in thinking his first wartime furlough home would be granted in a couple of months.

Several men in our communications unit, including myself, were sent to radio school at the permanent buildings of Fort Bliss. Corporal Pitts would be attending the same training facility.

It was a gratifying change to eat in the Fort Bliss cafeteria. Besides the meals tasting much better, we were using real chinaware plates and drinking from glass containers. It was far more pleasant than using the GI metal fold-up mess gear and the lip-burning aluminum drinking cup from our canteen kit. When completing meals at the cafeteria, someone else washed the dishes. At the "Heights" when finishing our meal, we would take the metal mess gear outside of the mess hall to a location where four large containers were positioned. The first held scraps of uneaten food. A local hog farmer would pick up the scrap food containers each day to "slop" his pigs. The next three metal containers were heated over a fire. One receptacle held hot soapy water where we would utilize a wooden-handled miniature floor mop to remove food debris from the mess kit. The other two large containers of hot water were for rinsing and sterilizing the eating utensils.

During the schooling at Fort Bliss, we were learning how to send and receive messages in the Morse code. Morse code is an audible system of sending and receiving dots and dashes by radio. All messages were sent and received in five letter (or numbers) groupings. This procedure was designed for cryptography (code) purposes. As usual Bud always kept me entertained with his impromptu sense of humor. One specific transmission message sent by him stated, "KENDR INKAB EERAN DP38-" (Ken, drink a beer and pee 38) The P-38 was a twin-boomed military aircraft.

Upon our return to Logan Heights, we commenced numerous rigorous field exercises in New Mexico. Our artillery battery would form into a convoy position and depart for gunnery practice at the New Mexico gunnery range.

For this specialized training we would be utilizing live ammunition to shoot at a canvas target towed by an aircraft. The airplane and target were disassociated from each other by a light weight cable. The distance separating the target from the aircraft was controlled by the aircraft crew. I wondered if any previous gun crews had ever fired on the plane by mistake. After all, planes were the intended ultimate target of antiaircraft artillery. The length of the cable between the plane and the cloth target appeared to be directly proportional to the experience of the gun crews. Gun crews doing the firing must have been carefully assessed for gunnery expertise by those operating the aircraft used in towing the canvas target.

Tall wooden observation towers enabled artillery officers to safely observe, through their field glasses, the effectiveness of the antiaircraft fire as it hit or missed the long fabric target. After the completion of firing, the target was released by the plane's crew and dropped for further analysis by ground crews.

Bud and 37531447 were serving as communication operators. Our job was to pass pertinent information between the tower and the gun emplacements firing the .50-caliber machine guns and the forty-millimeter Bofors weapons.

We soon would discover commissioned officers also had a pecking order of command. Generals were to be feared by lower ranking commissioned officers. Dog Battery's Second Lieutenant Freeman was observing the weapon firing from a position in the towering wooden structure. He would determine the effectiveness of gun crews from Battery D.

During the firing exercise Bud received an esoteric message informing us a general was in the vicinity observing the results of the firing practice. This important bit of intelligence went to Lieutenant Freeman and to about every other place on the firing range. Bud was extremely thorough and highly dedicated with his communicational duties.

The lieutenant, while peering through field glasses, kept inquiring continuously if we knew the whereabouts of "the general". Second Lieutenant Freeman was a top-notch officer of Dog Battery. He always treated enlisted men in our battery with the belief that each man was highly important and special for the success of the mission.

The ascension up the lofty observation tower was achieved by climbing a tall wooden ladder attached to the rear portion of the enclosed structure. Blind to the three of us in the observation tower, the huge general had stealthily climbed the ladder to our observation position. We were not aware of his presence in the vicinity until Bud and I noticed the high-ranking army officer slip silently through the door opening. Lieutenant Freeman was intensely occupied studying the moving tow target as the general positioned himself directly behind the unsuspecting section gunnery officer.

Military regulation for such a situation, would require any person of lower rank observing the presence of a high ranking officer, to quickly shout a loud "Attention!" The exception to this regulation was: "If you are actively involved with important relevant military duties, you are not required to indicate the presence of a ranking officer." Bud and I were more busy with "important relevant duties" than we most likely would ever be during future stints of our military training.

While devoting complete attention to observing the frontal target activity, Freeman once again inquired, "Do you see the general in the area anywhere?"

An unusually long loud silence followed.

The general broke the spell of the temporal hiatus, as he softly inquired, "What would you like to ask the general, lieutenant?"

Freeman did an "about face" and with total disbelief perceived the close proximity of the large rugged-appearing general. Neither Bud nor I could recall what Lieutenant Freeman replied in response to the general's query.

After the welcomed departure of the general, the battery lieutenant still in a state of distress, mumbled repeatedly, "I know I'll be reclassified and reduced one grade in rank." The towering general must have had a terrific inner feeling of hilarity after departing the tower area. Much to the relief of the lieutenant, Bud and 37531447, the good second lieutenant was never demoted. Perhaps the general noticed the tow target had numerous holes caused by gunners of Battery D and – being a general – realized what was really important and what was not.

At other times our military unit would journey to some very desolate regions in the New Mexico desert for additional field training exercises. The antiaircraft weapons would always be placed in camouflaged tactical combat positions.

This portion of sandy desert topography contained large amounts of chaparral, including greasewood (creosote bush) and sagebrush. Years of windy conditions had formed numerous high mounds of sand covered with differing species of chaparral. Rattlesnakes and numerous varieties of scorpions also made the area their habitat. The rattlesnakes were almost as large and long as Texans described them. Several remote bivouacs sites produced frenzied shouts of, "There is a rattlesnake over here." "Here is another one." This was followed by, "There are a couple more over here." The presence of the vipers usually resulted in a sleepless night for the men. To my knowledge, no artillerymen from Dog Battery ever received a wound from any of the highly venomous desert dwellers.

Our communication crew would excavate the center of the large mounds of wind-blown sand that natives of the area referred to as "boondocks". When the boondock had a large enough area removed from the middle section, our communication equipment would be placed snugly inside and the entire boondock would be covered with camouflage netting and the previously removed chaparral.

The interior was hollowed out large enough so at least three men could squeeze inside. Only the radio antenna would be visible from the outside. John Henry Boss usually assisted us in lifting the equipment into position as well as demonstrating his natural born skill of providing disturbed species of scorpions with new homes – elsewhere.

The soldiers in charge of laying the telephone field wire networks were using the Dodge "carryall". PFC Garfield usually was the culprit "guiding" the vehicle. We often wondered if Garfield was in reality, a secret test driver working for the Chrysler Corporation. He thrived, almost to the point of drooling, in discovering the most damnable and unnecessary route to shepherd the sturdy four-wheel-drive military vehicle. During Garfield's fiendish navigational habits, the two soldiers riding in the back of the truck would direct a squadron of awesome descriptive expletives in the direction of the continuously laughing maniacal driver. The two soldiers in the rear of the vehicle unreeling field wire, were always hanging on for dear life while unwinding the bouncing, cumbersome and non-anchored heavy steel reel of communication telephone wire – onto the rough New Mexico desert terrain.

On one occasion, the captain misread his map and erroneously placed the entire battery of guns on "the make believe" aircraft runway that we were supposed to "protect". Even our communication position was on the mythical landing field. We were ordered to move off of the phantom airfield and repeat the operation – correctly! I was rather certain that the battery captain took a verbal reaming out from "higher ups" over his tactical training blunder. Field problems were designed to train commissioned officers as well as regular troops.

At the beginning of an additional training exercise, commencing at Logan Heights, a very memorable event unexpectedly unfolded during the forming of a military convoy. The convoy would consist of troop-carriers, tow trucks for the Bofors, field kitchen units, a water truck, ambulance and other assorted vehicles. Such convoy forming always managed to confirm the old military axiom, "hurry up and wait". Perhaps destiny was the culprit providing the commissioned officer in charge of the battalion convoy to have the rank of Major and the last name of Mumaw (pronounced "moo-maw"). It also was the period of time when civilian radio stations were playing the tune *Pistol Packin' Mama*, a national wartime novelty hit record. The refrain words of this old Texas two-step tune were:

> "Lay that pistol down babe, lay that pistol down.
> Pistol packin' mama, lay that pistol down."

In this small niche of our country's wartime history a waiting soldier in the back of one of the troop-carriers would wile away the monotonous period of waiting by presenting an impromptu vocal rendition of this song. He did, however, alter one important word during his spur-of-the-moment performance. He interchanged the word *Mumaw* for *mama* as he explored his newly discovered vocal talent. Other waiting soldiers, by their laughter, only encouraged an encore that was upgraded a couple of decibels. Some soldiers in the truck noticed the major approaching and the crescendo of gaiety trickled to a dreadfully foreboding silence. The soon-to-be unlucky soldier could well have been rendering his finest vocal version of the tune. He was placing additional emphasis on the alternate word for "mama" by making use of the major's last name. The soldier suddenly stopped singing and was looking directly at the "not too amused" battalion executive officer. The major promptly ordered, "Private, sing that song once more." The major then added, "It is one of my favorite tunes." The highly embarrassed private gave a rather wimpy audition using the "mama" word. The major didn't go for this correct version and sharply ordered the embarrassed soldier, "Sing the song using the exact words you were using when I was approaching this vehicle!" The artilleryman, now feeling thoroughly "trashed", meekly complied with the major's direct order. Before Major Mumaw departed, he inquired the name of the soldier and informed the budding vocalist, "When you get back to Logan Heights you will have latrine duty for the following two weeks."

Upon return to Logan Heights the major personally checked to make certain his edict was carried out. For two weeks the soldier cleaned the toilet "bowls", scrubbed the urinals and mopped the floor of Dog Battery's donicker.

Antiaircraft military convoys would usually move out of Fort Bliss in battery strength. Headquarter section would be first, followed by other batteries in alphabetical order. The last to depart the staging area would always be Dog Battery. Dog battery was always last – even when it came to giving out food rations. When it came Dog Battery's turn to draw its rations it seemed as if the supply of tender choice cuts of lamb had run out and we received tough goat meat as a replacement. Other battery soldiers always made the most out of the ignominious last place rating for Dog Battery.

Most convoys leaving Logan Heights were rather lengthy. Each driver was required to maintain a hundred yard distance interval between each military vehicle. Realizing the convoy would be travelling on a two-lane public highway after leaving Fort Bliss, each departing battery was directed to implement a ten-minute delay before following the preceding battery. This mandatory delay would enable the small amount of civilian traffic to pass the slower moving military convoy more safely on public roads.

Our battery commander, Captain John Hansen, would be in the lead vehicle, a three-quarter ton weapons carrier. The vehicle also would transport Bud and 37531447 as radio operators. The captain's driver would be the fun-loving PFC Garfield.

The anticipated moment for our departure from camp arrived. The lead conveyance began to move out as other units of the artillery convoy fell in line and neatly maintained the mandated 100-yard interval between each vehicle. At the last crossroad leaving Fort Bliss's military reservation was the road leading to the fort's laundry facility.

The Dog Battery captain was in a near "dream-state" type of mesmerism and appeared to be mentally preoccupied. Perhaps he was thinking about his important task of leading this "colossal" display of military might – the infamous "Dog Battery" – out upon the domain of the public highway.

Passing the final crossroad leading to the laundry area the captain, experiencing immense relief knowing the convoy was finally on its way, reached into a stash of cigars stored in a front pocket of his officer's uniform. Husking the wrapper from one of the cigars, he promptly inserted the status symbol into his mouth. Using his special silver-plated lighter, he soon had the cigar effulgent. Shifting his body around to make himself more comfortable in the seat, he now had moments to relax and possibly reflect on his skillful ability as a self-satisfied leader of fighting men.

Unanticipated trouble occurred at the laundry crossroad. Everyone in our lead vehicle, except the captain, noticed the unrehearsed happening about the same time. The driver of the military vehicle following us was being inattentive and did not notice a truck, similar in appearance to the captain's vehicle, cut through the convoy (against army regulations) and make straight for the fort's laundry facility. The unobservant driver of the Dog Battery troop carrier fell into position behind the vehicle that had wrongfully cut through the convoy. Other drivers of the entourage made the same erroneous turn until all of Dog Battery was rapidly closing in on the Fort Bliss laundry. None of us in the leading vehicle found any reason or sufficient courage to disturb the doyen leader of Dog Battery from his self-imposed euphoric trance.

I began thinking about one of the battery soldiers who earlier had written a note to the laundry and pinned it to his soiled underwear. The complaining message requested more soap to be used when cleaning his olive drab shorts because they had not come back clean. When his laundry was returned, the soldier discovered a note had been pinned onto his shorts. It stated, "Use more paper!" I wondered if the laundry worker writing the note viewed this surprise invasion by Dog Battery as an all-out frontal assault launched with the intended purpose of seeking retribution for advising the soldier to "use more (toilet) paper!"

During this "lost convoy" episode, I was positioned on the outside of the Dodge 4 X 4 between the spare tire and rear fender. My location was almost directly to the left of our chauffeur, PFC Garfield. Bud was near the radio inside

Left: Pfc Garfield and an unidentified El Paso or Juarez senorita
Arcade Photo; Lenke Collection

Right: Bud Pitts, A WAC and her date and 37531447 at Hot Springs, New Mexico
Ken Lenke Photo

the rear of the vehicle. About all of Bud I could see, due to the personal gear surrounding him, was his steel helmet covering most of his head except for the facial portion. His visage was now blessed with a very wide grin as we exchanged glances. The soldier from Casper was highly amused at our "large" convoy consisting of one vehicle.

Garfield, with hypnotic eyes glued straight forward, was tightly clutching the steering wheel of the military vehicle with his now white knuckles clearly visible. The short stocky PFC was driving as if the flat straight New Mexico highway stretching miles beyond, was the torturous twisting steep pathway full of numerous hellish switchbacks leading to the summit of Colorado's lofty Pike's Peak.

The captain was a man of confidence. Civilian occupants of approaching autos would patriotically wave at our vehicle as the commander, puffing strongly on his stogie, returned their waves. I then noticed just an ever-so-slight turning of the captain's head toward PFC Garfield as he confidently inquired, "How does the convoy look, corporal?"

I was the only corporal in that direction. It was up to me to break the bad news! Bud's grin had now become unusually large. He undoubtedly was relishing every moment of my immediate great discomfort. I reluctantly replied to the captain, "Sir, the convoy is not in sight." Captain Hansen suffered a traumatic transition from his dream world to the reality of leading a phantom convoy. Neither Bud nor I could ever recall with certainty, exactly what happened to the cigar the captain had been smoking.

The men on the "laundry invasion exercise" soon discovered their error and were rapidly retreating from the camp laundry. With feet heavy on the accelerator pedals, the lost convoy came into full view and took their correct positions behind our once lonely military vehicle.

We returned to Logan Heights after several days of field activities. When Saturday arrived, Bud and I each received one of the very few weekend passes issued. The two of us crossed the border into Juarez, found a place where we could relax over whiskey sours, have a huge T-bone steak and joke about our one-vehicle convoy.

We also wondered just how much longer we would be stationed in the "Lone Star State" of Texas.

43

Postscript

37531447 never could determine if any planes, pulling tow targets, had ever been accidently shot down by any antiaircraft action on the New Mexico gun range.

Some fifty-plus years later, a destroyer's gun crew did accidently shoot down a U.S. Navy A-6E Intruder aircraft (June 3, 1996). The aircraft was towing a gunnery target 1,600 miles west of Hawaii. The two crew members ejected safely from the aircraft and were rescued in good condition!.

I found this incident to be quite ironic. The 22mm shells had come from the Japanese destroyer *Yuugiri*. The Japanese vessel was participating in joint maneuvers called "RIMPAC" (Rim of the Pacific), with the United States military.

****

The Dodge military vehicle we used most of the time was called by many terms. Sometimes it was known as a "four by four", other occasions it was a "powerwagon", "carryall" or a three-quarter ton vehicle. In military "lingo" it was classified as a WC50 Dodge three-quarter ton six-cylinder weapons carrier.

****

There were two renditions of the tune *Pistol Packin' Mama* recorded about the same time. One version by Bing Crosby with the Andrews Sisters. The other recording of the song was made by Al Dexter, a singer of country music. In Texas the Al Dexter version was decidedly more often heard.

****

The term "boondocks" may have originated in the Philippines when U.S. Marines were fighting insurgents in that country back in the early 1900's. It could have been a corruption of the Tagalog word *bundok* – meaning "mountain".

****

The live alligator exhibit no longer exists at El Paso's *San Jacinto Plaza.* Information provided (1997) to the author by Peggy Boone, Tourism Sales Manager for the El Paso Convention and Visitors Bureau, states the live alligators have been removed. The "Texas Monthly Guidebooks" highlighting El Paso, mentions the alligators at *San Jacinto Plaza.*

"Stroll to the center of the plaza to view *Plaza de Logartos,* a fiberglass memorial to some of El Paso's best-known residents. For the better part of the twentieth century, the alligator colony at *San Jacinto Plaza* was an El Paso trademark. Almost any old timer, Paseno or El Paso visitor, can recall the reptiles, which arrived out west as a practical joke. Native El Pasoan Luis Jimenez designed and sculpted the larger than lifelike work, which was dedicated in June 1995."

****

Coming from rural Kansas, I had never seen alligators. I certainly never expected to see my first 'gators in the desert region of El Paso. The alligator colony I used to watch in *San Jacinto Plaza* in downtown El Paso evidently started out as some type of joke. According to El Paso historian, Leon C. Metz, "Two alligators came in a cigar box about 1883, and alligators were a fixture in the park until the 1950's when they were removed."

The alligators seemed to prosper. Historian Metz writes, "The alligators seemed happy and content, even though during cold weather they resented being bound with ropes and gunnysacks and at night lain behind pot-bellied stoves in one of the numerous nearby saloons. In the morning, after the sun had warmed things, residents carried the unprotesting bundles back to the pond, broke the ice, untied and unwrapped the 'gators and tossed them back in the water." I am not certain how long the ritual of collecting them and placing them behind stoves lasted. When I saw them they were by no means –

Kenneth L. Lenke

small in size. I also believe there were more than two of the reptiles in the *Plaza de Logartos* located in the *San Jacinto Plaza*.

****

El Paso is steeped in history. Texas historian, Leon Metz writes, "In 1598, Juan de Onate crossed the Rio Grande River and called the crossing place *El Paso del Rio Del Norte*. This is the first mention of a place using the words 'El Paso'.

In 1659, *El Paso del Norte* was built around the *Mission of Nuestra Senora de Guadalupe* (Our Lady of Guadalupe). *El Paso del Norte* is now called, Juarez, Mexico."

El Paso was first called Franklin, New Mexico (Territory). During the Civil War, the citizens of Franklin, New Mexico, voted to become part of Texas and the Confederacy. It was a time in history when the flag flying over Fort Bliss was not the flag of the United States.

****

El Paso's *Hotel El Paso del Norte* is presently called *Camino Real Hotel*. It has been lavishly remodeled in recent years. The Tiffany stained glass dome, that was once part of the hotel lobby, still remains. Beneath the twenty-five feet diameter customized Louis Tiffany stained glass dome, is the hotel bar. Among the list of famous guests staying at the hotel were: Pancho Villa, Charles Lindbergh, Eleanor Roosevelt, Will Rogers, General Pershing, Amelea Erhart, Bob Dylan and Presidents; Taft, Hoover, Nixon and Bush.

Chapter Five

Advanced Basic Training

Military base passes issued at Logan Heights were valid for a fifty-mile radius from El Paso. The fifty mile limit was not germane for traveling fifty miles into old Mexico. In Mexico, only the city of Juarez could be visited.

Bud and I soon became indifferent with the mundane passes to visit El Paso. There were so many military personnel in town it was difficult to believe you had actually left Logan Heights. It also appeared to us that the civilians of El Paso liked the money military men from Fort Bliss added to their coffers. We also had more than a slight impression that townspeople, for the most part, seemed to lack any genuine warm feeling towards servicemen. Undoubtedly there were numerous caring people in the border city. It just seemed difficult to find them with so many service men and women in the metropolitan area. Other large military bases most likely had a similar situation. The etiquette of some soldiers would often create many unwanted problems for the local citizenry.

Both of us grew weary of Juarez. Both of us tired of being pestered about some pimp's "sister" (always a virgin) who wanted to "sleep" with us. Outside of the good T-bone steaks, Juarez was just too much of a hassle. In addition, I felt fairly certain Bud's assessment was well-founded in believing Mexican bartenders were "watering down" the whisky sours. I doubt if it was any different with many bars located on the U.S. side of the border.

My Wyoming friend and I soon made an interesting discovery. Civilians living in rural areas of southern New Mexico were far more friendly towards military personnel. This was especially true for communities positioned along the *Rio Bravo del Norte*, better known to *Norte Americanos* as the Rio Grande River. We would often overextend the fifty-mile radius limit of our pass privilege whenever we visited the smaller communities of Hatch and Hot Springs, New Mexico.

We both would take great pleasure in sleeping on real hotel beds instead of the narrow steel camp cots in our living quarters at Logan

47

Heights. When staying overnight on pass, we always requested one of the corner rooms in the hotel. The windows could be thrown wide open on two sides of the room and we would indulge in the gentle cool nighttime breezes sweeping in from the direction of the verdant Rio Grande River Valley. For us, New Mexico was truly "The Land of Enchantment".

Upon acquiring T-4 rank stripes we would be called by the title of "Sergeant". This promotion in rating also placed a few more two dollar bills in our pockets.

One of our highest priorities was to avoid unwanted difficulties. We were surpassing the imposed fifty-mile radius travel restriction distance from Fort Bliss. It also was of extreme importance to return to Logan Heights before our passes expired. Not having transportation of our own, we relied on public transportation which in most cases would be commercial bus lines. Waiting for the last bus to bring us back to El Paso was extremely chancy due to wartime maintenance problems. Often buses would have all available seats and standing room filled to capacity.

When wearing my dress uniform, which included a recently purchased billed dress cap and leather garrison belt, I imagined how handsome I would appear when granted my first furlough home. In a way, I was acting somewhat similar to Captain Hansen when he was savoring his convoy of one solitary military vehicle. The exception – 37531447 could not afford his type of expensive wrapped cigars.

One morning while visiting Hot Springs, Bud and I struck up a conversation with another soldier and his date, a WAAC (Women's Army Auxiliary Corp). We sauntered over to a nearby café to have lunch. It was Sunday morning and a "no liquor day" as possibly decreed by local or state laws. Bud jokingly asked for beer but the café owner informed my friend, "Sorry. It is a 'dry' Sunday."

Activity was extremely slow at the café. To the surprise of all of us, the owner returned from the rear of the café and placed a case of gratis ice-cold beer on our table. Perhaps the law implied it was unlawful to sell alcoholic beverages, but it may have been legal to give it away. By this time I had come to the conclusion if I didn't drink so much beer, I most likely would not become ill. When placing the beer on the table the smiling café owner declared, "It is quite likely that no one else will show up." We thought he was a prince of a guy for being so darned pleasing to all of us. This happening was quite a contrast when compared to the seemingly lack of friendliness from the citizen population of El Paso.

Approximately halfway through the case of beer, one other customer did enter the café. It was the local priest from the Catholic Church. The café owner promptly locked the door following the arrival of the clergyman. The four of us thought we were in big-time trouble since we had the case of beer, displayed in open view, on the table and it was a "churchly"

Ken Lenke Photograph
"37531447" Russell A. "Bud" Pitts (Circa 1943)

day. We glanced over at the priest and each time he returned our questioning gaze with a kindly warm smile. The priest's demeanor appeared to be communicating to us, "Carry on."

It was a delightful experience visiting with the other soldier and his date. After posing for a few photographs, we bade the couple farewell. We thanked our gracious host, nodded our smiles toward the priest and reluctantly returned to El Paso. Several weeks later, my Wyoming friend and I were issued a Saturday pass expiring at 2400 hours military time. We purchased round-trip bus tickets to Hatch, New Mexico, knowing full-well we had to be back in Logan Heights by the "witching hour" for Cinderella or we would be suddenly transformed back to the rank of Private.

Upon arriving in Hatch we met a friendly civilian possessing an estimable automobile with an ample supply of gasoline. Our new friend informed us about a western-type dance taking place at the even more distant – Hot Springs. He invitingly remarked, "Let's go over there and see what's going on!" Bud, hesitating somewhat, replied, "I don't know. We are on a pretty tight schedule and have to be back in El Paso before midnight." The owner of the automobile convincingly assured us, "I will bring you back to Hatch in time for you to catch the last bus to El Paso and you will make it back before midnight, trust me." We found little reason to doubt his word as we piled into his sleek sporty car.

Arriving in Hot Springs, we immediately inquired about the starting time of the dance and then proceeded to a nearby saloon. My intuition and new sergeant's stripes kept informing me, "Don't try to keep up with Bud with his consumption of whisky sours." I was still remembering the inadequacy of my drinking ability at Fort Leavenworth. Bud and our newly garnered friend kept the barmaid busy. Eventually, we retreated from the saloon and advanced toward the location of the dance.

Once at the dance hall, there appeared to be ample supply of willing dance partners available. Many of the local men had also gone to war. I never could get the hang of dancing to either popular or country western music. In civilian life, I preferred to roller skate at small skating rinks. Even my fiance once remarked, "You can't even keep time to the beat of honky-tonk dance music!" I was not offended by her remark as it was definitely an accurate assessment of my dancing ability.

Bud and our new companion were enjoying the dancing as well as an occasional drink. I was clock watching and becoming nervously concerned that we might not make it back to Hatch in time to intercept the last bus to El Paso. I made a few futile half-hearted attempts to get the two of them out of the dance hall so we could start on the return journey back to the small town of Hatch. To make matters worse, Bud unearthed time to get into an altercation with a second lieutenant over one of the young ladies attending the dance.

The owner of our transportation staggered over to join in

Ken Lenke Photograph
Bud Pitts (next to auto) and "37531447"
Along the Rio Grande River in New Mexico (1943)

Ken Lenke Photography
Communications Section of Battery D 839th Antiaircraft
Weapons Batallion (1943)

on the fracas. When the lieutenant noticed his notch of inebriation, an invitation was extended by the young officer for both of them to step outside where he would promptly resolve the issue. I had known Bud too long to ever know him not understand any situation in which he found himself to be involved. Our New Mexico friend was definitely crocked, but Bud was just being downright cantankerous.

Vigorously striding toward the huddled group milling at the edge of the dance floor, I calmed the young officer and explained we were leaving. He sagaciously re-negotiated his previous plan of battle. I also convinced Bud it was time to start back to Hatch. The car's owner fumbled around in his clothing and following a drawn-out search – eventually located the correct pocket holding the keys to his expensive vehicle. Bud sat up front with me while our "sidekick" slumped into a supportive corner of the rear seat of his car. Volunteering the chauffeuring duties, I calculated we should make it back to Hatch with possibly an hour to spare.

The narrow two-lane road, leading to Hatch, had some lengthy grades and an extremely narrow center line – usually not too visible. Similar to "Lucky Strike Green" (the green color on the outside of a package of Lucky Strike cigarettes), white striping paint had also "gone to war." Before traversing too many miles, I alarmingly began to notice the water temperature gauge was approaching the red danger zone on the instrument panel. Compounding this unwanted problem, the engine oil gauge was indicating rapid dwindling of presure.

Our host's vehicle was beginning to slow down from acute overheating. I noted another car passing us on one of the steep grades. In the semi-darkness, I observed a door on the auto, now ahead of us, open on the passenger side and the weak headlights on "our" limping vehicle caught the glimpse of what appeared to be – a body being unceremoniously shoved out over the road embankment. The auto then accelerated and sped away. We never stopped to investigate this possible foul play.

Attempting to relate to the car's owner the serious status of his automobile, 37531447 informed him, "This damn thing is in desperate need of engine oil." The chap just waved off the critical piece of information and mumbled, "Keep driving."

With the auto's engine inoperative, we coasted into Hatch approximately a hundred yards shy of the local bus depot. The dense acrid smoke now pouring from the hot tinkling engine compartment, strongly hinted the motor of our new-sprung friend's beautiful automobile was completely "totaled".

We hastily waved good-bye to the lonely figure, still awash and hunched over in the back seat of what, at one time, was a elegant vehicle. It was providential that the bus to return us to El Paso was just arriving. This would be our last trip to Hatch, New Mexico. We always were a little apprehensive we might bump into the owner of the auto. In all fairness to the man from New Mexico, he kept his word. "I will bring you back to Hatch in time to catch the last bus to El Paso…"

Bud and 37531447 had managed to foil the military pass deadline of midnight – once again!

At Logan Heights our communication instructor had befriended a small mutt dog in the tar-papered communication shack. The staff sergeant had named the dog "Meeka" which may well have been the old Spanish word *mico* which means "monkey". The sergeant and his dog would often trek to the Post Exchange together. Our cadre instructor carried the dog under his arm and a small round tin plate in his hand. Each time he purchased a beer, he would pour some of the bottle's contents into the tin plate for Meeka. Bud and I would always have a good chuckle when they returned to the communication shack. Neither the dog nor the sergeant could walk in a straight line.

Whenever the call for breakfast sounded, Meeka would usually lead the charge of soldiers to the correct entrance door of the mess hall. Bud and 37531447 were always close behind. The only time she let us down was the morning we had the rarest of opportunities while in the military – to enjoy fresh eggs cooked-to-order. She led us to the wrong door and to the shameful last place position in the chow line. Later on, Meeka had a litter of pups under the communication shack. This event led to an edict from Major Mumaw to get rid of all the dogs including Meeka. Neither Bud nor I could ever ascertain the final fate of the dogs. We both felt certain the communication sergeant found good homes for them.

The month of December and Christmas day was fast approaching. This would be my first Christmas away from home. Letters arriving from my fiance had slowed significantly and Bud had gone home on furlough. I was feeling very lonely and depressed. I was having deep resentment toward all the circumstances which had positioned me in such an untimely scenario.

Utilizing my pass to visit El Paso Christmas Eve, I observed countless reminders of the Yule season surrounding me. Decorations, holiday music and bell ringers only seemed to make matters worse. Extreme loneliness prompted me to purchase a bottle of gin. Placing the vitreous container securely inside my coat, I made the return trek to my bunk at Logan Heights.

I pondered briefly, wondering if my father would listen to the radio recording of *Silent Night* performed in the German language by the late contralto, Madam Schumann-Heink. He had done this each Christmas Eve for as long as I could remember. It was sort of an annual "rites of passage" for him, remembered by me – but not comprehended.

Depression and homesickness finally got the best of me. The unpropitious decision was made to start on the gin. I was the only one in the building at the time. The last thing I recall about Christmas Eve was the gin bottle about empty and I was puzzling why I hadn't purchased a larger-sized bottle. I impatiently consumed the gin "straight".

My Christmas Eve hiatus must have been ugly. I had not removed my clothing and unknowingly had urinated in them. In addition, I upchucked without knowing much about it. It was remarkably fortunate I had not departed from this world. I sensed a near-death experience.

Sergeant Keane apparently entered the tar-papered shack later that evening. It was Keane, "our father image", who found me, changed my clothes, washed my bedding and cleaned up the mess. I was supposed to be on KP duty on Christmas day, but no way could I do it. I still was one sick guy. Keane pulled my KP duty and later in the day fixed me some hot soup.

Christmas night I was back on the mend. If there are angels on earth, Sergeant Keane was one of them. When I had recovered sufficiently, Keane made known to me, "I suspected Christmas eve was going to be bad for you by the way you were acting." He continued in his fatherly way by telling me, "I am glad you had the good foresight to return to Logan Heights before beginning on the bottle of gin." The kindly sergeant never asked me the reason for my depression, but I expect he knew I had not received mail lately from my fiance and Bud was home on furlough.

Some time after New Year's day and a few more field maneuvers in the cold desert, I was given a long-awaited fourteen day furlough. I knew this would be my last trip home until the war reached its conclusion or I lost my life. The time spent at home was enjoyable, but all too short.

Most of the chronology of the furlough was with my fiance and a lesser amount of time was spent with my parents. I enjoyed being with my fiance and she again urged me to get married. This would be the second time I would say "no" to her. Perhaps I was just scared about responsibilities of becoming married or perchance insight concerning my dilemma was red-flagging me and warning about some unknown future problem.

On departure from Emporia, for return to Fort Bliss, I stood on the open end of the last railroad passenger coach and waved good-bye to my mother and father until we were out of sight of each other. It must have been very difficult for my parents to watch me leave. I suspicioned they had read enough between the lines to understand that I possibly would be participating in active combat duty on some distant war front.

My fiance was not at the railroad station to bid me farewell.

Upon returning to Logan Heights, the battery still participated in occasional field problems, performed more firearm drills and were definitely issued fewer passes. The attitude of the unit seemed to have changed during my absence. Dog Battery was pulling more duty than other units, grounded more often to perform close order drills and food was noticeably not as good.

On one occasion the captain ordered the staff sergeant in charge of the kitchen, who at the moment was occupied flattening food tin cans with an axe, "Put your axe down and report!" The sergeant paused briefly before placing the axe down to give the captain the mess report. The commanding officer may have been somewhat apprehensive about the next usage intent of the makeshift can smasher. The battery chef was a hard working soldier who took much pride in his culinary duties. He was well-liked by the men.

Several days later the first sergeant called an unusual meeting of all noncommissioned officers. His opening remarks were almost as startling as the time of our first battery formation. Using his slow Cajun drawl he tersely stated, "The penalty for mutiny during wartime is, execution by a firing squad."

This unusual verbal narrative received my full and undivided attention! He continued, "The battery commander is not performing his job the way it should be done. Dog battery is being crapped on." He added, "The captain is refusing to listen to any suggestions or complaints." The top kick then inquired, "Are there any noncoms here from PFC ranks to Master Sergeants who would fall out for the next commissioned officers' battery formation if I asked you not to appear for the formation?" To a man, all of the noncoms declared their intent was to remain in their quarters or at other duties at the next called formation.

When the whistle blew to call the formation, not one single non-com appeared, including the first sergeant (this fact was verified by privates who did muster the formation). I thought of the consequences of my action but also remembered my first pass to El Paso the Cajun top kick had presented me.

The communications noncoms met with our cadre leader. The communications sergeant always had a peculiarly unusual mannerism of leaning his head ·back toward his right shoulder whenever he was bored or wanted to make a point. He displayed the "maps" the captain had drawn for our use on maneuvers. The sergeant had saved all of these maps and adamantly declared, "These are not maps – these are cartoons." We viewed them and agreed with our leader's candid assessment. It was the communication sergeant's ability to know how things should work that always put together a brilliant communication setup, not the captain's maps.

The first sergeant was soon called into the captain's command post. I do not know what took place at this meeting. I do know the Cajun top kick won the skirmish of the only United States Army rebellion that I had knowledge of while serving in the military service. The old army first sergeant clearly understood how "things" worked within the military. I surmised the captain did not wish word to leak out to his peers or superiors about his little incident for fear of being relieved from command on the grounds, "unable to control soldiers under command".

There were additional moments of excitement every now and then. One hapless battery soldier was diagnosed at the base hospital as having both gonorrhea and syphilis. At the morning formation the top kick informed the men who the unfortunate soldier was by name and in no uncertain terms, advised us how to avoid this stupid type of health problem.

After the first sergeant completed his remarks, and while still standing formation, the captain made the following caustic remark, "Sergeant, that was poor politics to use that soldier's name in front of the men in this formation." Without a single blink of hesitation the first sergeant fired right back, "Sir, I am a *soldier* not a *politician*." The formation promptly ended.

The captain's remark to the top kick might have been an attempt for the commissioned officer to get back into the good graces of the noncommissioned officers of Dog Battery.

Such was army life in Battery D of the 839th Antiaircraft Battalion. Bud and I continued to kid around about transferring to a paratrooper unit. I treated it as a jest and laughed off the absurd flight of fancy.

There most likely comes a time, based upon how ornery the men of any military unit become, that foretells when a unit is ready for combat duty. My percipient intuition suggested time was rather close at hand for Dog Battery and the entire battalion.

One Monday morning while it was still dark, Bud and I hurried over to the communications shack to check on the radios. What we discovered was quite a surprise to us. The communication sergeant, the only person usually sleeping in the communications shack, had passed out in his bed from the effects of libations and a night of partying. On the floor was a mostly naked Hispanic woman holding onto the sergeant's hand and repeating continuously, "Jeemy, I love you." The only problem with these beautiful sounding words of endearment would be that the fully dressed sergeant was incapable of hearing them.

Also on the floor was a soldier not familiar to us. He was taking advantage of the woman's body. The unfamiliar soldier most likely was a friend of the communication sergeant from the Panama days. In twenty minutes or so, a formation would be called. Bud took charge of this serious and – somewhat comical situation. The woman was obviously quite frightened and quickly responded to urgent instructions. She rapidly dressed into the basic essential undergarments. Borrowing the cadre sergeant's heavy wool overcoat and fatigue hat, we hastily shrouded the woman with these ill-fitting military garments. She carried the remainder of her clothing and purse under her arms.

Bud somehow managed to "shoplift" the Dodge carryall, sans tarp, from the motor pool. We propped the woman firmly in the middle space between the two bucket type seats of the military vehicle. With the aura of unmistakable authority, Bud began driving on some alternate routes while I officiously saluted all commissioned officers encountered on the journey to the main gate area. It was the location where civilian workers enter and

Ken Lenke Photograph
Communication shack on the left and 37531447's "home" on the right. Cobb seated on bed, Com Sergeant seated on steps and Al Gempler standing in doorway. Logan Heights at Fort Bliss, Texas

Ken Lenke Photograph
"37531447" On pass at Hot Springs, New Mexico. "Out of Uniform" wearing a
WAC hat and purse

leave the base. Much to the surprise of those waiting for bus transportation into El Paso, we unloaded our human cargo, reclaimed our *guest's* temporary overcoat and hat and forthwith vanished with the truck.

During our absence, the cadre sergeant's male crony had departed. At the formation beginning to take place, we informed the top kick the com sergeant was not feeling well. Everything worked out to perfection. We were rapidly learning the art of how to cover for each other within the "system".

Once again we found ourselves performing field problems in the New Mexico portion of Fort Bliss. Our position maps were decidedly more skillfully drawn, the captain was performing a professional job of leadership and harmony slowly returned to Dog Battery. On the following field exercise among the numerous boondocks of New Mexico, I was by myself and engaged in splicing a broken communication wire leading to the command post of Dog Battery. Without notice, a jeep appeared from out of nowhere. Glancing at the vehicle I noticed it was displaying an emblem having one or more stars. After observing at least one star any additional stars were not relevant. Stars indicated a general was in the vehicle.

The general motioned me over. He then enquired, "Sergeant, where is the command post for Battery D?" We had been informed earlier our position would be infiltrated by "enemy" soldiers to check out our security. Fearing this was an attempt to breach security I replied, "I don't know where it is, Sir." Following several more fruitless exchanges regarding the location of the CP, the general lost his patience. Shouting loudly he exclaimed, "I am General _____ (no name remembered) and soldier – I am ordering you to tell me the location of the Battery D command post!" Definitely deciding not to push my luck, I carefully directed him to the CP some 150 yards distant. Once there, the general reprimanded the battery captain for not having the command post adequately camouflaged! I remained judiciously silent as to how the general located the CP.

Our communication sergeant had been instructed to inform us to use the phone lines only for important conversation and to tell the men to refrain from using so many expletives while utilizing the field telephones. At our regular briefing, the communication sergeant relayed the request and petitioned us to use restraint when choosing words for the artillery telephone network. A soldier, coming from the Brooklyn Borough of New York City, decided to pick up the field phone and listen to the "traffic". We all took turns listening to find out what was taking place. This type of activity was similar to the old party line telephones in rural areas of the United States.

When the soldier from Brooklyn started to listen in on the network, he apparently heard profanity still being used. The Brooklynite came unglued. He pressed the butterfly switch on the hand set while shouting into the EE8A military telephone, "Hey uze goddamn guys, quit your goddamn swearing on 'deeze' fuckin' phones! You ain't supposed to be 'uzin' 'dat' fuckin' talk."

Our fearless leader, upon hearing this outburst from the newest member of the communication section, looked directly at the soldier and scornfully inquired, "P-r-i-v-a-t-e, what are you doing?" Assuming the body language of a snitch waiting to be rewarded with praise from the sergeant, the private triumphantly replied, "After 'uze' told 'doze' guys to stop 'dare' fuckin' cussin' on 'duh' telephone 'netwoik', they were doing just 'dat'…and I told 'em not to do 'dat' 'kinda' shit no more!"

With much disbelief of what he had just heard, the sergeant cocked his head toward the right shoulder, looked directly at the private and through his piercing blue eyes sarcastically replied, "And private, just what kind of language did you use to tell them they should not use profanity?" There was a period of silence as the com sergeant walked slowly away shaking his head, leaving the soldier from Brooklyn standing in total disarray, wondering what in hell he had done wrong.

On the same field exercise, Bud and I also had a small crisis. The desert weather had turned quite cold. Our radio setup was in a five man pyramid tent having a small heating stove. Before going to the breakfast chow line, we gathered some greasewood (creosote bush) and tossed it into the stove to help keep the tent warm during our absence. Upon our return to the canvas shelter we noticed many holes burned through the top of the squad tent from falling glowing embers. Considerable conversation took place among the commissioned officers deciding if the two of us should be required to pay for the tent from our $50.00 a month salary. We both considered we would have to do our own laundry for quite some time. We most certainly would not have enough money left to pay for having it done at the fort laundry. Fortunately for both of us, the incident was analyzed by the battery officers as an "unfortunate accident". Perhaps the decision was another effort by the captain to indicate to battery personnel he was doing a superb job of commanding – the way it should be done. Bud and I were elated with his final decision.

Several weeks later I was assigned to take the radios to a distant remote area in order to calibrate their frequencies and report via radio all aircraft flying toward El Paso. The antiaircraft artillery back at Fort Bliss could practice at the make believe effort to shoot them down. We were given a vehicle and a GI trailer. A new soldier to our communication section did the driving. It was to be a three-night mission in the cold New Mexico desert. 37531447 would enjoy the solitude of the lonely remote location.

He would soon be on the receiving end of still another completely unexpected surprise!

Postscript

In 1950 the name of Hot Springs, New Mexico was changed to the name of Truth or Consequences. Ralph Edwards, MC of the *Truth or Consequences* network television show, had told a nationwide media audience, "If any town in the United States will rename their town 'Truth or Consequences', I will come to that town once each year and produce my television show." He apparently kept his word and produced the TV show once a year (until the quiz show was terminated) in Truth or Consequences, New Mexico.

The once small laid-back town of Hot Springs where Bud and I visited during our period of basic training while at Fort Bliss and now called "Truth or Consequences", is officially listed (1995) as having a population of 11,000 people.

****

If it appears strange to the reader that we would open the windows of our hotel room, one must remember the air conditioning process

65

was still in an infancy stage of development and most places did not have this convenience at the time.

****

The communication cadre sergeant's dog "Meeka" was a bitch. She would be given the Spanish feminine gender name of *mica* The letter "i" is pronounced in Spanish like the English letter "e" as in the word "eat". The cadre sergeant most likely had been in Panama long enough to have acquired a good knowledge of both Spanish and monkeys.

****

I often wonder if Captain Hansen had some type of domestic problem to deal with in addition to his military duties. This might account for his short period of unusual behavior. He was a human being just like all the rest of us and he could well have had an extra burden to carry which we knew nothing about. Whatever the problem might have been, he handled the ordeal. This is not only the trait of a good man – it also is a mark of a good commissioned officer in The United States Army.

****

It was customary for "old army" noncoms to keep written communications passed to them by commissioned officers. It was a way of "keeping their 'butts' covered". The communication sergeant was "old army" and had saved all of the captain's field exercise maps.

****

Perhaps another reason for the anxiety of my mother and father while home on furlough was due to the fact that they had two sons wearing the military uniform of the United States Army. My brother, Ralph, also served in Europe with the United States Army and the 94th Signal Battalion attached to General George Patton's 3rd Army.

****

I can recall my father, who was a railroad engineer employed by the Atchison, Topeka and Santa Fe Railroad, telling me (on the only furlough home during the conflict) he thought he recognized me on one of the many troop trains that he pulled during the war. He related to me his great disappointment when he walked over to see me – only to realize it was some other young soldier and not his son.

My railroad engineer father was responsible for safely transporting many military units, military equipment and countless freight cars loaded with dangerous munitions during the long period of warfare. Three other brothers also worked for the Santa Fe Railroad system during the war. Stewart was a clerk. Howard was the head brakeman on freight trains.

Another brother, Don, operated a switch engine in the Emporia, Kansas railroad yards. On one occasion during the war he switched a troop train coming from Fort Riley, Kansas, utilizing the Missouri, Kansas and Texas Line – to the Atchison, Topeka and Santa Fe Line – where it was picked up and sent on its destination by a steam engine operated by my father. Sabotage of tracks and rolling equipment by enemy forces was always a realistic possibility.

****

In 1996 I asked my older brother, Milton, about Madam Schumann-Heink. He told me that the old Uptown Theater in Strong City, (population of less than 1,000) Kansas, was designed as an opera house and was simply called "The Auditorium". The limestone Auditorium with mahogany and oak opera chairs, a piano with all the latest attachments and the building designed for outstanding acoustics was dedicated on April 19 and 20 of April, 1901. On the night of the 20th, Marshalls Band played music ranging from the descriptive conglomeration *Nigger in the Barn Yard* to *Grand Selection from '11 Trovatore* by Verdi.

Madam Schumann-Heink actually performed on the stage in the Auditorium as well as John Philip Sousa's band. My father most likely attended Schumann-Heink's performance in the building. He had to be careful not to tell anyone about listening to her sing

67

(recorded) the Christmas song *Silent Night* in the German language during the war because of his German ancestry.

****

It was rumored at Fort Bliss that Major Mumaw was married to one of the Schlitz girls of the brewing company. I am not certain if the scuttlebutt was true; however, in 1995, the only still actively flying World War II Liberator bomber visited the Scottsdale (Arizona) Airport. Painted on the outside of the huge plane were the names of other WW II Liberator bombers. One was named *Pistol Packin' Mama* and another was given the name of *Paper Doll.*

Gazing at the nose section of the bomber, I observed a painted sexy appearing portrait of a beautiful young woman and the logo of the "Schlitz Brewery". I thought it to be a significant coincidence!

Chapter Six

A Change in Military Assignment

The highest type of friendship is the relation of
"brother-friend" or "life-and-death" friend. This bond
is between man and man; it is usually formed in early
youth, and can only be broken by death.
—Ohiyesa (Charles Alexander Eastman)

The unexpected distant sound of an approaching military vehicle caught my ear. I was currently positioned somewhere in the desert region of southern New Mexico in the general vicinity of El Paso, Texas. As the olive-drab truck arbitrated its way around the chaparral-covered boondocks of the area, I was able to recognize the beaming face of my communications partner, R.A. "Bud" Pitts.

Both of us were in the eleventh month of military training with "Dog" Battery of the 839th Coast Artillery Battalion stationed at Fort Bliss, Texas. Through the seemingly endless months of basic and advanced training, Bud and I had become good friends. Together, we had learned Morse code, how to calibrate radios, establish telephone networks requiring miles of field wire, how to throw live hand grenades, and shoot a variety of weapons from .45-caliber pistols to .50-caliber machine guns. We had even experienced nighttime infiltration exercises where we were graphically taught with live ammunition – the importance of keeping our heads and butts close to the ground.

On the lighter side of army life at Fort Bliss, Bud and I mastered how to cross the border into old Mexico to visit Juarez, steer clear of the places of ill repute, consume whiskey sours, order large steaks at Mexican eateries – questioning if they came from animals meeting their fate at the nearby circular arena devoted to bull fighting. Perhaps the most important skill, we leaned how to cross the maze of border check points guiding us back into the United States and to the tar-paper-covered shacks of Logan Heights that we called our domicile.

I was greatly surprised to eye the four-wheel drive weapons carrier since another day of assignment duty was required before returning to Fort Bliss. As the military vehicle approached closer, I wondered what breed of message my grinning colleague was bringing. Noticing his broad cheerful smile, 37531447 reasoned his distinguished friend was undoubtedly bringing some genus of gratifying intelligence.

When the truck finally came to a halt, I greeted my familiar friend and inquired, "What in the hell are you doing out in the damned alien place by yourself?" Bud appeared to be "bursting at the seams" to enlighten me about the nature of the unforeseen visit. He jubilantly replied, "You and I are being transferred out of the Coast Artillery." Before having an opportunity to voice anything, he continued his version of the "town crier" by further elucidating, "I *forged* your signature and army serial number on the transfer papers!" My Wyoming friend consummated his recitation by triumphantly proclaiming, "Now we can get out of Texas!"

Vaguely recalling our previous conversation on the topic of "How to get out of Texas" during a session of consuming whiskey sours in a side-street bar in Juarez, Mexico, I didn't figure Bud was all that serious about wanting to get out of the State of Texas. I had realistic reasons doubting if "old R.A." would even remember the absurd "whiskey talk" conversation which took place in the small dingy smoke-filled Juarez "grogshop".

I rationalized this was now the moment to ask my trustworthy and faithful "old" comrade from Dog Battery, at least one pertinent question – one beaming a ray of light on this newly-sprung bit of information currently providing me with a few bad "vibes". With a degree of heightened misgivings and equally fearful of even wanting to hear his reply, I dared to ask, "Bud,…transferred to what?" My esteemed "friend", still wearing the trademark version of his wide grin, proudly proclaimed, *"To a combat infantry division!"*

37531447 immediately sucked in an extremely long deep breath of fresh New Mexico air and briefly speculated if he should still consider the Wyomingite as a friend, the enemy, or even an acquaintance. This bit of new and distressful information did have its good side. At least my "sidekick" didn't forge any papers with my name and serial number for joining the paratroops.

With adrenaline fully aroused, I commenced flowing over thoughts of a new military adventure in some other place – out of

Texas. Leaving my mission co-worker still in charge of our assignment, I tossed my military gear between the two front bucket seats and crawled up into the spot usually reserved for Captain Hansen. We immediately headed back in the direction of Fort Bliss.

Arriving at Logan Heights both of us busied ourselves by packing all gear not necessary for the train trip to our unknown destination in our duffels and dropped them off at a predesignated area to be loaded separately. To my dismay, there appeared to be quite a large number of duffel bags being shipped. Most of the pile appeared to be from members of Dog Battery. Many of the departing soldiers were from our original noncom cadre that had been stationed in Panama. The top kick and our communication sergeant were not among those departing Dog Battery.

Everyone leaving Logan Heights and the antiaircraft battalion was granted pass privileges for both El Paso and Ciudad Juarez. Bud and I opted to visit the border city of Juarez. My friend soon was engaged in a marathon contest with whiskey sours and in the process – the drinks would prove to be the winner. I had a feeling one of us should be sober enough to safely navigate our return through the border check points and back into the United States. I recruited myself for this responsibility.

Bud was in an argumentative "gear". He felt as if our Mexican bartender had been – once again – "watering down" his whiskey sours. This turn of events indicated it was time to exit the lonely bar and begin our return trek to the relative safety of the United States side of the border. Successful with the return to El Paso, I "accompanied" Bud to the bus station to await transportation back to Logan Heights.

Considerable time remained before the mandatory hour of return to camp, We both stayed in the bus terminal until my Wyoming friend had an increased perception of his whereabouts.

At one point a major from a military police unit approached and asked, "Sergeant, what is the difficulty with that soldier?" He was nodding his head in Bud's direction. I replied to the officer, "Sir, we have just returned from Juarez and my friend had a little too much to drink." I quickly added, "Sir, I will make certain he returns to camp without any problem." The major replied, "O.K. soldier. I'm glad to see you taking care of your buddy." The major, seemingly immersed

71

in a much larger problem, abruptly turned around and hurriedly walked away.

Bud was never much of a behavior problem when drinking. During his rare times of excessive indulgence he was always able to wear an unusually peaceful and impish smile on his countenance.

I soon would discover the reason the military police major was walking a tour of duty. Most of Dog Battery's old army cadre had participated in a rather raucous celebration in El Paso. They might have believed they were back in the jungles of Panama. The military police had contacted our battery commander about his band of hunnish revellers.

It is not certain how the old cadre of "urban warriors" got back to Logan Heights. They most likely were escorted by the MP's. I'm confident Captain Hansen was awaiting their arrival back in camp. All of the errant soldiers were somewhat corralled and promptly reduced to the rank of Privates. The captain ordered rank chevrons to be removed from the uniforms of the "new privates". Many of the former cadre noncoms did not wait for their stripes to be neatly cut from the uniforms by battery commissioned officers and the first sergeant. Instead, the old army soldiers aggressively opted to remove them. During their zeal to dislodge the rank stripes, some of the shirt sleeves would become badly shredded or completely "amputated". Spare uniforms had already been sent ahead in the duffel bags.

This tacky-appearing group would shortly be boarding a Texas and Pacific Railroad Line military troop train that would transport the former antiaircraft soldiers to an undisclosed destination.

Bud and I arrived back in camp shortly before curfew. The commanding officer did not find any reason to bust us. We resembled two angelic Sunday-school kids just returning from church services. We walked in without weaving or staggering, our army uniforms were in neat order, and perhaps of most importance – not being escorted by military police.

We definitely would miss the battery's commissioned officers as well as the first sergeant and the communications staff sergeant. Captain Hansen had taken a genuine liking to both Bud and me. The captain's leadership was professional and he had become an outstanding commanding officer for the antiaircraft artillery battery.

Those departing Fort Bliss, soon found themselves aboard a troop train. We were informed our group would be on the train for at least two and a half days. Sergeant Pitts and I felt confident we had witnessed the last of the Lone Star State for the duration of our military service. Soldiers demoted by Captain Hansen would "memorialize" this important event with continuous consumption of "liquid refreshments" until reaching our appointed destination.

Instead of using Pullman Company sleeping coaches, we were using a relatively new type of railroad coach called a "GI Sleeper". This type of "coach", not much larger than a common railroad boxcar, could accommodate up to thirty-nine persons sleeping in three-tier bunks. During the daytime the upper two bunks could be folded back and bottom bunks became park-bench type of seats.

We continued the rendezvous toward our unknown distant destination. Additional troop cars were attached to the train. Troops utilizing these cars came from other military bases along the route.

When the train stopped at San Antonio, a railroad trainman informed me the mid-morning stopover would be for two hours. I intentionally left the train in an attempt to find an "Army" store. Most large cities near military installations had such emporiums. If the outlet could be located I could procure some new shirts to replace some of the severely decimated clothing for the sleeveless unfortunates who had been demoted at Logan Heights.

Successfully locating the army clothing store, I purchased what few shirts possible with my limited funds and returned with the precious bundle of clothing to the location of the troop train. I became very alarmed and was in a state of near panic when observing only empty tracks where the troop train should have been. I was now either an unwilling deserter or absent without leave. Either way, it seemed apparent I would eventually wind up as a prisoner in some damned army stockade.

I hastily queried a nearby railroad worker as to what had happened to the troop train. I was very certain my return was well within the two hour period of time for the stopover. Tensions were partially relieved when the workman informed me, "Your train was switched from the Texas Pacific Depot to another depot in San Antonio." I thanked him for the information and hailed a nearby taxicab.

Pleading with the driver of the taxi, "Would you take me to the other San Antonio railroad depot so I can catch my troop train?" I am quite certain the cab driver was noticing my stressful sense of urgency. Even after informing him I didn't have much money, he replied, "Hop in soldier." He added with a chuckle, "I think I know where you need to be."

Arriving at the other depot location, I was thoroughly relieved to observe the waiting troop train. Pulling out what little change still in my possession, it was offered to the cab driver. He laughingly informed, "Soldier, the taxi ride is on me." I quickly expressed my gratitude to the cabby, dashed toward the train and climbed aboard just moments before its departure.

Handing out what new clothing had been purchased was a pleasant event. Even if the number of shirts fell far short of supplying all of the "impoverished". My effort was rewarded with a well-needed toddy from the continuously celebrating group of old army soldiers.

We finally reached our final destination in the wee morning hours. I sort of remember army trucks poised to transport us to our new military base. I definitely remember recalling some one dressed in an officer's uniform declaring, "Welcome to the 103rd Infantry Division of the United States Army and to Camp Howze, Texas." In total disbelief I turned toward Bud and whispered, "Shit. We're still in T-e-x-a-s!" It may have been one of the rare moments when Bud did not have a grin on his face.

The officer continued his "welcoming" discourse by informing our assemblage, "You are – beyond any doubt – the sorriest appearing group of soldiers I have ever observed in my entire lengthy time as a career army officer!" We did appear rather ragged. Our formation was not too straight or steady in any direction but at least we were all standing. This cutting assessment of the officer's newly arriving "combat" group of men for the 103rd Infantry Division was unconditionally justifiable.

Bud later informed me Captain Hansen had told him, "I am sorry to see both you and Sergeant (37531447) leave the antiaircraft battery. It will be a difficult task to find replacements as dedicated with unit responsibilities as you two have been.

****

According to information received from Mr. Roy Pickering, Director of Libraries for the San Diego Railroad Museum, San Diego, California, troop movement by rail was secret and highly confidential.

"All railroad personnel were to give troop trains special attention! Movement of troops were confidential and no information should be given out pertaining to same. The train personnel handling should understand that they should not discuss the train's movement with any person."

The cost to the government for berth space (each night) was:

> tourist – lower berth $10.25; upper berth, $7.85
> standard – lower berth $15.35; upper berth, $11.70
> three-tier bunks (G.I. Sleeper) - $6.05

Pullman porters (predominantly, if not all, were black men) were to be allowed four hours sleep period the first night. Conductors were given four hours of sleep the first night and six hours each night thereafter. The Pullman Company handled all of the details of the troop movement.

A typical troop train might have one baggage car, two troop kitchen cars, thirteen tourist cars, and one standard car (I surmise the standard car was used by ranking officers since the berth rates were highest in cost!). One notation on the troop train orders from the Pullman Company stated: "Car 'Courland' is in standard service. See to it that first class service (is) rendered." Rank had its privileges!

****

It was not unusual for troop trains to be turned over to a series of different railroad lines during lengthy distances of wartime troop movements. For example, a troop train leaving Camp Carson, Colorado, having the ultimate destination of Camp Kilmer, New Jersey, could be routed on the Atchison, Topeka and Santa Fe Railroad to Denver; the Chicago, Burlington and Quincy Railroad to Chicago; The Erie Railroad to Waverly and the Leheigh Valley Railroad to the destination of Camp Kilmer. I have no idea to what Railroad Line we were turned over to when in San Antonio.

****

Texas is indeed an extremely large state. Traveling on the troop train for the two and a half days and still remaining in Texas proves the point. It was even more ironical to find out we would be in a military camp named in honor of a former commanding officer of Fort Bliss – Major General Robert L. Howze.

****

The beginning chapter six and chapter eight quotes are excerpted from THE *SOUL OF AN INDIAN*, edited by Kent Nerburn © 1993. Reprinted with permission of New World Library, Novato, CA 94949, www.nwlib.com

Prologue (Chapter 7)

The following is a true story about men coming from differing walks of life and from all parts of the United States. They came to form a new infantry division. Some were professional soldiers, others were enlistees and the remainder were draftees.

There were occasions when this human melting pot brought about open conflicts among the soldiers. This was the situation for one infantry company that was part of the 103rd Infantry Division of the United States Army in World War II.

The 103rd Division was eventually sent to the European Theatre of Operations for combat duty. On November 11, the old Armistice Day, the division engaged the real enemy near St. Die, France. From here to the end of the war in Europe, these soldiers, who had trained in the swamps of Louisiana, the prairies of North Texas and the desert regions of West Texas and New Mexico – would become mountain men.

They would fight from the Vosges mountains of France to the towering Alpine mountain passes between Austria and Italy, where the conflict in Europe finally came to conclusion for this United States infantry division.

Chapter Seven

Camp Howze, Texas

The heart has its reasons which reason knows nothing of.
—Blaise Pascal

The 59,850 acre (93.5 square miles) military infantry training facility was named Camp Howze in honor of Major General Robert L. Howze, Indian fighter and former commander of The Fort Bliss military facility (1919-1925). The camp utilized training sites close to Lake Murray, Honey Grove, Decatur and in the vicinity of the Red River of the South – a natural boundary separating the states of Texas and Oklahoma. Camp Howze was located in North Texas near the small community of Gainesville, and not too distant from the larger cities of Dallas and Fort Worth, Texas.

In addition to the arrival of new members from existing military training sites to fill the 103rd Infantry Division's numerical quota, a fairly large group of men came from colleges or universities where they were attending Army Specialized Training Programs (ASTP).

37531447 was rapidly processed and assigned to a platoon of a heavy weapons (.30-calber machine guns and mortars) infantry company and taken to the platoon barracks. Russell Pitts was placed with a rifle unit, Company G of the 409th Infantry Regiment. It would be the first time the two soldier buddies had been assigned different military units during their military training.

At Camp Howze, a soldier from the infantry command post accompanied me to my new quarters located in the platoon's barracks. Not observing any other soldiers inside the long wooden-framed structure, I inquisitively asked my pathfinder, "Where is the rest of the platoon?" He officiously replied, "They are on maneuvers near the Red River along the Texas-Oklahoma border." He hastily added as he departed, "They should be returning before daybreak."

Chosing a vacant lower bunk at the far end of the building,

ASN 37531447 at Camp Howze, Texas (1944)

Plattoon Barracks at Camp Howze, Texas (1944)

relatively close to the "john", I proceeded to make myself comfortable in my new quarters. I considered myself extremely fortuitous to have the entire barracks to myself for a pleasant night of well-needed rest.

Almost asleep, I was startled by the creaking barracks door slowly being opened. Someone carrying a flashlight appeared to be purposely searching each bunk area. The continuously probing beam of light eventually focused on my bunk and halted any further movement. In a fatherly tone of voice, a soft-spoken soldier introduced himself, "I'm the platoon sergeant from the next barracks over." The soldier than admonished, "If I were you, I would not stay in this building tonight." He continued, "You may sleep in my platoon barracks located adjacent to this building – if you wish."

This strange invitation didn't make much sense to me. All I really desired was to be left along to enjoy a quiet restful night of peaceful sleep. I politely replied, "Thank you sergeant for your concern. I know I will be just fine here." The platoon leader then counseled, "Be careful. I hope you will have a good night of rest."

After the uninvited soldier departed from the building I began to speculate about this rather unusual invitation to spend the night in the neighboring barracks. Was this quiet speaking serviceman privy to knowledge about a situation which could place an innocent neophyte to the infantry platoon in some type of jeopardy? Perhaps there was some other explanation for the sergeant's extraordinary adjuration. I soon dismissed a series of speculative scenarios from my thought processing machinery and my tired body finally succumbed to slumber.

Close to the hour of midnight, I once again was awakened by the sound of the building's screaking door. With all the oil in Texas, I silently questioned, "Why in the hell hasn't somebody someone oiled the fuckin' door?" A small contingent of soldiers, three or possibly four, entered and without shilly-shallying, walked the full length of almost completely darkened structure. They halted at the bunk area of the barrack's absent platoon leader. His bunk was next to the end wall of the building's sleeping quarters. It finally occurred to me that something interesting was about to unfold.

Much similar to the actions of a well-trained medical team of skilled surgeons, the intruders immediately commenced to "operate". The dress uniforms of the absent platoon leader were swiftly dissected

– freed from staff sergeant's stripes, buttons and decorations. Many stitches would be required to mend the uniforms. Mess gear was drastically "restructured", shower shoes firmly "sutured" to the wooden floor with nails and a hammer brought by the "medical team". The platoon leader's foot locker was not neglected and soon became the object of primitive experimental exploratory "surgery".

I became considerably more attentive when one of the "surgeons" took the sergeant's spare trench-knife in hand, raised it high over his head, and with an arc of sudden swiftness and power, drove the sharp pointed weapon downward against the wall where a photograph of the "patient" was positioned. The location the knife entered the likeness of the platoon sergeant suggested the patient wasn't likely to survive the operation.

The group silently departed as suddenly as they had entered. My curiosity finally got the best of me as I cautiously slid out of my bunk for a closer inspection of the "operating room". I discovered the knife had been driven not only through a photograph of the absent sergeant, but the point of the sharp steel blade went completely through the wall partition and protruded into the toilet and shower room on the opposite side of the wall. I was rapidly forming the impression that this particular platoon sergeant may not be a very well-like individual. I also began rethinking the wisdom of my choice to sleep in the building for the duration of the night. It was, however, far into the night and I decided to stay. Perhaps the few remaining hours of darkness would be uneventful and peaceful repose would come at last.

Approximately an hour later the building's squeaking door announced another intrusion. In lumbered the shadowy hulk of a huge broad-shouldered soldier. His over-sized arms made him appear even larger. His legs appeared to be too short to balance his seemingly top-heavy upper body. He shuffled past my bunk and continued walking to the end of the barracks. I now realized this mammoth soldier was the "leaseholder" of the space that had been so methodically trashed. I didn't have the slightest clue how the gigantic man would react to the surprise "how-do-you-do" currently awaiting him.

With pulse rate rapidly accelerating, I mentally began making my escape plan from the building if danger appeared to be eminent. I earlier had recalled observing a big heavy iron poker by the large pot-bellied coal stove located close by. Perhaps I could use this object as a defensive weapon if need be. I firmly held my ground and continued to observe and assess this intriguing volatile situation.

To my complete astonishment – no words were audibly spoken by the sergeant as he scanned the damage and no sign of visible anger was detected. Adding to my further amazement, this huge man dropped down on both knees at bedside and in childlike fashion appeared to be praying. He spoke so softly I was unable to hear the words of his prayer. Completing his invocation, he removed his work uniform and fell fast asleep on what little remained of his bed.

My thoughts returned to the staff sergeant next door who had offered me safe haven. Perhaps he really didn't know this seemingly spiritual individual lying so quietly on his bunk. Perchance this wronged man had asked in his prayer for God to forgive the perpetrators for their odious deed.

Shortly thereafter, the remainder of the platoon returned from the maneuvers along the Red River and entered the building. I gave up on any thoughts for a quiet night of sleep.

The next sonance was the shrill bugle call *Reveille*. Everyone got dressed and proceeded to gather for the morning call to formation for the company commander's report.

When the moment arrived for my platoon's report, the captain called on the mountainous platoon staff sergeant. Double-timing, the sergeant strode forward, faced the captain and presented the customary salute which was acknowledged by the commanding officer. At this point the platoon leader did not give the customary, "Sir, all present or accounted for!" Instead he shifted his large frame to face the men of the heavy weapon company. I was absolutely dumbfounded at the words the platoon sergeant voiced:

"Last night when I returned from maneuvers and discovered what had happened to my personal property, I got down on my knees at bunkside and prayed to God about those soldiers who have already departed this camp and are to be replacements for infantry units fighting German soldiers."

With tears rampantly overflowing the sides of his face, he continued, "I prayed, with all my heart, to God that a German U-Boat (submarine) would intercept the troop ship they will be travelling on and – send it to the bottom of the ocean!"

I could hardly believe the words the huge man had just uttered. He had informed us about his prayer to God, beseeching divine help, to sink an entire troop ship with possibly thousands of other United States soldiers and sailors aboard. The purpose of the prayer was to allow the platoon sergeant the satisfaction of knowing those few men aboard, who had earlier vented their anger against him, would lose their lives and the sergeant would thereby have the gratifying satisfaction of a crowing personal revenge.

The infantry company was quickly dismissed from the formation noticeably absent of any comments from the company commander.

In the following days of infantry training I became more familiar with the platoon sergeant. I witnessed him use his size to intimidate others and began to have a better understanding why he wasn't particularly well-liked by the men in the platoon. The very fact he had the large photograph of himself taken in a San Antonio boxing ring mounted to the barrack's wall was an indication of premeditated intimidation.

I have to confess the staff sergeant was knowledgeable about platoon weaponry. I recall the platoon leader teaching us how to field-strip the water-cooled .30-caliber machine gun. With eyes blindfolded he could field strip the weapon and put it back together in record time.

On one particular occasion, the drill mission for the day was to use live ammunition and shoot at a radio controlled aircraft. In theory, if the drone aircraft were disabled by a bullet, a parachute would automatically gently lower the damaged plane to the earth for repairs.

My turn to use the weapon finally arrived. I had never fired the browning machine gun before, and I wasn't very confident about my ability to fire a weapon unfamiliar to me. Observing others ahead of me firing the machine gun, I was aware of a knob which had to be pulled back in order to place the first round inside the firing chamber. I wasn't certain how far the knob had to be pulled back to complete this necessary operation.

Evidently I must not have pulled the pertruding knob back far enough and damn thing jammed.

The herculean platoon leader grasped me up by the collar of my fatigue shirt and the seat of my pants and tossed all 130 pounds of me some twenty feet or so to the rear and in a rage shouted, "Get someone up here that knows how to use this gun!"

To be absolutely fair to the gunnery sergeant, I must mention that after others had their turn shooting at the drone aircraft, he came back to where I was now standing and proclaimed, "I'm going to show you how to use the Browning." After previously tossing me the seemingly long distance to the rear, he certainly had my complete attention. I felt as if everyone participating in the gunnery exercise now had their eyes glued on just the two of us. Perhaps it brought back their memories of the Biblical episode of *David and Golieth.*

While growing up I often had the opportunity to shoot at ducks and geese flying over the many cattle watering ponds in the Flint Hills. I knew you had to lead the rapidly flying birds. In this instance it appeared to me it was cheating to use tracer bullets to "guide" other bullets from the machine gun toward the direction of the flying drone aircraft.

Following the platoon sergeant's instruction, came the crucial moment to shoot at the approaching target plane. I am not certain if I was still annoyed at the sergeant, the Browning machine gun that had previously jammed or – the situation in which I had been placed. Perhaps I was angry over all three of the possible reasons.

Carefully squeezing the trigger of the rapid-fire weapon, it responded by sending an unusually long burst of bullets ripping into the intended target. As it was falling from the sky I placed another lengthy burst of bullets into the midget-sized aircraft making certain I had "killed" the damn thing.

Unfortunately, the parachute failed to open, and the craft was completely demolished when it made contact with the Texas soil. When hearing the authoritarian voice from an observer remark, "There goes twenty-five grand of taxpayer money shot all to hell", I thought for certain I was once again in deep trouble. To my bewilderment and complete surprise, the platoon leader began jumping up and down and hollering like a hysterical crazed person. At the same instance, he was "praising" me by bestowing numerous hefty sledge-hammer-like blows on my back. It was nice to see the son-of-bitch so fuckin' pleased.

My only other run-in with this noncommissioned officer occurred during a platoon "touch" football game. I had played quarterback on my high school football team and was small in size, but fast. The mammoth platoon leader was on the opposing team and definitely liked to carry the football. He became quite incensed with me because I could always catch him.

The size difference between the two of us finally got to his ego. When this seemingly top-heavy man hit the turf, not so much from my touch on his back but from his lack of balance, he became infuriated with me. The sergeant picked me up over his head and body-slammed me to the North Texas ground. It hurt so badly I struggled to hold back the tears, but I would be damned if I would give him the satisfaction of knowing he had painfully bruised me. All of the players intentionally walked off of the field after this incident leaving the big platoon sergeant all alone – to play with himself. 37531447 now had an understanding of why the previous group of soldiers trashed his belongings during the first night's stay in the barracks.

In the few weeks I trained with the heavy weapons infantry company, I discovered a rather unique way of avoiding additional confrontations with him. During some of our training forced marches, while balancing the tripod mount for the .30-caliber machine gun on my shoulders with one hand, I would take out my little Hohner (Tm) harmonica and play the old Bob Wills country tune, *San Antonio Rose*. The sergeant, upon hearing me play this popular song of the era, would predictably chime in with a fairly accurate imitation of a Bob Wills, "Aha Ha!". The tune apparently brought out the sergeant's Texas heritage pride as well as a big grin on his face. Texans enjoyed their country music.

During one these training marches I came to the conclusion those trashing the sergeant's belongings were most likely not from my platoon. I never had proof of this theory; however, I often observed the obvious open friction between the sergeant and other platoon leaders from the heavy weapons infantry company. I developed a highly confident opinion those perpetrating the deed that first night, most likely came from the platoon of the soft-spoken sergeant who advised me to sleep in his barracks.

One of the more interesting learning experiences was my introduction and training on a troop glider known in military lingo as a WACO CG4A Cargo Glider. The glider could carry close to sixteen soldiers including the pilot. The craft was ugly-looking in design but appeared to be air worthy.

Division troops were not taking turns by military units and I was pleasantly surprised to observe the smiling face of Bud Pitts. We would be in the same glider for the training.

Once inside the craft, the interior gave me a correct assessment that this training flight would take place on a very "low budget airline". The instrument panel appeared only slightly more complex than the 1930 Model-A Ford sports coupe that I had learned to drive while attending high school. The craft's green-tinted aircraft aluminum tubing was covered with coated fabric. Some of the interior structure was made with plywood. The glider was equipped with wheels and a tow hook on the front end.

Following the given instructions on how to use our primary parachute and the back-up emergency chute, we boarded the craft. Where I was seated I could gaze through the glider's windshield as well as observe the glider pilot. A large long nylon rope was fastened to the tow hook on the upper nose area of the glider. The opposite end of the rope was fastened to a C-46 twin-engine prop plane.

I was fascinated by the lift-off procedure. The glider remained motionless as the twin-engine plane lumbered down the runway and almost became airborne. The nylon rope attached between the two crafts lengthened a surprisingly long distance before the stretching stopped and the glider began to move. We became airborne without even as much as a hint of being jolted. The nylon rope returned to about its original length once we were off the ground.

The glider pilot kept the craft out of the propeller "wash" of the large cargo plane. Eventually we gained the planned altitude and the glider pilot released the tow hook holding the tow rope. The propeller plane carried the nylon "umbilical cord" with it as it flew away. It was an eerie sensation to hear only the rushing wind and the creaking noise the controls made as the pilot turned the CG4A back towards the intended landing area. When approaching the landing into the wind, a driver of a military truck chose an inopportune moment to move the vehicle directly in line to the CG4A's approach path and park the big truck. The glider pilot did some frantic hand and foot work to avoid hitting the conveyance carrier, thereby averting a catastrophe that would most likely terminate my military career. It was a rough but good landing – using plan "B", which meant we landed somewhat cross-wind at about ninety miles per hour.

Thankfully, I was one of the first to leave the craft. All inside the CG4A had the feeling they had damned near "bought the farm". This time I was not the only one hunching on the runway calling for "Rrrralph".

Following the glider training I never saw Bud very often. All evidence, rumors and activities of the 103rd Division pointed toward leaving Camp Howze and going to the European Theatre of Operations for combat duty.

One day, prior to going on another training exercise, I received a letter from the mother of my fiance. Enclosed with the letter was the engagement ring I had given her daughter. In the short letter she briefly explained that her daughter had married someone else having a deferment from the draft board. I wondered why my former fiance asked her mother to break the news to me.

With Bud gone, and my fiance married to someone else, I had a period of very mixed and tumultuous emotions. I was not a very pleasant person to be around. I felt combat oriented and was ready to start killing. At the same time I was extremely angry with myself.

It was uncomfortable for me to have the engagement ring back in my possession. The returned diamond ring was placed in my pocket as we began another military field problem near the Red River. We were using blank ammunition to repulse a counter-attack of "enemy soldiers". The military exercise reminded me of our home-made "rubber guns" we used as kids to shoot inner tube rubber bands at each other. The big difference now was, I was using a .30-caliber machine gun to shoot blanks at the "enemy soldiers" attacking our position.

My mind was rather absent of anything that made much understanding. I didn't sense as if I were a real person, or perhaps I was in a protective custody mental state without knowing it. I had the sensation I was about to "lose it".

Fortunately we soon had a break in our make believe war. I now had the perception of purposely being walked by an invisible force to where a lone tree stood. Once there, I removed my pack, laid down on my back and closed my eyes. Suddenly I became extremely aware of the sound of a brisk wind blowing through the leafy branches of the tree. I will never forget this unusual experience. It was as if some gentle hand had been placed on my head and I almost instantaneously dozed off into a deep sleep. When I awakened, I felt extremely calm. The realization that the actual duration of time I spent under the tree was less than ten minutes was just as puzzling as noticing the complete absence of any blowing wind.

Somewhere in the bottom of the Red River flowing between Oklahoma and Texas, there is a diamond engagement ring.

The field problem was not a lengthy event. We were critiqued on our performance in repelling an "enemy force" before returning to the barracks of Camp Howze.

Upon return to camp I was given orders to serve with Battery "A" of the 928th Field Artillery. My job would be that of a forward observer with the artillery. I would be working in front line situations with a commissioned officer who would call for artillery support for infantry when shelling was needed to eliminate enemy positions. My main duty would be to help locate enemy positions, briefly radio the map coordinates to our gun positions located in the rear area and help determine the accuracy of the artillery response to the request.

The time quickly approached when the 103rd Infantry Division would leave Camp Howze. My army friend, Bud, would be serving as a rifleman. His assignment would place him in one of the more dangerous positions ground troops could be during actual combat conditions.

Postscript

Army records would indicate the 839th Antiaircraft Battalion eventually departed from Fort Bliss's Logan Heights. It would pass through the Boston Port of Embarkation on December 2, 1944 and would arrive in England on December 12, 1944. The battalion then made the journey to France, arriving there March 4, 1945. Their August 1945 location was Schuefluige, Germany. I have no further information concerning the unit.

****

I have no additional knowledge about my former heavy weapon platoon leader. Later on, I inquired about the sergeant from some

103rd infantryman. Some heard rumors that he was never sent to Europe with the division and others thought he did go to France with the division. Other infantrymen heard rumors that the staff sergeant lost his life on the first day of action as the result of a severe back wound. I sincerely hope the first rumor was the correct situation.

****

I often wondered what operation the military had in mind when they gave the 103rd Division soldiers the special glider training. I also have a great respect for the skill of these unsung wartime glider pilots.

****

The CG4A glider was intentionally designed as an *expendable* aircraft. It was to be used in combat landing situations where a fifty-percent loss of pilots and troops could be expected. The CG4A was also capable of carrying something as large as a Jeep or other heavy equipment.

****

I was pleasantly surprised on August 21, 1996, while visiting the superb Desert Caballeros (Spanish word for "horsemen") Western Museum in Wickenburg, Arizona. There I discovered a descriptive plaque and an exhibit displaying a painting of a WACO CG4A combat glider of the World War II era. It was similar in appearance to the one Bud and I had taken our glider training ride at Camp Howze, Texas. Wickenburg was one of the glider pilot training sites during WW II. At the time of the glider training program the place was simply called "WW II Flight Academy". The inscription on the plaque read: "THEIR BRAVERY HAS HELPED KEEP THE UNITED STATES FREE."

****

The unit of measurement for the inside diameter of barrels (bores) of guns, artillery pieces and rockets is measured in metric units called millimeters or in caliber units based on the English inch unit of measurement. For approximation, an inch would be close to 25 mm. A 75 millimeter gun would have a bore diameter of almost 3 inches. A .50-caliber gun would have a bore of 50/100 of an inch (1/2 inch) or 12.5 millimeters.

Chapter Eight

Texas to Camp Shanks, New York

*All who have lived much out-of-doors, whether Indian or
otherwise, knows that there is a magnetic and powerful
force that accumulates in solitude but is quickly
dissipated by life in a crowd.*
> —Ohiyesa (Charles Alexander Eastman)

The translocation to the 928th Field Artillery came as a complete and pleasant surprise. I had not requested this change in military assignment and this time, I was quite confident Bud had not forged my name on the transfer papers. I surmise some commissioned officer had read my military training record. They may have recognized I was a skilled radio operator and my abilities would not be best utilized by operating a machine gun, carrying ammunition or transporting the metal tripod upon which the weapon was mounted.

A few days before my new duties with the 928th Field Artillery, Bud stopped by the barracks to brief me on the whereabouts of our old ack-ack (antiaircraft) battalion from Fort Bliss. Bud related they were presently located at Camp Howze. When it came to sniffing out information concerning happenings going on at a military installation, Bud had a sense of smell equal to, or possibly surpassing, a Tennessee blue-tick coonhound.

We decided to locate the members of our old outfit, Battery D of the 839th Antiaircraft Automatic Weapons Battalion. After a very lengthy hike, we ultimately ferreted out their location. We again saw Captain Hansen, Executive Officer First Lieutenant Pendell, Second Lieutenant Freeman, the communications sergeant, our "old" first sergeant and as many others as time would permit. Our visit was rather brief but pleasantries were exchanged and best wishes given all around. We never did find out what the old outfit was doing at Camp Howze. They were quite tight-lipped about the reason for their period of training at the Camp Howze infantry training site.

I never knew for certain the reason for the sudden transfer to the artillery unit. I would hazard a guess Captain Hansen and First

Lieutenant Pendell had something to do with my assignment to the field artillery unit. The only indisputable reason was – Battery A of the 928th Field Artillery needed a trained communication soldier for their forward observer team.

37531447 was delighted with this new turn of events. I was completely convinced the term "heavy weapon" implied the machine gun, iron tripod and supply of thirty caliber ammunition simply inferred "heavy in mass". The 105mm howitzer is a tow type weapon that could propel a four inch diameter projectile with outstanding accuracy. If need be, it could fire fifty rounds or 1.8 ton of projectiles an hour. This was more close to my idea of a real "heavy weapon".

The men of Battery A of the 928th Field Artillery were very friendly, appeared to work closely together as a team and possessed great pride in their military skills. As the "new kind on the block" they were happy to have me as a member of their artillery team.

Radio skills required in reporting aircraft approaching Fort Bliss, had been replaced with communication expertise in giving instructions to the 105 mm howitzer gun crews as to the precise location of enemy military targets in need of elimination. It would be front line duty. It did not take me very long to master the new operational techniques.

It was extremely gratifying to realize I most likely had seen the last of the enormous platoon sergeant from the heavy weapon infantry company. I would always remember the huge man as an individual having some type of bizarre functional disorder of the mind, who had been promoted to the rank of staff sergeant, and placed in charge of a platoon of soldiers. He was a military conundrum – I disliked the man for being an intimidating tyrant but admired the Texan for his technical skill in weaponry.

The days ahead would be disquieting inasmuch as the division would soon depart Camp Howze and be ordered to active duty. Due to reasons of wartime security we were informed not to send letters, telegrams, or use the telephone. In one way I felt lonely as hell, and at the same time, I was quite grateful having only family members and a few home-town friends left to worry about my future welfare. There would be no girl friend or wife to wonder what I was doing or worry about my well-being.

Every now and then a group of soldiers, including Bud, would hire a taxi to take us to "Big D" (Dallas) and return us to camp. The warning to not call home, mail letters, and send telegrams fell mostly on deaf ears. Most phone booths in Dallas appeared to be occupied by members of the 103rd Infantry Division.

Civilians in the Dallas-Fort Worth area appeared to be noticeably more friendly toward servicemen than the citizens of El Paso. My monthly pay had not caught up with me due to my rapid series of transfers. I was critically short of spending money. The USO (United Services Organization) in the vicinity was helpful. In their entertainment center, I could relax with a magazine, have a cup of coffee with home-made cookies, and even "plunk" out a few tunes on the old beat-up piano. The USO was extremely helpful during the war period. Persons connected with the organization did everything within their power to maintain military personnel morale at a high level.

One café in downtown Dallas had a sign out front on the sidewalk proclaiming, "This café will give a free meal to any GI wishing to come in for breakfast on a Sunday morning". After El Paso, I was somewhat skeptical about the offer. The sign meant exactly what it stated and I consumed a terrific free breakfast. In retrospect, there were many "soldiers" not in uniform, both men and women, serving unselfishly on the all-important "home" front.

Bud and I took one final visit to Dallas. Again we hired a taxi that was expense-shared with other division soldiers. Neither one of us had much pocket money. We didn't visit any bars, take in a movie or even obtain a hamburger. We spent most of our time in one of the parks of the area discussing our days spent at Fort Bliss, Texas and pondering the future.

It certainly was no secret in Dallas that the 103rd Infantry Division would soon be performing combat duty. We had been forewarned about females who would make marriage proposals to soldiers destined for active duty. These women were not the so-called "V-girls" (victory girls), teen-age girls – known as "chippies", patriotutes" or "khakiwackies", who felt it was a part of their war effort to provide free "pleasures" for service men. The older women were downright fraudulent schemers. The primary goal of these women was to wed as many departing soldiers as they could and have each GI Joe's $10,000 government individual insurance (death) policy changed over to them as the wife beneficiary. Bud and I were approached by some of these female con artists but neither one of us bought into their deceitful "program" of impropriety.

My last weekend pass granted at Camp Howze was to visit the nearby town of Gainesville. It was the closest city to Camp Howze.

My military pay had not caught up with me and the only money I possessed was some small-change in coins. The army provided free bus service to Gainesville and return; however I opted not to return to the camp for the night. Instead, I hiked out to a grassy knoll in a pasture, somewhere on the outskirts of Gainesville, where I spent the early cool October night absent of all other human beings. I had a comforting feeling being by myself under the nightime sky, so generously filled with brilliantly sparkling stars and an occasional streaking meteor. After fussing with myself for a time and wondering what fate had in "store" for me, I suddenly was aware of a having a comforting perception that I was not completely alone. The beautiful Texas prairie nighttime vista temporarily wiped away what worries I possessed and some type of magical spell coaxed me into a peaceful state of deep slumber. I returned to camp in the morning just in time for breakfast.

In the remaining days at Camp Howze we were issued new winter uniforms. We also spent considerable time packing and checking all of our equipment to make certain everything was in perfect working condition. Our "Cactus Division" shoulder patches, displaying a colorful Arizona saguaro cactus, were removed from our uniforms for wartime travel security reasons.

All indications strongly suggested the 103rd Division would soon become operational as a neoteric battle-ready combat group.

Division units were ordered to gather for a motivational speech to be presented by some unnamed general. We also were given specific instructions (ordered) to be good listeners, and above all, we were supposed to be model combat-ready soldiers. This last comment when interpreted out of military language, means: "Do not do or say anything stupid!" The order also appeared to have a highly unusual wording which almost came extremely close to using the unmilitary-like word "please".

The motivational speaker was none other than the infamous Lieutenant General Ben Lear. The general was the same man starting

World War II's first major rhubarb for the home front of the United States, when he "severely" disciplined a quartermasters group. The soldiers were returning to Camp Joseph T. Robinson, Arkansas from lengthy maneuvers in Tennessee. Some members of the unfortunate group had allegedly directed a few "cat-calls" at some girls strolling near a golf course where the general was beginning a round of golf. Some of the remarks were directed toward the general (who also happened to be their commanding officer) who was playing "out of uniform" (dressed in civilian clothing). Lieutenant General Lear was a career soldier who had come up through the ranks and was presently in charge of all United States Army ground troops.

We eased through this diminutive crisis without a hitch of any kind. I do not recall any specifics of what the general told the men of the 103rd Division. I only remember what he said at the occasion seemed to make good sense for combat-bound fighting men.

The last memory of my stay at Camp Howze was cleaning the barracks for a "white glove" inspection. Our division would soon be boarding a troop train which eventually would transport us to the vicinity of our point of embarkation. I have an almost complete hiatus about the troop train ride to our new destination. It was as if this period of time was intentionally blocked from my memory for some unknown reason. I can only recall several happenings that took place during this troop movement.

One memorable incident took place as the troop train neared Paducah, Kentucky. An artillery soldier seated opposite me leaned over and stared wistfully out of the train window and sadly lamented, "The house where my wife and kids live is…is right there." He slowly swept his hand in the general direction. It took an unusually long time before he lowered his arm pointing to a place – now no longer in view. I noticed a moistness in his eyes as he gradually straightened himself into his previous position in the seat. I was very thankful the troop train would not be passing through my home town.

I also recall doing calisthenics on station platforms in some of the places where there was a water stop for the steam engine to a change of train crews.

The only other lasting memory of the trip took place when the troop train stopped at Indian Town Gap. It was located somewhere in or near the Pennsylvania Allegheny Mountains. The steam locomotive had to stop to take on boiler water. The citizens of this western Pennsylvania community were waiting for us. Through the open coach windows, they were handing the soldiers what appeared to be – a lifetime supplies of baked cookies, pastries of all kind, candy and reading materials. Sugar was rationed at the time and I do not know how they managed such an effort. It was a great boost to our morale.

At the conclusion of our long train ride, the troops arrived at Camp Shanks, New York. The camp had excellent food and sleeping quarters. I was delighted to discover my tardy back pay had caught up with me. Almost everyone was granted pass privileges to visit New York City.

We were once again cautioned not to mention anything which could give information, aid or comfort to our wartime enemy. We were definitely forbidden to mention we were staying at Camp Shanks, even though the army busses taking us to visit New York City had a well-lighted display above each vehicle windshield with the words, "Camp Shanks".

When arriving in the "big city" I found the location of the nearest roller skating rink. The rink was like a spacious place, gaudy with lights and having a huge pipe organ being played by an organist who was providing the skating music. The rink was almost beyond the wildest imagination of this small-town lad who was only accustomed to midget-sized rinks and raspy-sounding recorded skating music.

I was pleasantly surprised when asked by a young lady, also skating at the rink, "Would you like to be my skating partner for the 'Ladies Choice'?" I accepted the polite request and while skating, I naively mentioned to the girl, "You really talk funny-like." Her pronunciation of words was quite similar to that of the Brooklynite communication lineman private who had chided those using profanity on the phone during advanced training at Fort Bliss; however, this girl did not use any expletives.

The young lady politely related to me, "I live in Brooklyn." This Kansas Jayhawker concluded everyone in Brooklyn,—where ever that was – talks the same strange way. I felt the evening was a continuation of my on-going worldly education.

The two of us had a very pleasant session of skating and trivial conversation. She finally asked me, "What part of the country do you come from?" I replied, "I come from southeastern Kansas." She then

95

laughingly proclaimed, "You really have a cute accent." The reality of the real world and my wrist watch, unfortunately, suggested it was time to return to the bus marked "Camp Shanks".

I had one other pass to visit New York City and was excited about the possibility of skating one more time at the fabulous roller rink. Perhaps the young lady from Brooklyn would once again be there. Without prior warning, a short crisp announcement came over the camp's loud speakers. The message stated: *"All pass privileges have been cancelled for members of the 103rd Infantry Division!"* The loud speakers crackled one more: *"All 103rd Division members are ordered to immediately return to and remain in their barracks!"*

No one had to be told the reason behind this unwelcome and sinister-sounding bit of new information.

Postscript

The following quote has been included in its entirety because of its special interest to me as well as to the reader. I do not wish the event to become more lost history of WW II. The article is also an excellent example of wartime journalism.

ARMY

Yoo-Hoo!

Along busy Central Avenue, on the outskirts of Memphis, Tenn. rolled 80 trucks of the 110th Quartermaster Regiment, making slow progress through Sunday traffic. In the cabs and on the hard seats behind sat 350 soldiers, ties discarded, collars open under a blistering sun. After the manner of the U.S. soldier, model 1941, or the Roman soldier, B.C. 100, they were also making merry by waving at girls, shouting boisterous pleasantries at civilians. They had a right to be cheerful, they had just finished more than a month's hard work in the Second Army maneuvers in central Tennessee, and done a good, cheerful job of it.

Past the first tee of the Memphis Country Club the convoy moved at a snail's pace. Along the walk bordering the course strolled a group of girls in shorts. From the trucks came a drumfire of soldiers' shouts – "Yoo-Hoo-o-o" – "Hi, baby" – a fanfare of whistling.

"Tis He!" On the first tee, hard by the street, a leathery-faced golfer was getting ready to tee off. "Fore" shouted a soldier. The golfer turned and glared at the trucks. Thereupon the soldiers let him have it: "Hey buddy, do you need a caddy?" The man on the tee handed his driver to a caddy, jumped a three-foot fence, stalked to the convoy. A command car in the column jerked to a stop, and its officers piled out to face an Awful Fact. The golfer was Lieut. General Ben Lear, commander of the Second Army, director of the maneuvers from which the 110th had just emerged.

Ben Lear was a first sergeant before he was an officer, and what he had to tell the 110th's officers sizzled with first sergeant's wrath. When all the burning words had been said, Ben Lear told the convoy to move on, that it would hear from him after it got back to its home station at Camp Joseph T. Robinson, 145 miles away.

The men of the 110th, like the rest of the soldiers, know Ben Lear (in uniform). They know him as a ranker who lives commendably close to his troops, a rugged soldier despite his 62 years, a great believer in spit-and-polish. They know and generally approve his dislike of sloppy soldiers, his decisive action (Time, June 23) to clear his Second Army of incompetent officers so that its outfits' can grow into first-class fighting units. They know him, too, as a commander too much preoccupied with small details.

Tough Touch. But tough and touchy as Ben Lear is, no soldier of the 110th was prepared for the tough touch that awaited them when they pulled into Camp

97

Robinson toward sundown. The General's order: that the 110th return at once to Memphis and stand by. They were to get mass punishment, the innocent with the guilty.

Toward midnight the trucks were loaded again and the convoy was off. To rest the drivers, it stopped three hours on the way, resumed the journey by dawn. Before noon the 110th had pitched tents on Memphis airport, was waiting for the lightning to strike. It struck soon. To the airport came Ben Lear in person, read the riot act again – "disgrace to the army...loose conduct and rowdyism...breach of discipline." Then he announced sentence. After a night's rest, the 110th would head home. And on the way every man in the outfit must march 15 miles.

To the Second Army's hard-bitten infantry outfits this would have been a breeze. To the truck drivers, clerks, typists, mechanics of the 110th it was no such thing. But the General had spoken.

Next day, the hottest days in two years (97 degrees) the trucks rumbled off, crossed the river, stopped beyond the Arkansas flats, let all but the drivers out. Five mile ahead the drivers stopped, got out, started to march. Through the morning and afternoon the trucks were leapfrogged until everybody had his dose. One man just out of the hospital at Camp Forest, Tenn. soon fell out, was trucked into Camp Robinson. During the day about twelve others fell out and were picked up. The stragglers and heat-stricken took emergency treatment from a dentist and a sanitary officer who were also being disciplined. The rest ate plenty of salt against the heat, filled their canteens silently at wayside towns while the citizenry eyed them with sympathy.

But the 110th battalion took the whole business as soldiers should. When civilians were not around, they laughed and kidded, sang snatches of songs, tried to improvise on an old theme "General Lear missed his putt, Parley Voo—..." And when they finally got back home they grinned at the gibes of other soldiers. They did not seem to feel they had disgraced the Army.

Goat vs Rowdies. Neither did some Congressmen who roundly trounced Ben Lear off and on the floor. Texas' Paul J. Kilday sent a hot note to the General demanding an explanation. Ben Lear replied, "I am responsible for the training of all elements of this Army...Roudyism   can   not   be tollerated...Circumstances   called   for   immediate action." Arkansas' William Norrell demanded a Congressional investigation ("He apparently is engaged all the time in playing golf"). Illinois' Everett M. Dirksen said he did not know "whether public funds are to be expended so that grouchy, golfing old generals will develop a lot of sour-puss soldiers." Missouri's isolationist Senator Bennett Champ Clark called Ben Lear "a superannuated old goat, who ought to retire."

The controversy spread like a heat wave...The Arkansas Department of the Army Mothers' Club demanded Ben Lear's removal. The Knoxville (Tenn.) *News-Sentinel* printed a letter From an Army mother, "Maybe General Lear got his rule book mixed and read the one from Russia", and the paper invited its readers to say more about the Memphis Incident. Cantankerous Westbrook Pegler defended Ben Lear on the probability that "the obstreperous haberdashers and grocers" of the Quartermaster outfit had used lewd Language to Memphis' shorts-clad girls – an unfair and also incorrect assumption. The hubbub became so regrettably loud that the Army had to act. From Washington it announced that Ben Lear had been ordered to make an explanation. Until it arrived, the Army would say nothing. Under the circumstances there was not much to say. Ben Lear might have well been over-severe; his sentence had the stigma of capricious anger, wounded vanity. But his objectivity – better discipline – was good. Many an officer thought it better to forget the whole business than make a nationwide song & dance about it. But the nation thought differently. It was the first time U.S. citizens had a chance to make a song & dance out of anything connected to World War II and they made the most of it. They saw nothing wrong with yoo-hooing and proceeded to tell the Army so, with many a yoo-hoo.

But in the Army, a general is always right. The basis of all discipline is: "orders are orders". In the view of professional officers, Ben Lear was not dishing out punishment as a champion of U.S. womanhood, nor because a soldier threw him off his golf game. He saw it a breach of discipline, and smacked it good & proper. That he smacked it harder than good and proper was – in a professional's view – beside the point.

Meanwhile the hooraw had proved embarrassing not only to Ben Lear but to the 110th and the Army. Last week in Olympia, Wash., soldiers from Fort Lewis tossed out mash notes to girls ("Please write to this lonely soldier," etc.) tagged with the postscript: "Don't tell Lieut. General Ben Lear." From 70 noncoms of the 250th Coast Artillery went a challenge to the 110th to a 15 mile marching race. Wrote the 250th: "If we don't finish first without having to write to our Congressmen, we'll let you yoo-hoo at us." At a bathing-beauty review at the El Paso (Tex.) Country Club, brimstony Major General Innis Palmer Swift, commander of Fort Bliss (and one of the judges) watched the girls prance by and owlishly hooted "Yoo-Hoo." And out of the Memphis Incident came World War II's first nickname for a U.S. outfit: the 110th's marchers became "The Yoo-Hoo Battalion."

****

The people in Pennsylvania who treated the troops so graciously, were able to make the cookies only because they either cut back on the use of their allotment of sugar or did without. Later I found out the community was largely made up of merchants, farmers and coal miners – hard-working mountain people who were vary caring for others.

It is amazing to know the sacrifices people made on the home front in making their contributions to the war effort. Unfortunately, there were also some insidious merchants who raised prices for military personnel or were involved in the illegal business of buying or selling goods in violation of government restrictions imposed for price control or rationing.

****

The amount paid to a named beneficiary of a soldier killed in time of war was mostly based on the $10,000 government life insurance certificates of policy. Payments were made only to beneficiaries named in the policy and relatives who can be named were limited. The beneficiary named by the soldier received payments of $55.50 a month upward for twenty years from the time of his wartime death. This would generate close to $13,320 over the time period of the payments. This amount was well worth the risks involved for a young women to marry more than once service man bound for combat duty. If the "wife" was married to three soldiers at one time she would "win" the most if all three of her "husbands" lost their lives. If two of the soldiers she married were killed, it was not a great problem to claim the one returning...as the husband. The worst case scenario for the big city female scam artist would possibly be having all three "husbands" return from the war at the same time!

In addition to the certificate of insurance payments, the "kitty" could be spiced up a little by the six-months gratuity pay, in the amounts of from $300 to nearly $470, depending on the rating (rank). These amounts were adjusted upward for overseas service and would be six times the base pay of the man killed in service connected duty. The further adding of the arrears pay of the deceased and possible other private life insurance benefits, the amount received could add up to a tidy sum.

Although scenarios most likely varied, the ploy used in Dallas on Bud and me went on this order: "You brave guys are going overseas and we want to do 'our part' in the war effort. You might never return from battle so let's get married right now and afterwards we can have a 'good time' in bed." Terms would require us to change the name of the beneficiary of the insurance certificate from perhaps a mother (in my case) to that of the new "wife". Bud's insurance beneficiary was his father.

Modern day computers most likely would have made the fraudulent insurance scheme impossible to carry out.

****

The term "GI Joe" was a term given to an individual army soldier. It seldom was used to refer to a sailor or a marine. The "GI" portion of the term most likely originated from the phrase "Government Issue". "Joe" was used in making reference to any army male.

****

The communication training skills I acquired at Fort Bliss, Texas, typifies the desire of their training personnel to deliver extremely high quality instruction – the norm for Fort Bliss and the commissioned officers in charge. I never encountered any radio or telephone communication problems when changing from the Coast Artillery to Field Artillery assignments.

****

After these many years, I would wager the young lady I skated with in New York City, most likely knew about as many expletives as the soldier coming from Brooklyn. She just didn't use them on the occasion.

Chapter Nine

Ocean Convoy to Europe

The division's point of embarkation would be New York City. Even with more than my share of frustrations during basic training, nothing up to this moment would equal the fiasco about to descend upon me. Duffel bags were constructed having both a webbed carrying handle as well as a shoulder strap. In the army, equipment having any type of a handle, indicated the item was designated "portable" by the "military powers to be". Theoretically it could be carried by a foot soldier and – it commonly was shouldered.

At Camp Shanks our weighty duffels were lined in the order of the alphabetized artillery battery roster. While standing directly behind my duffel a number was chalked on the duffel bag corresponding to an identical number chalked on the front of my steel helmet.

We were wearing winter olive-drab wool uniforms, steel helmets, helmet liners, field jackets and heavy wool overcoats. Each man was shouldering the heavy M-1 .30-caliber rifle. My pack contained additional clothing – including "long johns", wool socks, a rain coat, personal gear and a wool blanket. We were issued one canteen of drinking water and a gas mask carried in a canvas cloth bag also having a shoulder carrying strap.

In addition, we were required to wear a damned necktie that appeared to add considerable psychological mass to our already sizeable burden. I seriously doubted if the enemy would be impressed by the neckties. We definitely were not going on some type of invitational pilgrimage.

I pictured myself resembling one of the Mexican burros observed on the back streets of Juarez, Mexico, packing a voluminous load of mesquite tree firewood much larger than the burro. I was elated to learn our duffel bags with handles would be sent ahead.

Division members boarded a train at the camp's railroad spur for the brief trip to the Weehawken ferryboat dock. Daylight had fallen victim to darkness by the time we arrived at the ferryboat terminal. I was utterly aghast upon noticing the cumbersome duffel bags with their two carrying straps awaiting us. I shouldered the bulky duffel along with the rest of my burden. Neither the desert sands of Texas and New Mexico nor the sweltering humidity encountered on forced marches at Camp Howze would compare to the tortuous physical challenge endured while traversing the seemingly endless distance through the ferryboat terminal building. I was believing the gravitational pull on the mass of equipment I was lugging was causing my ankle shin bones to rake the floor of the terminal's seemingly infinite concourse. Despite the cool autumn weather everyone was in a full sweat when finally reaching the ferryboat loading zone.

We were boarding the *Weehawken* ferry for the crossing of the Hudson River and eventually would be docking at the final embarkation staging location. Once again we became struggling mokes during the debarking process from the ferryboat – now firmly tethered to the south side of Pier 51 along the North River.

Stately women, from the American Red Cross, were on hand to offer us hot coffee, doughnuts, writing stationary, and decks of playing cards. I was grateful for the coffee, doughnuts and writing material. The small deck of playing cards was purposely avoided. My mental calculator was flashing significant data informing me the deck of cards would add just enough mass, to my already weighty burden, that it most likely would break this "burro's back.

The moment predictably arrived signaling the boarding of our troop transport. In the darkness we could not visualize the size of the vessel that would transporting us across the Atlantic Ocean waters. I sensed a discomforting awareness when realizing these final last few steps to board the troop transport could possibly permanently sever me from the land called, "The United States of America".

The number 37531447 was read from the battery roster. I laboriously lifted the heavy duffel bag and precariously struggled my way up the cleated narrow gangplank leading steeply upward toward the darkened bowels of the ship. The boarding process awakened memories of loading range cattle from stockyard holding pens into railroad cattle cars for the trip to market. Instead of using electric shock cattle prods to speed the loading for an impatient train crew, it was the sharp-tongued loading officers bellowing out words to the boarding soldiers to, "Hurry it up!" During such moments the gear we were carrying would, without notice, become completely uncontrollable wild-thrashing demons. The gas mask strap would snag on an immovable object, the M-1 rifle "goosed" the soldier ahead, the duffel would attempt to smash into the face of the man behind and the bulky pack would become an octopus whose tentacles eagerly grasped onto anything located in the narrow passageways other gear had dared chance to miss.

With military idioms being shouted and curses uttered, we

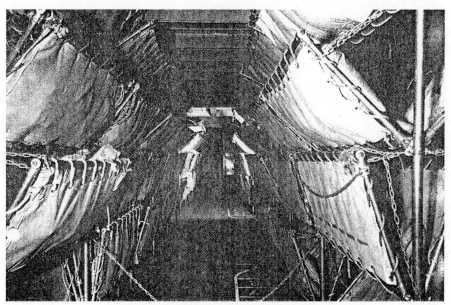

National Archives Photo
4-tier Bunk Quarters Aboard Troopship

were being compressed into a miniscule area, having a further diminutive space, containing a canvas cot laced to a steel frame. I wearily shoved the duffel bag to the top of the cot, hunched my way into a position which would allow me to remove the webbed straps holding the pack to my aching sweaty body. Following verbal instructions I secured my rifle to the far side of my cot with the provided twine cordage. I now wait for the next major catastrophe to strike. It would prove to be a very short-lived pause.

We were now being apprised our bodies had been erroneously guided to the wrong location in the lower portion of the troop transport. We were ordered to immediately vacate the site and quickly move to the correct portion of the ship.

By the time I had my oversized pack strapped onto my body, untied the M-1 rifle, grabbed the gas mask and cartridge belt with my canteen of emergency fresh water and hoisted the duffel bag, I was in a nasty mood and completely ready to kill all of the sons-of-bitches who had started the damned war. Words are not adequate to describe the challenge of this relocation mandate. We had to pass through oncoming soldiers in the ship's narrow passageways, who in turn, were attempting to push their way through us. They were just as frustrated and burdened. The scene was reminiscent of a large group of doomed prehistoric animals trapped in the sticky Pleistocene Epoch *"La Brea* (tar) Pits". Somehow we miraculously extricated ourselves and both groups safely made the migration to their amended quarters.

The canvas bunks were four tiers high. I felt good fortune had once again favored me when I was assigned to the top canvas cot. I could reach up and touch endless maze of piping between the deck above and myself; however, I had not given much sound thought about this seemingly bit of good fortune. I had ignored the important scientific principle – "warm air rises". It would carry with it all of the body odors, passed flatulence and recycled stale air. A somewhat measurable benefit of having the top cot position would be – no other persons would be above me when or if they became seasick. My tiny sleeping space would become a private territorial habitat until our unknown destination would be reached.

Prior to boarding the vessel, we were handed a card that was supposed to be carefully read by all enlisted men coming on board. I placed the card in one of my jacket pockets for the time being and vowed to read it later. Once settled in my bunk I remembered the card and removed it from my jacket pocket. It turned out to be a "Guide for Enlisted Passengers" aboard the *Monticello*. It started out by informing those boarding:

"This is a ship of the U.S. Navy; not an Army transport nor a Merchant Marine Ship. It is manned by Navy Personnel. Observance of the following rules will make the voyage easier and safer for passengers and crew."

DON'T tamper with your life belts. Wait for instructions for their use.

DON'T hang heavy bags from thin brackets, wire or piping. These will break and cause floods or fires.

DON'T throw gum, cigarettes, paper or anything in the urinals. They will stop and overflow.

DON'T throw rubbish in toilet bowls or troughs, particularly magazines, same reason.

DON'T dirty bunks with shoes or otherwise. On return trip same bunk must be used for sick or wounded.

DON'T lean, or put hands against paintworks unnecessarily. It will have to be scrubbed by you or someone else before leaving ship.

DON'T tamper with red CO_2 fire extinguishers. If valve once opens entire load discharges and can't be refilled at sea.

DON'T smoke in compartments after darken ship. It ruins your air.

DON'T tamper with air scoops in Compt. C-1. If you do they may emit light.

DON'T cut hair in compartments. Use latrines or ladder trunks. Loose hair spreads disease.

DON'T try to open any outside port while ship is darkened.

DON'T congregate in ladder trunks or passages. Keep them clear for emergencies.

DON'T sit or stand on life rafts on deck. It tears them apart. You may need one.

DON'T throw trash or butts in drains or drinking fountains.

DON'T waste fresh water. Use salt water whenever possible. All fresh water is made on ship.

DON'T cut holes in ventilating ducts. This is pure sabotage. It holds the ship in port to repair holes and renew ducts. Also, you are cutting off air from someone else. Fresh air must come in at bottom, and exhaust from the top.

DON'T use urinals to vomit, use latrine troughs or toilet bowls.

DON'T run drinking fountains. The longer water runs, the warmer it gets.

DON'T throw trash on decks. Use cans provided.

DON'T use life belts for cushions or pillows. It ruins them. You may need one.

DON'T crowd in port holes. It cuts off air for others.

DON'T wear hats or helmets to mess.

DON'T take food from mess hall. It breeds rats and roaches.

DO obey all orders promptly.

DO wear life belts when ship is under way except in bunks.

DO keep decks as clean as possible.

DO put out cigarettes before throwing in cans.

DO be considerate in mess halls; move over and make room.

DO use ladder furthest to right in ladder trunks.

DO keep passageways clear and quiet during Ship's General Drills, General Quarters, (Battle Stations), Fire, Prepare to Abandon Ship Drills.

DO report all difficulties to your compartment officer.

DO leave mess hall promptly after cleaning your tray.

DO keep your head covered in the sun. You are in the tropics.

DO when tiers of bunks join, sleep with your feet towards the other man's feet.

DO watch your money or valuables. Don't' wave them around in public.

DO keep your canteen filled in case you must abandon ship.

DO if abandoning ship, always jump feet first.

DO keep life rafts tied together.

DO have all bottom bunks triced up for inspection, and cleaning.

DO use pack for pillow, tie bag to post at foot of bunk, Sling rifle with twine to the unused side of bunk, horizontally.

DO keep shoes on but unlaced for Prepare to Abandon Ship drill.

I soon discovered my new lodging space in the ship was close to the middle. In rough seas this possibly would be a better place to be than the bow or the stern of the vessel. This central area location definitely would minimize the up and down motions of the troop ship during periods of high seas. Perchance it also might minimize the degree of seasickness certain to be encountered during the lengthy ocean crossing.

Excitement soon was replaced with boredom. Many soldiers were playing cards or writing letters to acquaintances back home. One enterprising infantryman, having a bunk located along the route to the ships mess, would wile away time practicing counting his numbers up to ten. He very carefully counted each soldier in the mess line until reaching the tenth man. 37531447 was the tenth. Without asking why he was counting he remarked, "Statistics indicate one man out of every ten will contract syphilis while in France and you…are the tenth one."

Our ocean voyage took place in the season of the year when the Atlantic Ocean was prone to be stormy. Our odyssey encountered one of the roughest storms even veteran navy sailors assigned to the *Monticello* could remember. Winds reached minimal hurricane velocity. The troop ship's bow would dip down

National Archives Photograph
U.S.S. Monticello (Notice deck gun on the stern)

into such a huge water wave trough it would cause the stern to come out of the water. During this event the screws (ship's propellers) would push atmosphere instead of ocean water. When this occurred the vessel would groan, creak and violently shudder.

When winds diminished sufficiently, we were allowed back onto the top deck. The waves were still high enough that the small S.S. *Santa Maria*, also carrying units of the 103rd Division, would temporarily vanish from view. It made me appreciate being on the much larger *Monticello*. I also was gratified knowing I was not a sailor aboard the small-sized navy escort destroyers.

My bunk was fairly close to the ship's outer hull, and I could hear the swishing sound of water rushing by the steel plates of the hull as the convoy charted a zig-zag course to confuse Nazi U-Boats. The rushing water would cause me to reflect upon the words spoken by my former platoon sergeant of the heavy weapons company at Camp Howze, Texas, when he gave his fervent prayer. I kept wondering if a German torpedo was on the way to strike the *Monticello*. This disconcerting thought seemed to intensify on Friday, October 13th, when the convoy was just south of the Azores. This thorny vagary completely vanished when I developed a severe case of seasickness. At the time, death seemed to be more of a logical choice.

On one occasion while sampling fresh sea air, I noticed two burning vessels on the starboard side of the deck. Perhaps they had become victims of Nazi U-boat attacks. The burning ships brought the reality of real danger considerably closer to all aboard. When moving from our sleeping area our life jackets always went with us.

Enlisted men aboard the *Monticello* were offered two meals each day. The lines for the "stand up and partake" meals became much shorter when the big storm struck. Some men were too sick to attempt the food line, while others would start the risky trip only to upchuck on the enclosed passageways where others had to walk. Many making it as far as the eating area would "lose it" the moment the smell of food was intercepted. All foul odors eventually seemed to rise over my bunk and form an odoriferous sewer line thermocline in the humid stale air.

For safety and security reasons the ships in the convoy traveled in a darkened posture, port holes were sealed and no electric shavers were allowed to be used. The little motor in the razor could possibly send out electrical disturbances that could help the enemy locate the position of the convoy.

Latrine facilities were double rows of parallel troughs that appeared to be made from fifty-five gallon steel drums cut in half longitudinally and with ends removed they had been welded to each other. They reminded me of troughs made by ranchers to feed livestock. Each steel barrel would provide two sections of the long welded trough of the latrine. For seating purposes, two iron pipes were welded parallel on the top of the barrels. These pipes were spaced about a foot apart and would provide a seating area for defecation purposes as well as something to hold onto during acute reactions to seasickness.

One end of the trough was slightly higher than the opposite end. On the high end of the primitive toilet facility, a rather large continuous volume of sea water was pumped into the trough causing human waste (or vomit) to be flushed by gravity flow to the lower end of the long barrel latrine where it would flow through piping directly back into the ocean waters.

Each row of the two back-to-back latrine troughs could accommodate approximately twenty soldiers at a time. Every so often some diabolical demented pervert, often from the *Monticello's* crew, would crumple a fairly large wad of toilet paper, set it ablaze with a cigarette lighter and drop the fiery torch into the latrine's high end. This action would allow the flowing water to transport the blazing package of mischief beneath unsuspecting soldiers seated on the two pipes. As the blazing inferno passed under the "victims" they would immediately – and in turn – stand up. The victimized soldiers appeared to vaguely resemble the synchronized movements of the New York Radio City Rockettes chorus line.

The 409th Infantry Company Bud Pitts had been assigned was also on the *Monticello*. We had several opportunities to meet and recall the past, joke about the present and ponder the future. For the most part, we just engaged in small talk.

A convoy travels only as fast as the speed of the slowest ship in the group. The destroyer escort, stormy weather, and our ever changing course had apparently kept us safe from German U-boat "wolf packs" that continuously prowled the shipping lanes of the Atlantic Ocean searching for prey.

The rough weather eventually gave way to calmer waters and sunshine. The large war-time convoy soon entered the Straits of Gibraltar. It was the first land observed since leaving New York. While approaching the Rock of Gibraltar 103rd division soldiers took turns going topside to see the famous geological natural wonder. The convoy continued past the "rock" and headed into the Mediterranean Sea where it paralleled the shore line of North Africa. I could make out the white buildings partially making up the city of Oran. I noticed other African cities but did not know their names.

Africa soon disappeared from the scene when the convoy turned to a more northerly direction. A mistral, a strong cold north wind blowing toward the Mediterranean Sea coming from the Rhone River Valley of France, struck our convoy. It did not have the tenacity or continue as long as the Atlantic fury; however, the water became rough enough to commence another round of unwelcome seasickness.

When the warm Mediterranean sun came out from behind the storm clouds, personnel on topside could observe the coastline of southern France.

After fifteen long days out of New York, the *Monticello* entered the war battered port of Marseilles where the ship navigated around considerable war wreckage in the harbor and docked. Debarkation commenced immediately and 103rd Infantry Division soldiers stepped upon French soil for the first time. For many, it would be the only time.

Postscript

The United States troop transport *Monticello* was the former Italian cruise liner *Conte Grande*. It was constructed in Trieste, Italy and launched June 29, 1927. In 1940 the ship was laid up in the harbor of Santos, Brazil when Italy entered the war on the side of the Nazis. On August 22, 1941, it was taken over by the government of Brazil. It was then purchased April 16, 1942 by the United States and commissioned the same day in Brazil. The vessel was renamed the *Monticello* (AP-61).

The *Monticello* sailed north for conversion to a troop transport at the Philadelphia Navy Yard. The conversion to a troop transport was completed September 10, 1942. She left New York on November 2 for the invasion of North Africa, carrying troops to Casablanca. Returning to New York, she again sailed on Christmas day transporting men for the various commands of the China-Burma-India Theatre to Karachi, by the way of the Panama Canal, Australia and Ceylon.

The transport returned to the port of New York April 24, 1943, carried reinforcements to Oran (Africa) on two voyages, then sailed from Africa to San Francisco by the way of the Panama Canal. Through the first half of 1944 the vessel carried men from San Francisco to California ports, Australia, Hawaii, and numerous bases of the south Pacific. In June of 1944, she commenced the first series of trans-Atlantic voyages, bringing troops to help win victory in Europe. On October 6, 1944, she sailed for France carrying 391 officers and 6,415 enlisted men, mostly from the United States Army 103rd Infantry Division.

In 1949 the vessel was returned outright to the Italian government and was once again given the name *Conte Grande* where it was refurbished as a cruise ship for the Italian Line. Its first post-war voyage in 1949 was from Genoa, Italy, to Buenos Aires, Argentina. It took turns sailing in winter to South America and was used in the summer time, in the northern hemisphere to travel to New York City.

When the *Andrea Doria* collided with the Swedish ship *Stockholm*, the *Conte Grande* filled in for the sunken *Andrea Doria* and was sailing the North Atlantic during 1956. It made its final cruise to Australia in 1960 before returning to the shipyards at La Spezia, Italy, where it was scrapped in 1961.

****

Convoy U.G.F.-15B, Task Group 69.7
NYC Port of Embarkation to Marseilles, France
Transported troops of the 103rd United States Infantry Division during World War II

DATE: October 6, 1944 to October 20, 1944

ESCORT: U.S.S. *BUTLER,* U.S.S. *GENTRY,* U.S.S. *TRAW,* U.S.S. *MAURICE J. MANUEL,* U.S.S. *NAIFEH*

CONVOY: *GENERAL J.R. BROOKE, GENERAL W.H. GORDON,* U.S.S. *MONTICELLO,* U.S.A.T. *J.W. McANDREW,* U.S.S. *MERAK,* U.S.A.T. *HENRY GIBBINS,* U.S.A.T. *GEORGE WASHINGTON,* S.S. *SANTA MARIA,* H.M.S. *ENGADINE,* U.S.S. *SOLOMONS*

CONVOY COMMODORE (UGF-15-B):
   Captain H.W. Pillsbury, U.S.N. in U.S.S. *GENERAL J.R. BROOKE* (AP132)

CONVOY VICE-COMMODORE:
   Captain B.B. Lanier, U.S.N.R. in U.S.S. *MONTICELLO* (AP61)

FORMATION OF CONVOY:

   Column 1

   U.S.S. *GENERAL W.H. GORDON* (AP117)
   U.S.A.T. *J.W. McANDREW*
   U.S.S. *MERAK* (AF21)

   Column 2

   U.S.S. *MONTICELLO* (AP61)
   U.S.A.T. *GEORGE WASHINGTON*
   S.S. *SANTA MARIA*

   Column 3

   U.S.S. *GENERAL J.R. BROOKE* (AP132)
   U.S.A.T. *HENRY GIBBINS*
   S.S. *MORMACMOON*

Column <u>4</u>

H.M.S. *ENGADINE*
U.S.S. *SOLOMONS*

****

In the process of transporting the 103rd Division the men of the 103rd were pretty much kept in the dark about any details or happenings in the process of moving the division and its equipment across the waters of the Atlantic Ocean.

The *Monticello* had mounted deck guns. When the convoy was under way, we had heard the guns firing. At the time we did not know what the intended target might have been. Fifty some years later the deck log of the *Monticello* indicated it had been sessions of target practice.

The entire operation was highly complicated operation. It could be likened to moving at one time, a city having a population of 16,000 people, including their vehicles, and other necessary supplies from United States to Europe. It was vital to the safety and success of the mission for everyone involved to do their job and cooperate to the fullest extent.

There was good reason why it was essential to load the division troops as rapidly as possible. In an operation of this magnitude schedules had to be maintained without delays. This fact was undoubtedly the reason for officers exhorting us to quickly board the largest ship in the convoy – the U.S.S. *Monticello*.

For late arriving sailors returning to the *Monticello* from shore leave, Captain B.B. Lanier of the United States Naval Reserve, dealt swift punishment. Errant sailors were made "prisoners at large" and placed on a diet of bread and water with a full ration every third day until their sentence had been carried out.

When the men of the 103rd were aboard the *Monticello* and while the ship was still moored to the port side of Pier 51, the New York Central Railroad ferryboat *Utica*, engaged in landing troops at the end of Pier 51, North River, was swung by the strong ebb tide down stream. In spite of the efforts of the attending tug the ferryboat struck the port quarter of the *Monticello*. A part of the wooden upperworks of the *Utica* was stoved inward. The *Monticello* had the paint scratched. A subsequent examination of our ship by a diver indicated the ferryboat had neither struck underwater body, propellor, nor rudder.

Most of us were never aware of the full extent of protective security given to the transporting of the 103rd Infantry Division to France. Air coverage, when feasible, was also provided by numerous air units.

A partial summary of Convoy U.G.F-15-B, Task Group 69.7 as taken from the log of the *Monticello*:

OCTOBER 5, 1944 – COMMENCED EMBARKING MAIN BODY OF ARMY PASSENGERS AT N.Y.C. PORT OF EMBARKATION

OCTOBER 6, - UNDOCKED FROM SOUTHSIDE OF PIER 51, NORTH RIVER. PASSED THROUGH ANTI-SUBMARINE NETS. FORMED INTO CONVOY. AIR COVERAGE BY TWO NON-RIGID AIRSHIPS AND A PB2Y CORONADO WINGED AIRCRAFT.

OCTOBER 7, - PLANE COVERAGE BY PBM MARINER FROM BERMUDA

OCTOBER 8, - DAYLIGHT PLANE COVERAGE BY PBM MARINER FROM BERMUDA

OCTOBER 9, - GUNNERY PRACTICE. AIR COVERAGE BY PBM MARINER FROM BERMUDA

OCTOBER 10, - NO PLANE COVERAGE. REFUIELING OF ESCORT SHIPS

OCTOBER 11, - HIGH WINDS. SEVERAL SHIPS OUT OF STATION. MEASURE TAKEN TO AVOID COLLISION

OCTOBER 12, - HIGH WINDS AND SEAS. ACTUAL WIND 68 KNOTS (78.2 M.P.H.) ALL SHIPS LABORING HEAVILY. 1440 WINDS AND SEAS MODERATE

OCTOBER 13, - CONVOY REDUCED SPEED TO 8.8 KNOTS. REFUELING FOR ESCORTS

OCTOBER 14, - CONVOY SPEED UP TO 14 KNOTS

OCTOBER 15, - AT 0914 PASSED ON STARBOARD TANKER *WILLIAM MCKNIGHT* AND S.S. *HARVEY GIBSON* BOTH VESSELS ON FIRE DUE TO COLLISION DURING STORM. EACH SHIP ATTENDED BY A DESTROYER

OCTOBER 16, - PLANE COVERAGE BY ONE OR MORE B-24 LIBERATORS

OCTOBER 17, - PLANE COVERAGE BY B-24 LIBERATORS AND PBY CATALINA. PASSED THROUGH STRAITS OF GIBRALTER. H.M.S. *ENGADINE* PROCEEDED TO GILBRATER

OCTOBER 18, - NO PLANE COVERAGE TODAY. CROSSED MERIDIAN OF GREENWICH. U.S.S. *MERAK* PROCEEDED TO GIBRALTER

OCTOBER 19, - SHIPS IN CONVOY CHANGE STATIONS. NO PLANE COVERAGE. HEAVY SEAS FROM MISTRAL

OCTOBER 20, - SHIPS ASSUME SINGLE FILE FORMATION INTO PORT OF MARSEILLES. DOCKED END OF MOLE "A" IN BERTH 2-A STARBOARD SIDE OF MOLE. COMMENCED DISEMBARKATING TROOPS OF THE 103RD INFANTRY DIVISION TROOPS AT 1435

****

The H.M.S. *ENGADINE* was a British vessel. Gibralter was most likely a home port for the ship.

****

The two ships I observed burning were not torpedoed. They had collided during the storm. Until I read the deck log of the *Monticello*, some fifty plus years later, I had erroneously believed they had been victims of a German U-boat attack.

****

On the same day the 103rd Infantry Division disembarked from the *Monticello* at Marseilles, France, the ship was made ready to receive another group of military personnel. At 1620 military time, the work of loading German Prisoners of War and a U.S. Army military police detachment had been completed. Fifty-five minutes later, the loading of 23 officers and 644 enlisted men from the French Army had also been completed. During World War II the *Monticello* played a key role in the long hard road to bring about final victory.

****

In reading the rules for soldiers aboard the *Monticello* (the list of "do" and "don'ts") you will notice the rivalry among the various branches of the military was quite prevalent. The Navy wanted you to definitely understand you were aboard a Navy ship and not a Merchant Marine or U.S. Army troop transport. Division soldiers purposely annoyed sailors by calling the navy vessel a "boat" instead of a "ship".

****

Following the surrender of German forces in World War II, Hermann Goering, Chief of the German Air Force, was extremely critical of Adolph Hitler for the Fuhrer's refusal to order the capture of the Rock of Gibralter early in the war. The seizure of the Rock of Gibraltar by the Nazis would have closed a strategically important supply artery for the Allies using the Mediterranean Sea to reach North Africa, southern France, Italy and other combat zones of the region. It most likely would have altered plans for the *Monticello* to reach Mediterranean ports.

****

The infantryman aboard the *Monticello* who was wiling away time by pointing out every tenth soldier, proved to be wrong. I never fell victim to syphilis or any other of the "social diseases".

Chapter Ten

Bivouacking on the Mediterranean Sea

The fifteen days aboard the troop ships had taken its toll on the army men. Seasickness, dysentery, lack of sufficient exercise, foul air and enemy U-boat concerns were just some of the evildoers adding to the problem of maintaining top combat-ready physical fitness for the 103rd Division soldiers.

After debarking the *Monticello*, we were ordered to commence a lengthy march with full field packs. We also were provided uninvited information revealing the chosen route would be uphill for the entire distance. We were introduced to a new international unit of measurement of distance – the *kilometer*. My mind was trying to assure me the distance of thirty-two kilometers was approximately the same distance as twenty miles. At the present moment neither unit of distance measurement offered much in the way of any tangible gratification for 37531447.

It was a wonderful feeling to be back on solid land once again. Unfortunately, our legs were not responding very enthusiastically to the idea of walking in a straight line. Most of us had acquired "rubbery sea-legs" while crossing the stormy ocean waters while aboard the troop ship. Our lower extremities, already weakened from inactivity, had to be retrained to walk on stationary solid ground. It was an exemplary bit of Divine Providence to learn our hefty duffel bags would be trucked.

Among my first thoughts after getting off of the troop ship was wondering if the Shriners were having a convention close to the dock area. Brightly colored fezes were being worn by numerous black men in the port area. If indeed the Shriners were having a convention, this would be the first black Shriners I had ever seen. I was informed those wearing the unusual-appearing headgear were most likely from Morocco. I immediately concluded these men were bilingual since they were speaking fluent French language. A short moment later I had a brief talk with myself and accused 37531447 of being one stupid shit. French was their national language and it was quite unlikely if many spoke much English. I was beginning to realize I was in a foreign country – far distant from my home in the Flint Hills of Kansas.

The Port of Marseilles was protected from low-flying enemy aircraft with numerous silver-colored zeppelin-shaped barrage balloons. Each of the hydrogen filled unmanned blimps, strategically located, was tethered to a point on the ground or water by a metal cable. The heavy cable was designed to discourage ground-level bombing or strafing runs by enemy aircraft. The metal cable would damage aircraft propellers or create catastrophic structural damage to the aircraft.

Shouldering my heavy pack I fell in line with comrades from Battery A of the 928th Field Artillery and commenced the late afternoon elevated climb through the winding cobble streets of Marseilles. I was struck with the realization that not one solitary individual I had known in civilian life would have the slightest clue as to where in the hell I was. I was also somewhat perturbed by the vast time difference between my present location and the old home town in Chase County, Kansas. It was more difficult to imagine what friends and loved ones were doing at this very moment in time. I was undoubtly feeling very lonely, pensive and not taking my life too seriously.

The periods of loneliness would make numerous return trips throughout my tour of combat duty. This type of "I don't give a damn" attitude would cause me to take risks not exactly deemed rational for a trained soldier wishing to survive the riggers of combat. It appeared as if I would have two wars to fight – one with the enemy and the other – with myself. It would be during such times I would have thoughts about my former fiance and longed for support for the additional hardships I was beginning to face. The event under the solitary tree at Camp Howze had dulled the real pain; however, she still would enter my thoughts from time to time. Her marriage to someone exempted from military service still made me ill-natured at times.

The uphill march continued as dusk turned to darkness and the unlighted port city of Marseilles slowly faded from view. Many men from my artillery unit were becoming fatigued and were lagging behind. I continued walking as if I were an automaton having the number 37531447 stamped on my "mechanical" body.

I now became aware of hearing voices no longer familiar to me. In the near blackness of the night it was impossible to recognize faces. I was definitely walking with strangers from a 103rd Division infantry company. Soon the distance separating the infantrymen would become greater.

I was beginning to have occasional doubts if anyone was still walking ahead of me. Every so often my combat boot would hook onto a strip of long narrow fabric. I reached slowly down in the darkness and retrieved one of the "trip" devices. The "thingamajig" turned out to be a United States Army top-secret combat "weapon" which was supposed to terrorize the enemy into surrendering. Preceding infantrymen had been discarding the neckties they had been ordered to wear. Finding an occasional necktie on the ground was solid evidence I was till on the correct route. My necktie also was aborted in an effort to guide those behind, if indeed, anyone was still walking on the trail. In all honesty, I just wanted to get rid of the damn thing. My body was aching and the stench of two weeks without a decent bath or shower began to apprise me of the truthful status of my personal hygiene. The partial starry sky gave way to dark threatening rain clouds. Soon large drops of cold rain announced their arrival by playing a steady rhythmic staccato on the topside of my steel helmet. At least I was becoming drenched with fresh rainwater and it actually felt wonderful.

Continuing my zombie-like motion, I came to the realization I had not scraped up any recently orphaned neckties. It appeared as if everyone, including commissioned officers, had called a halt to the operation and were bedding down for the remainder of the night. I too, stopped, removed my weighty pack, unfastened the water-saturated woolen blanket from the pack, folded it in half and shook out as much water as I could with a snapping wrist action. I then pulled the damp blanket over me. Before calling it a "night", I laughingly considered I had been in France for less than seven hours and was already "missing in action" from my artillery unit. I periodically dozed off until daybreak.

As the day dawned and the warm rays of the sun came out from behind the dark bilious rain clouds, I became absolutely absorbed in the "fairy book" vista appearing before my searching eyes. There, right in front of me, was the beautiful deep-blue Mediterranean Sea, complete with a small off-shore island having a large castle nestling on the highest hill. The scene could have been straight out of the Grimms' stories of childhood folklore.

During the night we had unknowingly traveled along a bluff overlooking the sea. The awesome panorama we were viewing presented a deceptive portrait of tranquility, peace, and beauty. It was extremely difficult to perceive human beings, as well as other living creatures, dying along frontal combat lines a relatively close distance to the northeast of Marseilles.

Covering approximately fifteen miles of the total distance to our bivouac destination, my cramped stiff legs reluctantly carried my body the remaining stretch of upward-sloping terrain We eventually regrouped into our correct military units.

The uphill march to the staging area would be appropriately remembered by soldiers wearing the resurgent saguaro cactus shoulder patch as "The Death March from Marseilles". Every one of us survived this "special event" of our notorious decathlon having its beginning in the snake and mosquito infested swamps of Louisiana, the wind-blown boondocks of New Mexico or the North Texas plains near Camp Howze.

Our first assignment would be pitching tents on the windy treeless coastal plateau overlooking the Mediterranean Sea. Erecting a "pup" tent is usually a fairly simple task; however, while driving the first tent peg into the ground, a chalk-like limestone layer an inch or so beneath the damp wind-blown sandy soil was encountered. The wooden tent pegs splintered and were of miniscule help in supporting the shelters. Everyone pitching tents encountered the same frustrating difficulty. An alternative solution to the problem was to find stones, large enough, for use in attaching the supporting tent ropes.

With canvas shelters somewhat secured, we were ordered to dig trenches large enough to be used as protection against a possible strafing attack from enemy planes. This was a realistic possibility. While hiking in the dark to our bivouac one of the barrage balloons, protecting the harbor on Marseilles, had been shot down by enemy aircraft. The burning balloon left behind a fierce fiery trail marking its final decent to destruction. Later a lone German reconnaissance aircraft had dropped a magnesium flare for the likely purpose of taking a photograph of what was taking place on the ground. If the aerial photo was ever developed, German intelligence would most likely be rather puzzled by our highly unusual unorthodox nighttime military field tactics.

The effort to "dig in" was an exercise in perseverance. Our GI picks and shovels were hardly an evenhanded match against the chalky limestone that was resisting each energetic ringing blow. We continued with the chiseling process until we had foxholes carved into the rocky layer and blistered hands. Shortly after the completion of the protective shelter a heavy rain descended from the sky. Rain and surface runoff completely filled each hole brimful with the liquid. The water-filled holes offered precious little protection from any strafing enemy aircraft but could have served well for a communal bathing. Perhaps the bivouac area had been selected by the enemy.

I am not certain how long we stayed at this staging area. On the second night Sergeant Greene, a noncom in charge of one of the 105 millimeter howitzers, along with one of his gun crew members, left camp in search of "liquid refreshments". The two men evidently had befriended the contents of a flask they managed to discover. About 0200 hours (2:00 A.M.) a terrible moaning and groaning began in the sergeant's tent. It was the keening sound of a "dying person" who had swallowed something possibly chemically related to hemlock. These awful sounds of misery would keep the entire battery awake for the remainder of the night. A fortnight later I would be hearing similar cries from the battlefield injured and dying.

The staff sergeant quickly recovered; however, the unscheduled event led to a stern lecture by the battery's captain on the subject of "Liquor Consumption." We were strongly urged by the commanding officer to read bottle labels before consuming their uncertain contents.

Our heavy equipment, including the howitzers, trucks, Jeeps, and our duffel bags had been unloaded from other ships of our ocean convoy to Marseilles and were beginning to arrive at the bivouac location. During the time of our forthcoming military equipment, many of us were granted passes to visit Marseilles. These passes would provide us with an opportunity to converse with the French citizenry. We could also practice speaking the language by making use of our newly issued French language phrase booklets. In addition, it would provide us experience learning how to use our rather skimpy supply of newly-issued colorful French paper "invasion" currency.

The paper money was almost as bright as the blue, red, green and purple hair styles displayed by the port city's *mademoiselles.*

In the port city we could illegally buy a loaf of delicious French bread providing we closed the deal with a few cigarettes. We had been ordered to not purchase food from the French since their food supply was rather lacking. Apparently their supply of tobacco products was even shorter.

It was my first attempt drinking schnapps (a German liquor). I didn't care much for the schnapps as a drink; however, it worked fairly well as a fuel source for my Zippo cigarette lighter.

The trip back into Marseilles and return gave us a good idea of the difficulty and distance of our long uphill march to the bivouac site after disembarking from the troop transports.

Both of my visits into Marseilles were taken with a soldier from one of the howitzer crews. The Artilleryman's name was Bill McDougall. He was an easy-going chap with a terrific sense of humor. His laid-back mannerisms reminded me of my old army friend, Bud Pitts. PFC McDougall purchased a "FDR" (Franklin D. Roosevelt) style cigarette holder from an enterprising Marseilles shopkeeper. My companion rationalized he could obtain a few more puffs on his supply of Chesterfields (U.S. brand of Cigarettes) by using this distinguished stylish gadget.

Approaching a corner newspaper stand, McDougall confidently inserted a fresh cigarette into his recently purchases holder and lit it. He inhaled a long drag from the spanking-new cigarette and lowered the hand clutching the holder and cigarette to his side. We momentarily halted at the crowded newsstand to observe the latest headlines. Departing from the area my gunnery friend put the holder back to his mouth and took another long drag from the now-empty device. While looking at the newspaper headlines a tobacco-starved Frenchman had "picked" the holder clean from its freshly mated cigarette.

Meanwhile, back at the staging location, most everything was in order for our departure to forward positions. As we struck camp the weather began to change for the worse. Our convoy formed and would soon depart from the unusually beautiful Mediterranean bivouac site.

My thoughts became a repetitious collage of happenings of my life up to this moment. I knew down deep inside I was still bitter and resentful over the seemingly bad turn of events with my former fiance. I wondered how I would handle this knotty problem during combat. I laid the nagging uncertainty to rest and slowly climbed up into the back of the waiting troop carrier. Soon our convoy began to move toward the direction of frontal battle lines.

Moments later, the sound of steady rain began to ominously fall upon the canvas cover of the troop carrier. The cold rain soon turned to sleet. The mood of the men appeared to change just as rapidly as the weather.

Facial expressions became somber and conversations were much shorter.

Postscript

While aboard the *Monticello* we did take an occasional shower; however, the water was from the ocean. Saltwater showers did little to make you believe you were better off afterward than before taking the shower.

****

I can still visualize the astonished expression on the mustached face of PFC McDougall when the friendly artilleryman realized he had been "sharked" by an unknown Frenchman deftly separating the cigarette from the "FDR" holder. We both often enjoyed many a chuckle over this incident in the days ahead.

****

Many years later while looking through the 103rd infantry division's *Report After Action*, I noticed photograph of a military vehicle transporting us to the battle area. The insignia on the tailgate resembled an elongated capital "X" with the top and bottom of the letter closed. It was similar to a straight line hourglass or two triangles with their apexes just touching.

In LaVan Martineau's book *The Rocks Begin to Speak*, he presents many interpretations of rock petroglyphs left behind by indigenous native people of the Southwest. The identical symbol painted on the back of the troop carrier showing the two triangles is similar to the ancient rock carving made up of two triangles (arrow points) that has the meaning "conflict" (war).

Chapter Eleven

Welcome to Combat

For the combat infantry rifleman, longevity is dismal for even the most optimistic. These soldiers fully understand the fragility of their existence. They constantly witness human dying, smell the dead, and themselves, cause swift dissolution. There is no beginning or end of the day for the rifleman. Only when complete victory over the enemy is achieved, can there be hope for a tomorrow.

—37531447

During the brief stay in the Marseilles countryside, the 103rd Infantry Division was "officially" welcomed to France by a woman known by Allied soldiers as "Berlin (Axis) Sally". Sally was the sexy-voiced radio "mouthpiece" of the Nazi propaganda department. The radio station was located somewhere in Germany and would broadcast recorded music, some from the "Big Band Era" of our high school days.

Undoubtedly the Germans knew the 103rd Division was on its way to Europe before we ever left Camp Howze, Texas. They certainly knew we were in New York City and were aware we were being transported across the Atlantic Ocean by Convoy U.G.F.-15B. Nazi U-boats were undoubtedly searching for us and would have much satisfaction if they could sink the largest troop ship in the convoy – the *Monticello.*

The Germans also were aware of our landing in Marseilles, France. This fact was confirmed by Berlin Sally's welcoming broadcast. The Nazi aerial photographic mission undoubtedly corroborated the division's presence in Southern France.

The purpose of the German broadcasts was not to be taken as an enemy gift to entertain American soldiers. The long interlude between each well-known tune was filled with Nazi propaganda. I couldn't help but recall the clear channel Mexican Border radio station "XELO" of my Fort Bliss days. There, it was little "country" music and lots of commercials and here – it was still a short-lived period of music mixed with ponderous doses of Nazi propaganda. The most often used Nazi tactic was informing us, "We (the Germans) do not want to do battle with you so you should go back home to your families. During your absence from your homes, your wives and girl friends are sleeping with draft-exempt defense plant workers."

Sally's honeyed voice didn't impress me. I had neither a wife nor a girl friend back home. I already was quite aware of who was sleeping with whom. It was highly doubtful if very many 103rd Infantry Division soldiers ever heard either the music or the propaganda. The majority of infantrymen did not have access to radios. Most military tactical radios did not cover civilian radio frequencies.

Among songs I occasionally would hear was *Paper Doll*. Especially remembered was the one line in the lyrics, "*I would rather have a paper doll to call my own, than have a fickle-minded real live girl.*" Perhaps the words struck a still tender segment of my deep inner feelings.

Berlin Sally also was informing division troops New York City had been destroyed by the German Luftwaffe (air force). 103rd Division men knew better since that had been their recent Port of Embarkation. There were often times when the German persuasion "mills" seemed to be out of sync with their own propaganda organizations.

Our military convoy continued the snail-paced journey through the rural French countryside. I was amazed to observe how near French villages were located in proximity to each other. Only a few kilometers (one kilometer = 0.6 mile) separated each small hamlet. My home town of Strong City, was located just across the Cottonwood River from the county seat town of Cottonwood Falls; however, most other rural towns in Kansas were a dozen or more kilometers distant from neighboring communities.

Every now and then, the army convoy would parallel railroad tracks along our route. Occasionally we would notice a French steam engine pulling "30 and 8" (thirty soldiers or eight horses) type train cars also transporting 103rd Division Infantry troops toward the front lines.

Acknowledging arm waves were traded between men on the train and the artillerymen in our motorized convoy. I could not ascertain how the exchange of greetings was to be interpreted. Was it a greeting of joy in seeing our own infantry troops or a *devoir* – suggesting the sadness of a final farewell? In a few short days many of the infantrymen possibly would be dead. At the time, it never seriously entered my youthful mind, I could also become a battle casualty of war.

When arriving in France, most of us believed the war with Germany had all but ended and our combat services would not be required. During one of our convoy stops provided to answer the call of nature, I observed some seasoned combat infantrymen marching to the rear for some R and R. I chanced to remark to one of them, "Is there anything left for us to do at the front?" A weary-appearing crusty combat infantry veteran paused, studied me momentarily and carefully phrased a brief, almost reverent, reply, "The war is not over and the guys up there can really use your help." The soldier's remark was by no means stated in a sarcastic or biting manner. I mulled the soldier's sincere short statement as his message began to reshape my previous attitude in believing the war was all but finished.

I was far too naïve to understand the magnitude of the problems facing us in the days ahead. I was not considering the Nazis had been driven out of North Africa, much of Italy, and western France. In the process of their withdrawal came numerous seasoned Nazi soldiers and salvaged weaponry. The fighting ahead would reflect the psychology of any people fighting to save their own homeland. Enemy supply lines were vastly shorter for the enemy, while our own supply line distance increased dramatically. The Germans, now desperate, would be defending Germany with great tenacity.

The weather appeared to become more disagreeable. The dampness of the rain, chill of the sleet and occasional snow, was beginning to make their unwanted presence known by the men riding in the trucks. My cold feet started to signal some serious problems concerning the inefficiency of our new winter clothing. This disconcerting belief was amplified by uncoordinated rest stops no longer coinciding with the need for more frequent body waste elimination due largely to the chilling damp weather.

Soldiers crowded in the truck took turns making the laborious trek to the tailgate of the moving vehicle prayerfully kneel down in front of the tailgate and "bless" the narrow French roadway with frequent "offerings" of recycled water.

The advent of diarrhea posed a more serious problem. Great skill and teamwork was required to hold the seated "victim" on top of the narrow steel tailgate of the moving truck while answering the unexpected rapid call of nature. It was an extremely delicate operation. We had to make certain the unfortunate soldier extended the highly important necessary distance over the frigid metal tailgate.

The most dangerous part of the exploit would take place when the "patient" had to make use of toilet paper while holding on to the truck with his only free hand. Curves in the road or rough spots only added to the degree of the challenge.

These episodes caused me give much credit to the military genius who recognized the need to maintain a 100-hundred yard interval between each vehicle. The football field distance between the vehicles was for security reasons to minimize damage from enemy strafing and shelling; however, the 300-foot distance was an added gratuity for drivers in each following vehicle. I mentally presented the inventor of the "windshield" with the *Nobel Prize* in the – "you pick a category".

The journey toward the front lines was a longer distance than we had been led to believe. At Marseilles the frontal positions were less than a hundred miles to the northeast; however, we now were going more northerly on an odyssey covering almost five-hundred miles.

Our convoy was passing through the city of Lyon, France and I considered the name to be a small coincidence. I had been inducted into the Army from the Lyon County Induction Center of Emporia, Kansas. The very name momentarily turned my memories back to the old haunts of my youthful days.

Members of the convoy were now beginning to notice some of the carnage from recent military action along the roadside as our military entourage of trucks, 105mm howitzers and Jeeps continued to the northeast. Burned military vehicles, mostly German, had been unceremoniously bulldozed off the narrow French road. Every so often a United States tank or truck could be identified among the burned and bullet-riddled roadside debris. This definitely was not training maneuvers. Recognizing the combat wreckage was increasing the already high intensity level of our ever mounting nervous anxiety.

The relatively flat countryside was gradually being replaced with high woodland hills. The small villages the convoy was threading through were showing evidence of even more recent warfare. Shattered roofing tiles, bullet pockmarked buildings and piles of fresh battle rubble were noticeable indications our frontal area destination would soon be reached. Caliginous forested mountain terrain was now replacing the medium-sized hills the convoy had been traversing.

Everyone became silent and seemed to be preoccupied with inner thoughts. There appeared to be a ghostly perception of unreality to what was taking place. It could be likened to having a disturbing dream and knowing you will mercifully awaken from the unwanted nightmarish aberration.

The early autumn daylight was being replaced with darkness as our motorized column of trucks, using the small dim blackout lights, slowly probed the darkened roadway leading to reserve frontal positions. The night became very quiet as the convoy vehicles carefully inched forward.

Suddenly a lightening-like bolt of brilliant light followed by a tremendous explosion took place near the left side of the truck. The though of being cold was instantaneously replaced by the urgent need to urinate.

37531447 had erroneously believed a huge German artillery projectile had come close to making a direct hit on the truck. The large explosion and flash of intense light had come from a United States Army weapon positioned close to the roadway. The outgoing missile was fired from a 155mm artillery piece called a "Long Tom". This weapon was capable of sending a ninety-five pound lethal charge accurately to a target almost fourteen miles distant. I soon would learn the difference between the sound of incoming and outgoing artillery shells.

Military scuttlebutt suggested we would be relieving a well-known infantry division and becoming operational with the United States Seventh Army commanded by General Alexander M. Patch. This grapevine rumor would prove to be accurate.

We were currently located in the foothills of the Vosges Mountains near the German-held French city of St. Die. The city was just north and west of the so-called "Colmar Pocket" bordering France and Switzerland. The 103rd Infantry Division would be relieving units of the U.S. Third Infantry Division – giving those weary fighting men a well deserved rest.

The truck slowly ground to a halt. We dismounted and were immediately informed about the danger of incoming artillery shells exploding at tree-top levels, sending their deadly jagged steel shrapnel in all directions. We spent the remainder of the night constructing log-covered foxholes or pulling sentry duty.

With the emergence of dawn our forward observer team would be establishing observation positions overlooking enemy defenses. The names of St. Die, Steige, Barr, Eafig and Selestat would become a memorable part of our geographic vocabulary.

Some major problems facing the 103rd Division would be the almost endless mountainous terrain, the Siegfried Line of enemy fortified positions, the wide Rhine River to cross and an usually bitterly cold wet winter. Floods, dysentery and inadequate winter clothing were among a rather lengthy list of lesser problems.

On the morning of November 11, 1944, soldiers from the 103rd Infantry Division were involved with the deadly and ugly business of killing and being killed.

Postscript

The song *Paper Doll* was recorded in the United States on February 18, 1942, by the black harmonizing group "The Mills Brothers". Over six-million copies of the record were sold.

****

The Third Infantry Division, replaced by the 103rd Infantry Division on the front lines, had commenced their combat action with the assault on North Africa on November 8, 1942. This action was followed by assaults on Sicily, Anzio and the Colmar Pocket of the Vosges Mountain region. The Third Division was never given any "cushy" assignments. The United States Army Infantry Division listed

4,922 men killed in action, 18,766 men wounded in action. 636 wounded died from battle wounds.

****

United States Army infantry divisions were supported by four division artillery (*divarty*) field artillery battalions. Three of the four battalions used 105mm towed howitzers and the fourth – 155mm towed howitzers. Each 105mm howitzer battery had six howitzers when at maximum strength.

Larger artillery such as the 240mm (eight-inch) self-propelled tracked howitzers were not part of supporting divarty but remained within the "corps" level of army command.

****

It is well within the realm of possibility, that the small group of men who vented their displeasure with the heavy weapons platoon staff sergeant at Camp Howze, were sent to the Third Infantry Division as replacements.

****

Axis Sally was the German counterpart of Tokyo Rose who also played recorded music from the Big Band Era while dishing out Japanese propaganda for troops in the Pacific Theatre of Operations.

Axis Sally was an American woman who broadcast propaganda for the Germans. Mildred E. Gillars, a native of Portland, Maine, and a former Ohio Wesleyan University student, went to Germany in the 1920's and worked as a singer. When the war began, she left a job teaching English to broadcast propaganda from a Berlin radio station. In broadcasts aimed at American troops in Europe, she taunted soldiers with tales of unfaithful wives and girlfriends back home. The troops dubbed her Axis Sally and scoffed at her while enjoying her jazz records and her frequent playing of *Lili Marline*, one of the hit songs of the war. Arrested after the war, she was convicted of treason in 1949 and sentenced to twelve years in prison. She was paroled in 1961.

****

The French railroad cars carrying division troops to the front lines were similar to the "40 and 8" type boxcars used in World War I. Since only thirty soldiers were allotted to each rail car the men had more room in which to move about.

Chapter Twelve

The Vosges Mountain Campaign

> *Had I but been born blind, I would not have caused*
> *so many deaths and so much destruction. At times I was*
> *the "god" who determined which enemy would live or*
> *which would perish. I was a forward observer for the*
> *field artillery. Yet, concealed across the battlefield was*
> *my foe counterpart and he would have to make the*
> *decision if I was to be spared or would be eliminated. I*
> *never found my adversary to be more charitable than I.*
> *—37531447*

Some units of the 103rd Cactus Division participated in action on the anniversary of the World War One Armistice Day of November 11th. The first combat mission undertaken by Battery A of the 928th Field Artillery Battalion would come several days later.

The battery would be lending artillery support for the 411th Infantry Regiment. The 928th Field Artillery would most often support the 411th Infantry Regiment. On other occasions we would bolster the 409th and 410th Infantry Regiments. It was doubtful if any of us realized how formidable the German-held territory of our first combat assignment would prove to be.

This section of the Vosges Mountains was extremely well fortified and largely defended by experienced German military units. The enemy had sufficient time to construct numerous defensive positions. Likely invasion routes had been meticulously zeroed in by enemy artillery, machine gun emplacements, tanks, and twenty-millimeter rapid-fire antiaircraft/anti personnel weapons. This awesome assemblage of weaponry was ready for use against our ground troops. In addition – roads had been mined, roadblocks constructed, lethal booby traps in place and concentrations of both heavy and light mortars awaited to deal dissolution for the infantrymen of the Cactus Division. If the soldiers of the 103rd Division could seize their assigned objective, it would open up a pathway leading to the Rhine River and the German homeland. Nazi troops defending this region were very much aware of the importance of holding onto the vital defensive high ground of the Vosges Mountains of Alsace.

Our FO (forward observer) group was made up of Lieutenant Whidden, Elsworth Lockwood from Hayward, California, Corporal Safford and 37531447. Field artillery battalions had enough men to allow rotation of FO groups, adding additional groups or changing the manpower makeup of individual FO units.

For the division's impending attack, Lieutenant Whidden would be the commissioned officer in charge of our small group of observers. The lieutenant was a natural leader who understood how to best use artillery against the enemy. If he had any fear it never did show. The lieutenant's primary goal was to help infantry riflemen survive by directing artillery fire on Nazi strong points of opposition as well as elimination of German artillery forward observer positions. Forward observers were the "eyes" for rear-positioned artillery gunners.

While moving onward on foot to our OP (observation point) we met a "Graves Registration and Body Recovery" team near the front line position. Using a Jeep and a military trailer they were picking up both U.S. Third Division and German dead from the recent previous battle. It was difficult for me to observe this warfare arena and realize such an unnatural event was actually taking place. The many bodies on the trailer were grotesquely cross-stacked like lengthy logs of firewood.

One of the soldiers with the body recovery team stared indifferently at me and lamented, "I don't mind placing our dead on the trailer, but it sure as hell bothers me to place one of these Nazi sons-of-bitches on top of our guys." The bizarre part about this unusual one-sided conversation was the soldier did not really appear to want a response to his unsolicited words. I nodded my head as if I fully understood the meaning of the commentary from the obviously stressed-out soldier and continued walking.

Another soldier from the Third Infantry Division, upon noticing me, approached and voluntarily exclaimed, "I sure am glad to see you guys!" His face was drawn and his eyes were almost completely expressionless. He did not have to tell me that he had been through some real rough fighting. I wasn't certain how I should reply to his remark or even if a response was required. I chose to respond to the

139

soldier wearing the striped blue and white division patch. "We'll get these Nazi bastards and then we'll go after those fuckin' Japs!"

37531447 most likely was attempting to bolster his own courage to help cope with a situation he had never before experienced. The rough expletives were just a component of the process.

I was not prepared for the rejoinder the Third Division soldier gave me. I feel certain he knew we were untested fighting troops as he crisply replied, "We have some Japanese-Americans with our division and let me tell you they are one hell of a fighting group and we are damn proud of them!" Attentively listening to his mini-lecture he added, "They are a gutsy group of fighters. Even the German soldiers respect their courage." It was the first good remark I had heard about American-Japanese (Nisei). I silently ended the brief dialog and once again commenced walking. My mind was still struggling to analyze the Third Infantry Division soldier's strongly worded statements. How could it possibly be we had Japanese-Americans fighting in the U.S. Army when I knew full-well the country had rounded up the Japanese-Americans and placed them in detention camps based on the belief they were both security risks and traitors? The United States Government had even confiscated their land and other belongings.

Eventually reaching our observation post, we began the process of searching for enemy strong positions. We located quite a number of suspected targets including machine-gun positions, artillery and mortar emplacements. In addition, we spotted several camouflaged German tanks. Map coordinates of all suspected enemy targets were relayed back to our rear area Fire control and eventually on to our howitzers. In the morning our 105's, along with other division artillery, would concentrate a barrage of fire-power on these worthy targets.

Preceding the actual infantry attack would be what is called a "rolling barrage" of our artillery that would place the explosive projectile rounds a relatively short distance ahead of our own advancing troops. We would have to inform the artillery batteries when to move the rounds slightly further ahead, or infantry platoon leaders would have to hold up their men in order to avoid being struck by our own artillery shells. The operation required a high degree of expertise and coordinated cooperation. The purpose of this artillery procedure was to detonate mines, destroy foot soldiers, eliminate rapid fire weapon outposts and keep the enemy pinned down. During a rolling barrage, enemy counter artillery was often mistaken for short rounds of so-called "friendly fire".

I made one of my first combat blunders before the imminent battle began. Noticing a highly worried 411th infantryman, I believed I could give him some reassurance if I told him our FO group had most of the enemy positions spotted for our howitzers. Unfortunately, there were far more Nazi strong points hidden from view.

Before the battle ceased, I developed a real good understanding in the difference between incoming and outgoing artillery rounds. I soon learned when to "hit the dirt" or ignore the enemy artillery rounds.

It would be an understatement to suggest "all hell broke loose" when the initial attack commenced. The 411th Infantry Regiment took many casualties during the battle. The infantryman I had tried to reassure earlier had survived the battle; however, his unit took heavy casualties and he lost many friends from his platoon. Later, when he spotted me, he sarcastically berated me by his cutting words, "So you had all the targets located, huh?" I did not attempt to answer the soldier. I never made any more endeavors to reassure anyone else throughout the duration of the conflict.

The "Grave and Body Recovery Unit" I had earlier witnessed picking up battlefield dead would be doing the same thing all over again. This time there would be one important difference. The dead United States infantrymen would be wearing a saguaro cactus shoulder patch and not the blue and white-striped Third Division insignia.

The 103rd Division's inaugural objective to take the high Vosges Mountain terrain was successful in military terminology if battle dead and injured were overlooked.

For the infantrymen there always appeared to be one more battle awaiting. For FO's it always meant one more isolated OP to maintain and perform a similar type operation all over again.

Most of the time we used radios to give the howitzer crews pertinent target information. When time permitted, we would also use small black insulated electrical communication field wire. We would string the wire from the OP to rear guns positions. It would create a telephone setup quite similar to the type we had used in antiaircraft training at Fort Bliss, Texas. It was far safer to communicate with the

EEA8 field telephone than the use of radios. Radio transmissions would help enemy counterintelligence locate our FO position by utilizing direction finding loop antennas.

Regardless of which system of communication we utilized, a high observation position was essential. When establishing an OP in a village, we always avoided the highest two vantage points and would opt for the third highest point. We witnessed many tall church bell towers disappear from view when destroyed by German artillery. The Germans incorrectly believed the tall bell tower was the most likely location of U.S. artillery observation positions. When the first highest point was destroyed, we down-graded our position to the next highest point if possible. I am certain we must have annoyed the hell out of the Germans as they attempted to wonder where our OP was located since we kept right on ordering more artillery strikes on their positions.

One fascinating situation occurred when our group located the OP in a three-story vacant building. The top-story room we were using contained a small wood burning stove and an ample supply of firewood. Corporal Lockwood started a fire in the stove so he could stay warm. The Germans evidently noticing this new smoke source coming from the chimney, decided the building would be a worthy target for one of their large SP (self propelled) artillery pieces. Upon hearing the SP gun fire, Lockwood led the charge down the narrow staircase leading to the basement. Somewhere between the first and second story, Corporal Lockwood stopped, turned around and rapidly disappeared back up the narrow stairway. At that moment the other two of us felt the building shudder after taking a direct enemy artillery hit. The rest of us continued the expeditious descent to the relative safety of the basement. We began to wonder what had prompted the Hayward Californian to return to the third floor. We began to express a degree of uneasiness about his fate.

We didn't have to wait very long before a healthy and grinning Lockwood showed up in the basement. Before we could ask him anything, he proudly announced the now old news, "A German artillery round hit our OP room!" His explanation for running back upstairs during the shelling was, "I didn't want the fire in the stove to go out while we were down here in the basement." The war paused for a few brief moments as we evaluated his exegesis.

During the lengthy wait in the basement the fire did go out. We decided to continue using the now – almost three story building, hopefully guessing the enemy SP gun crew believed they had successfully eliminated us with their artillery. We proceeded to pick out targets for our own artillery, one of which included the SP gun. We gave up on future stove fires for warmth. It just wasn't a very prudent thing to do.

Battery A of the 928th was commanded by Captain Hanlon. He was an excellent commissioned officer and was very much aware of my military training, especially those portions indicating I had some previous infantry training. He appeared to take a measure of comfort in knowing I was his Jeep radio operator whenever the howitzers would be moved to take up new firing positions.

There were times when I would be moving to a new OP and another FO would fill in as the captain's radio operator. His personal driver was Corporal A. P. Chipman, who hailed from the small rural community of Friendship, Tennessee. Chipman was well-suited to be the captain's chauffeur. He seemed to possess a photographic memory. It was standard operational procedure to have the captain locate new positions for the howitzers, return to the old position and lead the battery of guns to the new site. Chipman could navigate the Jeep through, over, or around the debris of war shattered villages and accurately make the return trip to lead the howitzers to their new sites.

Any type of equipment requiring an electrical energy source for operation, automatically indicated the usage of that particular apparatus would be performed by radio operators regardless of any prior training with the contrivance. This belief was similar to the military concept, "If it has handles it can be carried". One of my "inherited" duties was to operate the portable land mine sweeper and check the new gun placement positions for possible German land mines – prior to the positioning the howitzers in their new firing posture. I always had a large notch of apprehension during this sweeping process. The Germans were beginning to use plastic mines. The metal detector could not readily detect this new type plastic weapon. When I did obtain an indication suggesting the likelihood of a possible mine, I would use a slender four-sided French bayonet to probe the unidentified object at a low angle – an angle most likely to miss the detonator usually positioned on the top of the mine. Most of the "readings" located buried shrapnel. The mine sweeping operation was a task always receiving my full undivided attention.

On one noteworthy occasion the audible warning device on the electronic metal detector, positioned on my shoulder, began to alert me to the possibility of a mine-sized object under the surface of the ground. The object's shape, as indicated by the sweeping, gave me concern that the object might not be shrapnel. Gingerly probing at a low angle, I made contact with the buried object in question with the French bayonet and became quite puzzled.

The probe did not appear to be touching any metal. Carefully removing soil from the perimeter of the object, I came to a rubber-like material resembling a portion of an inner tube from an automobile tire. Further work uncovered a sixteen-inch section of an auto tire inner tube tied securely at both ends with cordage. Something heavy was positioned inside the tube. I cautiously untied one of the ends. Slightly lifting up the remaining tied end, a revolver and a small supply of cartridges slid to the ground. The weapon appeared to be in excellent condition and I decided to carry it since it might provide me with a small measure of extra security.

After a couple of weeks passed, I had an opportunity to test-fire my recently acquired pistol. The target of choice would be a tree stump located by a mountain stream. I took aim and gently pulled the trigger which would propel the lead bullet speeding on its journey. When the firing pin struck the rear of the cartridge the sound of a muted "poof", not the sharp crack of a healthy explosion, was duly noted. I was dumbfounded when I heard the sound of a small object strike the ground directly in front of my combat boots. The bullet only traveled slightly more than the length of the pistol's gun barrel before dropping to the ground. I fired one more round and this time the bullet lodged in the barrel of the revolver. The powder inside the cartridges had become damp during the entombment in the inner tube "coffin". The weapon was immediately dispatched into a nearby stream. I questioned, "What would have happened to me had I been forced to make use of the gun in a critical situation?". I disliked the logical return answer to my query.

While performing the dangerous mine sweeping operation, I never ever discovered a land mine. Looking at my unwanted hazardous occupation in another way – *neither did I ever miss one!*

One late afternoon the captain pulled 37531447's name out from the underside of his protective "steel helmet" to lead a group of our own battery artillerymen into a wooded area to check out the report of bypassed German soldiers. Frankly, I worried the most about being shot by my own nervous artillery members. The rumor proved to be false.

Moving ever deeper into the Vosges Mountains, the days and nights almost appeared to be one and the same. At times it was so foggy it was impossible to locate any enemy targets. It was at such a time when our vital OP phones became inoperative. This usually meant either an enemy shell had severed the thin black electrical communication line or the wire had been intentionally cut by an enemy patrol. It was my lot to follow the little black field wire through the fog-shrouded dark forest to locate the break and make the necessary repairs. Picking up my tools and extra loops of field wire, I began the lonely trek by myself, knowing full well that if it had been cut, there was the possibility of a enemy greeting party waiting for me to show up at the point of the line malfunction. I felt very much as if I were living on the thin edge of existence.

Hiking a couple of kilometers through the snow, I located the broken line. It had been cut; however, the other end of the line was almost touching. Usually when a communication line is cut, the enemy would remove a length of the wire just to make repair work more difficult. This was the reason extra coils of field wire were carried with wire repairmen. Had I interrupted recent activities of a nearby enemy patrol? Perhaps the enemy patrol had severed the communication line in numerous different places. The air temperature appeared to warm up considerably during the time used to splice the "broken" field communication wire. Seconds of time seemed like minute units of time measurement until the splice was completed. I checked the vicinity for other possible breaks. Finding none, I hastily departed the area and headed back to the OP.

This time luck had been with me. I celebrated my good fortune by removing a C-ration can of hash from my combat jacket and laboriously cut open the lid with cold numb fingers and the midget-sized can opener that came inside the boxes of K-rations. Removing a spoon I carried from the inside of my combat boot, I commenced the attempt to eat the hash. I had not noticed the fog had lifted and the air was so cold the hash had frozen inside my jacket pocket. Both the can and its contents were pitched, the spoon replaced to the outer inside of my boot and 37531447 continued the cold lonely trek back to the OP.

Arriving at the observation point, the smile on the faces of my friends told me the phone line was once again operative. It was kind of a double purpose smile as other forward observers were highly relieved to know I had safely returned.

Following several days at the OP our crew returned to the gun emplacements while another group took over observation duties. I was always highly annoyed to be informed by the mess sergeant to wait until the regularly scheduled meal time before I could obtain something to eat or even get a hot cup of coffee. It also bothered me that during my previous stay at the OP, new warmer winter trousers had been issued by the supply sergeant. The supply sergeant joyfully announced he had "saved" a pair for me. I was supposed to be overjoyed with my new size "forty-two" britches for my 135-pound body frame. My protesting complaint fell on the sergeant's seemingly deaf ears. The battery supply sergeant's clothing always appeared to fit as if it had been professionally tailored.

My new winter trousers were so oversized, even after the cuff area was tucked into my combat boots, the so-called "bloused" leg portion dragged on the ground. When Captain Hanlon observed my new wardrobe he suggested I should find something better fitting. The supply sergeant was almost my size, but the captain's remark was only a suggestion and not an order. I was certain I resembled one of the zoot-suiters observed at the Fort Leavenworth Induction Center.

Several days later I was presented a new pair of correct fitting winter trousers; however, they were not from the battery's haberdasher. They came from the supply officer of the Black 614th Tank Destroyer Battalion which was now operational with the 103rd Infantry Division. The captain was quite happy I had trousers that fit, I was delighted to have warm fitting trousers and our supply sergeant was bothered to no small degree about not knowing how I managed to obtain new correct fitting winter trousers without having to bend over to kiss his fuckin' ass.

Every time the large howitzers were moved forward after a recent battle, the burying squads would arrive to remove the corpses. Before they came, one member from our own battery howitzer crew took great delight in bayonetting dead German soldiers. He either was trying to be macho or most likely his "orbs were not orbiting". I found his actions to be completely repugnant. Later, upon return from another FO assignment, I was informed the "soldier" had been killed when he picked up a German booby-trapped German pistol. His parents back in the "states" would soon be receiving a telegram informing them, "…your son has been Killed in Action", etc.

The weather had now worsened and air temperatures were quite low. I found it interesting to think how human beings could almost become acclimated to the harsh mountain winter.

On my short stay with the howitzer crews, an urgent call came for an FO team to go to a frontal area near Metz (France) where the enemy was launching some probing counterattacks. I was not called to be part of this group; however, I was cognizant of the seriousness of the situation as well as the extreme danger of this particular mission. Corporal Lockwood was one of the assigned radio operators for the perilous undertaking.

Confronting the Hayward, Californian, I just right out asked him, "How many Lockwoods' are in your immediate family?" He appeared somewhat puzzled by the unusual question. His reply, "I am the only Lockwood other than my parents." The corporal hastily added, "Why do you want to know?" I quickly informed him, "My parents have six boys, and I would appreciate it if you would let me take your place as the radio operator for this assignment." I was surprised when the hesitating Lockwood reluctantly agreed to this hasty arrangement. I felt certain the corporal would be assigned a less dangerous mission. The California soldier was another terrifically talented FO from our battery.

Our FO crew would be led by Lieutenant Whidden and the OP location would be north of the Colmar area not too far distant from the approaches to the industrial area of Germany. It would be a difficult task in support of the 411th Infantry Regiment.

Arriving at the desired advantage position, we established the observation post. Lieutenant Whidden had changed his views considerably since our first possible enemy target of the war. I recall the first time when we observed German soldiers go into a building. On that occasion he did not call for an artillery strike, declaring that it would damage or destroy the building. Now a single German uniform would be cause enough for the officer to call for an artillery response.

Following a brief lull in activity, a small group of ravens landed in an open field between our wooded position and German held territory. I was both astonished and amused when I noticed the lieutenant seriously studying the small flock of birds. I was already reading his mind and knew exactly what he was contemplating. He turned to me and read off map coordinates for an artillery strike of one round for the ravens. He must have noticed the look of disbelief on my face as I radioed the necessary target information to fire control center.

Upon the completion of my brief radio transmission calling for an artillery strike, the now smiling artillery officer explained, "I just want to check the gun crews to see how good they are."

Moments later, the whining whooshing sound of a single projectile low overhead signaled the arriving large artillery round. It was right on target. The grinning lieutenant proudly proclaimed, "They are getting pretty damn good aren't they?"

German soldiers, undoubtedly witnessing this episode, must have come to conclusion American forward observers are crazy as hell! When our gun battery fire control unit wanted to know the nature of our target, I radioed back, "It appeared to have been some sort of *flying contraption* on the ground." My thoughts returned to Camp Howze and the taxpayers when I had downed the drone plane in my first practice session with the .30-caliber machine gun.

Again returning to where the battery guns were located, forward observers traded their heavy M-1 Garand rifles for .30-caliber light weight automatic gas operated carbines having a 15 round clip. It meant several less pounds to carry plus the carbine was much shorter in length and less awkward to manage when transporting the bulky communication equipment. We welcomed the exchange. I did not, however, welcome the report informing me Corporal Lockwood had been wounded by shrapnel while on a mission with another one of our FO crews. I was deeply saddened to know the corporal had been injured.

Postscript

The 36th Infantry Division (Texas National Guard) had one of its regiments cut off while in the *Foret Domaniale de Champ* on October 23, 1944 and was rescued by the 442nd Infantry Regiment which was made up of Japanese Americans (Nisei) during heavy combat on October 30, 1944. This action took place in the Vosges foothills (Bruyeres). The Texas unit that had been cut off and rescued by the Nisei regiment, was the 141st Infantry Regiment. The 141st was attached to the Third Infantry Division during the first part of September of 1944.

The 103rd Division entered combat on November 11, 1944. When I met up with the soldier wearing the Third Division insignia who informed me about the bravery of the Japanese-American soldiers, he evidently was either a member of, or a replacement for the 141st Texas unit, that the 442nd Nisei Regimental Combat Team had rescued! I feel certain this was the reason for the soldier's scholarly lecture to me regarding the exemplary fighting ability of the Nisei soldiers.

****

On March 21, 1996 I received an obituary notice from my Wyoming friend, Russell A. "Bud" Pitts. The obituary notice appeared in the *Casper Star Tribune* and told of the death of Masa Suyematsu at the age of 98. The obituary stated, "The deceased woman's two sons, Tosh and King, both served with the famed Japanese American (Nisei) 442nd Regimental Combat Team in World War II."

The death notice went on to relate, "Both brothers were wounded in the same engagement, the 442nd's breakthrough to a surrounded Texas Battalion (141st Infantry Battalion of the 36th Infantry Division) in northern France."

The obituary also pointed out, "In addition to two Purple Hearts, Tosh earned a Silver Star, Bronze Star and four Unit Citations with the 442nd."

After the conflict and a college education, Tosh Suyematsu served as Assistant U.S. Attorney General in Cheyenne, Wyoming, until his death in 1994.

Bud Pitts remembered both boys (Tosh and King) since they also attended Natona High School in Casper, Wyoming.

I am not certain if the word "battalion" used in the obituary is correct since I question if the word used should have been "regiment". I realize there were unit designation exceptions and this might well have been one of them.

****

After the Japanese bombing of Pear Harbor, Hawaii, the move to remove Japanese Americans (Citizens of the United States) from coastal areas along the west coast for reasons of national security and placing them in camps, such as the Heart Mountain facilities in Wyoming, the Manzanar relocation center near Independence, California, on the Gila Indian Reservation near Sacaton, Arizona or Poston (near Parker, Arizona), may have sounded reasonable on first glance. The move, after all, was U.S. politics of the time amplified by genuine fear of an impending uprising of the Orientals living on the West Coast.

Many possessions of Japanese-American citizens acquired through years of hard work and thrifty management, possibly were lost to masquerading opportunistic non-Japanese property "grabbers" operating under the premise, "the time was right" and concerns over national defense gave them the perfect alibi for such a fortuitous "patriotic" opportunity to increase their individual or corporate wealth.

The California Anti-Alien Land Acts of 1913 and 1920 denied the Issei – Japanese parents of the Nisei (legitimate citizens of the United States by right of birth) – the right to own land. *The United States Exclusion Act* of 1924 denying the Issei citizenship rights, automatically made them "enemy aliens."

****

Seldom is it ever mentioned close to 2,000 (the actual number may never be known) people of German and Italian ancestry were also interned. When the United States became actively involved in the conflict, war prejudices were often directed against Americans of Italian and German decent.

****

I still have great detestation for the Japanese surprise sneak attack at Pearl Harbor. I also realize the relocation camps for the Japanese-Americans forced them to reside in rickety tarpaper covered barracks (20 X 25 feet) with no privacy, no insulation, hot summers without cooling facilities, enduring incredible dust storms and shared communal bathroom facilities. Those living at Heart Mountain had the additional hardship of bitter cold of Wyoming winters. The hardships listed above were somewhat identical to those I encountered at Logan Heights during military training at Fort Bliss. Mary Ruth Blackburn of Ralston, Wyoming, notes the real difference at the relocation center at Heart Mountain, Wyoming, and Logan Heights at Fort Bliss. She rightfully points out, "A person can feel for the elderly and for the mothers with little ones. On top of that – these people came from a warm climate. Lack of warm clothing, shortage of coal (heating), and inadequate diets added to the stress of life in the camp."

I realize many basic privileges were taken away from those removed to relocation centers. In spite of the fact I endured the hardships of being uprooted from my home for three years, sent to a foreign land, oftentimes cold and hungry, usually provided with only primitive shelter and being shot at countless times, I do not resent the fact *survivors* of the relocation camps were given $20,000 in 1980 by the U.S. Congress as reparations. By 1980 many of the original internes, the ones most deserving and bearing most of the burden of the times, had died.

Perhaps the largest disparity would be, "My citizenship was honored by the United States Government while Japanese-Americans were stripped of their United States citizenship rights."

****

Preceding United States involvement in the war, two heavy weight boxing matches occurred between the African-American Joe Louis, "The Brown Bomber", and Max Schmeling of Germany. In the

151

first fight between the two men, Joe Louis was the loser in the 18th round of the fight. It was the first time Louis had ever been defeated in a boxing match. In 1938, (just prior to World War II) a re-match of the two world renowned pugilists took place. Max Schmeling lost this match in the opening round.

In recalling the strange paradox of this event, U.S. citizens of German ancestry had to "silently" root for the German boxer (if that was their choice) or risk being accused of being un-American and branded traitors of their nation. Other white Americans could openly "patriotically" cheer for "their nigger" even though African-Americans were considered by many of these *same* white people – unfit combat "material" for the U.S. military service.

****

The frivolity of Lieutenant Whidden directing a 105mm artillery round to be expended on a flock of ravens might be compared to a remark attributed to the German commander defending Aachen, Germany from the advancing Allied Forces. The German officer reportedly stated, "When the Americans start using 155's (Long Toms) as a sniper weapon, it is time to give up."

****

The small hinged can opener I used to open the can of hash was about an inch and a quarter in length and five/eighths of an inch wide. Instructions and diagrams were printed on the brown paper wrapper of the opener. Printed instructions are as follows: **"CAN OPENER DIRECTIONS"**

Open blade. Place opener as shown in the diagram. Twist down to puncture slot in can top inside rim. Cut top by advancing opener with rocking motion. Take small bites.

STERILIZE BEFORE RE-USE

Tie string through hole in opener to wash and sterilize with mess gear. If possible. When boiling water is unavailable, clean opener as thoroughly as possible and hold cutting blade over a match flame a few seconds before use."

****

When repairing the black communication wire the enemy had cut, I could have tapped into the line immediately after it was spliced to determine if the circuit was operative. At the time we did not have a "test phone" available at the OP for this purpose.

****

Although the 411th Infantryman I had tried to assure before our first combat survived the initial fighting, he later lost his life in subsequent battle action on March 17th, 1945. I have no other information about the regimental soldier. I deeply regret he was KIA ("killed in action").

****

The Nazis would make use of church towers for their observation positions causing them to make the erroneous assumption U.S. artillery observers also used church towers for the same purpose. It was unfortunate our artillery had to destroy many church steeples to rid them of the enemy.

****

Sound travels approximately 1100 feet per second of time. This often was faster than the travel time of an approaching projectile. This made it possible to often hear a distant large gun fire a brief interval of time before the actual arrival of the missile. The higher a gun muzzle was elevated, the longer it took for the shell to arrive since the travel path now became longer. The SP gun shelling our three-story OP (observation point) had to elevate its barrel to miss a nearby building "hiding" the low profile weapon from our view. Had the SP gun been able to directly fire at us, this narrative might not have been written.

Chapter Thirteen

Over the Vosges Mountains

> *Soil and moisture can be compatible when it comes
> to dealing misery. As ugly as the mud was for fighting
> the ground war, it was equally honest for friend and foe
> alike. Eastern Kansas black "gumbo" breeds a far
> worse concoction than the European variety.*
>
> *—37531447*

Fortunately, Corporal Lockwood's battle wound was not too serious and before long he was back with the gun battery FO pool, displaying his new Purple Heart Medal. The medal is presented to United States soldiers receiving battle wounds as the result of enemy action.

Lockwood earned the distinction of being the first forward observer in our artillery battery FO unit to be awarded the Purple Heart Medal. 37531447 was certain he had played an unintentional ignominious role in helping the corporal achieve the unsolicited award.

The weather in the Vosges most always seemed to be either foggy or snowy. To break this monotonous happening, some aberrant source must have contrived the slow continuous bone-chilling drizzle. Unpaved roads turned into quagmires causing much difficulty for even tracked and four-wheel-drive military vehicles. In some of the wooded areas combat engineers constructed corduroy (log) roads. Travel over such roads was a slow jolting tribulation. The muddy and damp conditions, along with the cold weather, was the leading cause of trench foot, a painful condition of the feet impersonating frostbite.

Following the return of Corporal Lockwood, we received an additional forward observer. The new man was Staff Sergeant Greene. The gunnery sergeant was the soldier having the unfortunate experience with alcoholic spirits when the 103rd Division was in the staging area outside of Marsielles.

Sergeant Greene was an accomplished artilleryman who called Athens, Ohio his home town. The big soldier became a member of our small fraternity of FOs due to an extraordinary circumstance. The sergeant's gun crew had fired their howitzer so many times in supportive action for division infantry regiments that the large howitzer had to be returned to rear echelon ordnance for extensive repairs. No replacement weapon was immediately available.

Sergeant Greene was so intimately attached to the 105mm weapon he broke down and began to softly sob as "his" howitzer was being towed away for repairs. After regaining his soldierly composure, Greene immediately asked for permission from the commanding officer to join our forward observer group. The sergeant's expertise in howitzer gunnery would make the Ohio noncom a highly valuable asset for our team of forward observers. Captain Hanlon approved the distraught soldier's request.

For a short duration of time our battalion was placed in a reserve military posture. With not much enemy action in our sector, we were taken to makeshift ranges to once again qualify (a method to check on our shooting skills) using our rifles and carbines.

Chipman, the Captain's Jeep driver was a pretty fair marksman with army rifles; however, I usually managed to outshoot him on the firing range. The soldier from Tennessee always appeared downright disappointed when my marksmanship score was higher than his tally. Taking prone positions along side each other on the firing range, we commenced our qualifying firing. I expended a few rounds into my target and then edged the carbine slightly to the right and squeezed off a couple rounds on the small bull's-eye of Corporal Chipman's target. Slowly moving my weapon back to my target, I finished the clip of .30-caliber ammunition. Corporal Chipman's face was really beaming when the scores were added up as he proudly exclaimed, "Yankee, you all got your butt beat this time!" Nobody apparently noticed his target had more bullet holes than it should and I had twice completely missed my range target. We both felt good about the exercise to successfully qualify but each for a different reason.

In addition to the small arms range firing some of us were selected for bazooka (rocket weapon) training. I was one of those destined to receive instructions on the use of the antitank weapon. Lacking prior experience in handling the bazooka, I became rather apprehensive about my ability to operate the rocket-like device. This is possibly a trait of individuals born under the sign of "Capricorn". A mental problem came into play when I understood how the shoulder positioned weapon operated as it was being loaded for firing.

The bazooka resembled a two and a third inch length diameter piece of thin pipe fifty-four inches in length and was rear-end loaded by another person. When the electronic trigger was activated the three and a half pound missile inside the tube would be rapidly accelerating – only a fraction of an inch from my head and exit the front of the tube on its speedy journey toward the intended target.

The selected impact site chosen for the bazooka's projectile was a rather tall tree stump some seventy-five yards down range. I was the last to fire the weapon and up to this point there had been some close misses but no direct hits. The instructor appeared to be somewhat distraught no one had scored a hit on the tree stump. Apparently I was his last remaining unlikely hope. I also was fostering an outlandish concern – wondering if the bazooka instructor was any blood relation of the platoon sergeant who gave me the "javelin" toss at Camp Howze.

Dismissing all apprehension about both the weapon and the seemingly distraught instructor, I placed the bazooka on my right shoulder, took careful aim and activated the electronic trigger. The projectile's trajectory was right on course and delivered an undeviating blow on the tree stump.

I realized it was just a lucky shot. I felt like a real smart-ass when I nonchalantly returned the weapon back to the now pleased instructor and scampered out of reach of any possible sledge-hammer-like congratulatory blows. I did not believe there was all that much difference between a near miss and a close hit. I just hoped no one would inform Captain Hanlon 37531447 was the only artilleryman to "dead-center" the target with the antitank weapon. He most likely would issue a call for me if the weapon were needed in an actual combat situation.

Our short duration of inactivity ended and we were ordered to establish an observation position near Ingwiller, France. We would be utilizing our pack-frame mounted radio sections and a Jeep to establish the new OP. Unusual enemy movement had been observed in the vicinity. Our forward observer group consisted of Lieutenant Whidden, Corporal Newkirk, and myself. Corporal Erickson, a splendid forward observer, would be the driver of the Jeep.

Nearing an open stretch of the road, we were halted by division military police. They informed us the road we needed to use was under sporadic enemy artillery fire. The lieutenant thanked the military police for their concern and motioned Erickson to proceed down the road. We were going to play a highly interesting game of "chicken" with German artillerymen.

This action is not as foolhardy as it first might appear to be. We previously had played this nervy "amusement" in reaching our necessary destination. It was during tense moments such as this present occasion, the bespectacled Corporal Newkirk would begin to softly vocalize the Mills brothers' hit song, *Paper Doll*. Newkirk always displayed a pleasant upbeat smile during his singing. It reminded me of how Native Americans would allegedly stoically remark, "Today, is a good day to die."

I never did ask the corporal why he always sang this particular song during such adrenaline creating moments. It seemed to be something both private and special to him. I wondered if he too, had received a "Dear John" letter from a wife or a girl friend. Perhaps the line in the song, *It's tough to love a doll that's not our own*, bothered Newkirk as much as it troubled me.

Our Jeep driver, Erickson, had remarkable savvy concerning the current situation. His Swedish eyes appeared to sparkle at the challenge. Heavy-footing the gas pedal to the floor he soon had the Jeep rapidly speeding down the exposed portion of the roadway. Erickson's timing was perfect as he suddenly slowed the vehicle almost to a crawl.

German artillery rounds slammed the area of the roadway several hundred yards ahead of our position. Erickson proceeded slowly for a brief period of time and then once again jammed the gas pedal of the Jeep to the floor, "vrooming" the vehicle to the maximum. Another salvo of enemy shells struck harmlessly behind us. We soon were safely out of enemy view on the open stretch of road. Newkirk marked the end of the miniscule crisis by halting his singing of *Paper Doll*. Following these brash episodes, Corporal Newkirk's smile always appeared to be slightly larger. I felt certain there was a reason but I didn't bother to ask.

Upon arriving near the vicinity of our new OP on the side of the wooded mountain, we parked the Jeep, put the radio packs on our back and began to trudge toward our new observation point. The path we were taking was less than two hundred yards above a German-occupied village. The only open area where the enemy could spot us was near a rock overhang. The lieutenant, Erickson, and Newkirk were walking in single file ahead of me. Without the slightest hint of impending danger, I heard the sound of a bullet pass very closely by my head. Bullets will break the sound barrier and make a sharp whip-cracking noise that you can hear if you are near the path of the fast-travelling slug. I instinctively dropped to the ground. Corporal Newkirk noticing me motionless on the ground was certain I had either been killed or seriously injured.

All members of the FO crew were relieved to witness 37531447 begin elbowing his prone body to safety. Reaching a relatively safe haven, I stood up to gaze back at the rock ledge. Where lichens covered the damp underside of the overhang was one very fresh bullet mark on the dark rock. The bullet had just grazed the top of my steel helmet. I was lucky to have been overshot by the sniper located somewhere below me. The tendency is to undershoot an uphill target.

This latest incident troubled me considerably more than

Ken Lenke Photograph (1945)
Forward Observers from Battery A 928th Field Artillery
L to R; Erickson, Newkirk, "37531447", Tyner and Greene

incoming artillery or mortar fire which is usually directed to "whom it may concern". In this case I was in the actual gun sights of an enemy sniper and I was the intended victim chosen to die. Luck had been with me during this recent unnerving situation and I vowed to never again complain about my five-foot six-inch stature.

Our forested observation position provided a good view and we kept pressure on Nazi positions with our artillery. Through our field scope (optical instrument) we located enemy machine gun emplacements on the edge the next town, vehicle movements, distant dummy wooden artillery pieces, and a small bridge crossing a mountain stream. The bridge had to be crossed by Germans bringing in supplies and reinforcements. Our artillery removed the bridge and hammered away at the other targets.

With darkness descending, we vacated our observation position for security reasons, leaving elements of the 411th Infantry in control of the area.

Returning to our Jeep our FO party departed to a nearby friendly Alsation village to rest until dawn. We spent the night in a rectory of the Catholic church. Outside, in front of the rectory, was the body of a Cactus Division infantryman. Alsation civilians had placed flowers near the body. It was still difficult for us to cope whenever we noticed one of "our own" whose life had been so abruptly taken.

All of us could have enjoyed a shot or two of cognac before retiring. On other occasions we discovered in this land, famous for numerous grandfather clocks, that these beautiful timepieces made excellent storage or hiding places for liquid spirits. We suggested to our lieutenant the possible beneficial merit of opening the front door of the rectory's grandfather timepiece just to check it out. Lieutenant Whidden vetoed the idea and admonished us, "The clock is sacred church property." In the wee morning hours a priest entered the room, opened the clock door, and removed two bottles of cognac. I thought of the kindly old priest Bud Pitts and I had seen in the café at Hot Springs, New Mexico. This time it was the padre who had the drinks.

In the morning we returned to our outpost. This instance each one of us assumed the "combat infantry crouch" as we sprinted by the rock overhang where I had been the target of a German sniper the previous day. No small arms fire came our direction as we hurried by the rock ledge.

We immediately were approached by infantry soldiers who had been on guard duty during the long cold night in nearby foxholes. They were informing us German engineers had spent much of the dark night repairing the bridge over the mountain stream. Carefully scanning the remains of the bridge with optical instruments, we did not observe any recent repairs to the structure. We were somewhat dubious about what sounds 411th infantrymen heard.

Once a target is spotted and a requested artillery response is carried out, it is a fairly simple matter to use the same location coordinates for additional precision shelling. We stayed later that day and waited until it was dark. Sure enough, we too, heard the sounds of construction equipment emanating from the general area of the bridge. The 411th infantrymen were jubilant to know we also recognized the sounds of repair construction taking place and the sounds they heard the night before, indicated they had certainly not fabricated a "fish story". We immediately radioed for a "fire for effect" on the bridge area. This meant all six of the battery guns would fire in unison at the target. After the covey of arriving shells exploded, we waited to determine if further German attempts to repair the bridge would take place. The night became silent. As we waited we did not hear any further sounds of construction activity emanating from the target area or anyplace else. We prematurely congratulated ourselves.

Exactly one-half hour later – and with great astonishment and total disbelief – the sound of construction once again was audible and another "fire for effect" was called for the bridge. The shells brightly thundered accurately upon the targeted bridge area. Again a half-hour of silence before construction sounds of hammers, saws and electric generators, once again interupted the dark silence of the night.

This time we did not call for artillery. Instead, we spent our time carefully listening to the noise of the construction activity. We began to note the sounds started to have a definite recurrent sequence. We sheepishly realized just how badly we had been duped by the crafty enemy. They were utilizing specially recorded sound effects suggesting ongoing repair work. The "special effects" were emanating from a sound-truck hidden far enough from the bridge that the vehicle would not be destroyed by our withering artillery barrage.

I imagined the Germans must have had a pretty good chuckle over their successfulness in knowing we had been "taken in". Our embarrassed FO team tried in vain to locate the source of the sound. It was a worthy target we would have enjoyed finding.

We returned to the town of Ingwiller for some possible days of R & R. I visited with an Alsation family. They spoke both French and German like most other people living in the region. I was really surprised when Bud Pitts showed up. He had noticed our battery's presence in the town and he kept asking where I was until he found me. I was extremely elated to know he was alive and well.

Both of us were invited to have dinner with the Yung family. Mrs. Yung (her husband was absent), along with her daughters – Jeanne, Marguerite, Marthie, Louise, Else, Anne and Mina saw to it that we had a great time. Even though they had little food, it was shared with us. Bud and I scrounged around and found ("liberated") cans of Spam, sugar, coffee and other food items from battery kitchen supplies for the family. The girls and their mother made snow ice-cream especially for us. It was a short but wonderful interlude from the war. These Alsations were very friendly to the Americans; however, their neighbors, an elderly couple, did not appear to be as friendly. The old man would not have anything to do with me and appeared to have much apprehension with my presence. He was old enough to have remembered World War I – when Alsace was part of Germany. The old-timer could well have been in the Kaiser's army fighting Yankee doughboys in that war.

One morning I noticed the elderly Alsation out in the courtyard attempting to cut firewood with a large two-man saw. I could see he was not making much headway with the wood cutting. I walked over to where he was sawing and silently took hold of the opposite end of the saw. Together, we cut quite a pile of firewood and it was the first time I had ever seen the old man smile. As I was leaving I noticed the oldster was still smiling as he said, "*Danke.*"

Later that evening, I heard a knock on the room door of my sleeping quarters. When I opened the door, the elderly man and his wife were standing outside. The woman presented me with a generous portion of freshly-baked delicious apple strudel. The rest and relaxation period was brief, but my experience with the Alsation people caused me to wonder why the world appeared to be so damned complicated and so screwed up.

I returned to my military combat duty until our division, along with other support forces, took control of the Vosges Mountains. The campaign had been costly in casualties for the 103rd Infantry Division. The German military did not believe American soldiers could come through the heavily defended Vosges Mountains. In a way they were absolutely correct in their belief. Instead of coming through the mountain range, the 103rd Infantry Division soldiers who had trained in swamps, deserts and the flatlands of Texas, *came over the mountains*.

Postscript

When we were in Ingwiller, Anne Yung (one of the younger girls) gave Bud a small stuffed toy. A goose with a small child having an arm around the neck of the animal. Bud carried Anne's little precious gift with him throughout the conflict. It came back from the war with my Wyoming friend.

****

The Alsation village close to the place where I almost became a sniper's victim was Offwiller. When a Nazi sniper had a confirmed kill of 50 enemy soldiers they were decorated with the Iron Cross Medal First Class and given twenty-days leave. Hitler always wore the Iron Cross Medal he obtained in World War I. There appears to be considerable doubt among historians as to how he was worthy of receiving the highly coveted German military medal.

****

General Dwight D. Eisenhower credited the bazooka as one of the four inventions doing the most to win the war. Others mentioned by the general were: the C-47 transport plane, the atom bomb and the Jeep. The bazooka was named after the musical homemade wind instrument played by United States radio comedian Bob Burns, who in turn, got the idea from a hand held funnel-like farm tool used for planting corn without having the person, planting the seed, bend over each time.

Chapter Fourteen

Alsace-Lorraine

Nobody knows the trouble I've seen,
Nobody knows – but Jesus.
Nobody knows the trouble I've seen,
Glory Hallelujah.

—Traditional Negro Spiritual

Alsace-Lorraine is a region of northeastern France, located between the Rhine River to the east and the Vosges Mountains to the west. This geographical sector was both good news and bad for the combat soldiers of the 103rd Infantry Division. On the good news side, the area was a grape-growing region producing excellent wines and champagnes. On the down side, the large grape vineyards often provided unwanted natural camouflage for enemy gun positions.

Sometime, in the not too distant future, our division would have to cross the Rhine River. The river formed a natural barrier defending the German homeland. I was apprehensive about the day we would have to battle our way across the wide north-flowing Rhine River.

On occasion, combat fighting would slacken due to foul weather and for the need of additional war supplies. It was during such a lull in fighting, Corporal Lockwood and 37531447 decided to explore a newly recognized wine cellar.

The underground wine storage structure was rather large when compared to most wine cellars previously "researched". Even with the wine cellar entrance door open, we had to use our cigarette lighters to read bottle labels. Without warning Corporal Lockwood, using a voice expressing a manner of alarm, loudly shouted, "Hey, look at this!" I hastily wheeled around not knowing what to expect. The corporal, who was standing closer to me than I realized, "caught" his front tooth on the barrel end of my shouldered carbine. The once grinning forward observer now had a front tooth – either half missing or half there. Through this abbreviated interval of distraction, I noticed he was placing one hand to his mouth and the other hand was securely grasping a bottle of Red Robin cognac. We exited the wine cellar with the corporal resolutely clutching the bottle of cognac. Lockwood hastened to a medical aid station for emergency dental attention. This latest venture did not amuse me and I felt very badly for the Californian. This was the second time I had brought the soldier unwanted bad luck. 37531447 was beginning to wonder if there might be a "third time" somewhere in his future. Perchance the corporal was also entertaining similar thoughts.

When Lockwood returned from dental repair, he hurried over to me and while flashing a wide grin displaying his repaired tooth, he proudly placed on exhibition for me to recognize, a Purple Heart Cluster. The cluster would be attached to his previous medal awarded for his initial battle wound. Lockwood had apprised dental personnel who treated him, "I was struck in the mouth with a rifle barrel as the result of unfriendly enemy action." In no manner could I fault the Californian for referring to me as the "enemy". This latest incident did not threaten our camaraderie. We still remained friends – even if he wouldn't share his prize bottle of cognac with me.

Later on, the two of us uncovered an old trunk in the attic of an abandoned Alsation house. Curiosity about what might be in the intriguing aged chest got the upper hand on us. We cautiously opened the large coffer and on the very top layer were bottles of cognac and champagne. Mixed in with the stash of "spirits" was a beautifully embossed bottle having an equally attractively French language label displaying an equally gorgeous nude female. We both wondered what type of liquor the latter bottle imprisoned. The thought about Staff Sergeant Greene's troublesome night from consuming some unknown potion in the Marseilles staging area, gave us respectable concern. We prudently decided to take a cautious approach to determine what type liqueur the bonny glass decanter held.

Our small treasure was taken to one of our French interpreters. He would translate the printed word on the eye-popping label and determine the genre of spirits in the container. Upon handing him the bottle and explaining our request, he immediately started cackling as he silently read the words on the label. Still laughing, our interpreter of the French language slowly started to hand back the bottle while informing us, "Uhhh…fellows…ahh…what we have here, is…uhhh…uhhh…a bottle of douche liquid used by women." He continued, *douche* means 'shower' in French." The language master was still chuckling and shaking his head as he returned the attractive vitreous container back to us.

We restored the bottle to its rightful position inside the aging trunk. It appeared to be rather lonely, all by itself, on the top layer of the attic storage box.

The brief duration of tranquility came to an abrupt halt. We were establishing new observation posts overlooking the Rhine River Valley. The Nazis opted to withdraw to new defensive positions along the Rhine. Fears about the crossing of the Rhine River once again surfaced.

Lockwood was part of our FO group as we were moving to a new observation station. While hiking to rendezvous with the rest of the battery forward observers, we spotted another elaborate-appearing wine cellar. We decided time would not permit us to investigate this underground structure. In addition, neither one of us cared about becoming the victim of an enemy booby-trap.

Fate, however, would cause us to almost enter this elaborate appearing cellar even though it definitely was not on our "first choice" list.

When passing by the cellar we were hearing a pounding noise originating from the inside on the cellar's massive wooden door. In addition, we could ascertain muffled sounds of an exceptionally hoarse voice uttering abundant English expletives. The heavily timbered door leading to the wine cellar was tightly secured on the outside with a metal drop bolt and a sturdy iron hasp.

Cautiously removing the bolt, we took defensive positions and shouted, "The door is open. Come on out!" The door slowly edged open and out walked an infantryman wearing the Cactus Division shoulder patch. Both of his eyes were desperately attempting to decipher who his liberators might be; however, the brilliant sunlit morning delayed the occasion momentarily. We informed him we were forward observers with the 928th Field Artillery. The released soldier expressed his gratitude to us for his newly-found freedom. The 411th rifleman related, "I was checking out this place last evening and some 'bitch' slammed the door locking me inside." We wished him well and laughingly continued on our way. We had liberated our first "prisoner of war" back to his infantry company. We both wondered how the soldier would explain his temporary absence to his company commander.

It was standard operating procedure for artillery to establish a point of reference for the howitzers whenever they had been moved to a new location. Such a reference point could be a isolated geological feature, a water tower, concrete high-line pole or some other man-made marker. This so-called "base point" is then used to mark the starting positions in degrees of azimuth and elevation for new artillery targets. Both of these adjustments were marked off in degrees or more often, a smaller unit, the "mil". If time permitted, each 105 howitzer would check this established point by firing several rounds to "fine tune" the accuracy of each artillery weapon. It was up to the FO's to radio or phone vital information assisting gun crews in making the necessary correcting adjustments on the howitzers.

It was highly unlikely an established base point would ever be the object of an actual enemy military target. Nearby shell craters in the area usually would indicate to a battle-wise soldier – it was or had been – a zeroed-in artillery reference point.

It was a moment of great disbelief for our forward observer team to witness a Nazi military staff car pull along side the established base point and come to a halt. A German, wearing the uniform of a Nazi officer, pompously stepped out of the vehicle followed by the rest of the enemy entourage. His demeanor reminded me of the lieutenant at Fort Bliss who had grounded me because of the length of my hair. They proceeded to intensely scan the area in our direction with their field glasses. The Nazis apparently were oblivious to the fact they were practically standing on the base point and completely unaware we were so close to them.

A radio call was immediately dispatched to the howitzers calling for a "Fire for Effect" on the "Base Point!".

A prompt radio reply came from Fire Control requesting us to, "Say again your last transmission." Not even the artillery Fire Control could believe we actually had a target at the base point. Once again, expressing a tonal sense of urgency, I transmitted, "Fire for effect!" The swarm of six howitzer rounds momentarily arrived and the object of the artillery mission disappeared in thunderous noise, flames, smoke and debris. The vehicle and its former occupants vanished. It almost seemed to be unfair to take advantage of the enemy's extremely bad misfortune. War, like the longevity of a combat infantryman, is oftentimes – quite uncertain.

We received one more transmission from Fire Control. It simply stated, "Stop by Fire Control on your way back." We felt certain they wanted clarification of the previous target. Lieutenant Segstruem, another top-notch artillery officer would make the report. The tall young and likable lieutenant had been in charge of our group on numerous other occasions. When returning from the mission, we stopped in at Fire Control as requested. The center was located in the town of Obermodern, France.

Remaining seated in the Jeep while other members of our FO group went inside the Fire Control headquarters, I closed my eyes to just "kickback", relax and enjoy the warmth of the late autumn sunshine. Slowly I became aware the sun was no longer shining upon me. Perhaps the late afternoon sky had turned cloudy. Slowly urging my eyelids apart, someone wearing outrageously large shoes was standing by the vehicle blocking out the warm rays of sunshine. I slowly inched my gaze upward and upward, until I discovered the kindly smiling face of a very large person staring down upon me. His size startled the "living shit" right out of me. The man was the so-called "Obermodern Giant". He appeared to take great delight in observing my initial reaction to his presence by the Jeep.

The huge Alsation's name was Georges Kieffer. He stood eight and a half feet tall and weighed 280 pounds. His shoes were size twenty-six. Georges was the local director for the *Forces Fancaises de l'Interiur* (French Forces of the Interior). The "giant" was a very interesting individual and once I calmed down, we enjoyed a rather pleasant dialog. He informed me, speaking in fluent English, "After the war is over I want to go to the United States to play basketball." The Alsation took great delight in slipping up on unwary division soldiers, just to observe their startled reactions.

All had gone satisfactory in the Fire Control when the lieutenant explained the nature of the target. The smiling commissioned officer returned, lifted his large frame into the Jeep seat and our entire assembly of observers hastened back to the battery area. I had mail from home and a box of cookies from my parents. The cookies were wrapped in a fairly recent issue of the *Emporia* (Kansas) *Gazette*. In the newspaper was a photograph of Georges Kieffer. I gazed at the photo with great disbelief over this unusual coincidence. The photograph of the Obermodern FFI Director apparently had been sent earlier to stateside papers by the news services.

One more time I found myself being assigned by Captain Hanlon to another exhilarating mission. The captain was still mindful I had participated in some infantry training. The battery commander informed me I would be a human route marker for a highly important night time army convoy. I would be transported to an isolated crossroad and dropped off to await the arrival of the high priority convoy. Existing road signs were often altered by German patrols causing U.S. convoys to be guided into an ambush. I definitely was not thrilled with the mission I had been assigned. 37531447 was well aware isolated route markers would often be captured or killed by having their throats slashed. Their uniforms would be removed to be worn by a Nazi soldiers. The pseudo-American soldier would then direct the convoy into its ultimate fate of destruction.

I breathed a huge sigh of relief when "scrubbed" from the assignment. My reprieve of salvation was extremely short-lived. 37531447 was now reassigned to "ride shotgun" on top of one of the trucks transporting the important cargo. The nighttime convoy would be passing through heavily wooded areas suspected of harboring bypassed well-armed Nazi troops. The cargo being hauled was high explosive artillery shells and gunpowder! I was wondering where in hell good news went.

Before long, I found myself perched atop the boxes of highly explosive ammunition and gunpowder. The convoy commenced the precarious journey along the heavily forested mountain road. Only the small black-out lights marked the position of each vehicle. So far, all had progressed smoothly for the convoy, almost too smoothly.

The trucks moved a turtle's pace as they approached a crossroad near the outer edge of a village and halted. Without warning a barrage of noisy enemy artillery landed rather close to the vehicles.

It was quite doubtful if the convoy had been spotted by enemy forward observers. It was routine procedure for both sides fighting to shell major crossroads every so often in hopes of achieving a "lucky hit" on a random passing target. Our artillerymen called such activity "programmed time fire". The Nazis were so punctual with their time fire that if it were programmed at half-hour intervals, we could use our wrist watches to accurately predict when the next shelling would likely occur. Our artillerymen usually just approximated when a half hour was up and then expend a few rounds. The guessed unit of time used by our artillerymen may have been more effective than the German precisely measured rhythmic interval.

When the incoming enemy artillery exploded, I could once more hear the wobbling, whining sound of the deadly jagged shrapnel passing uncomfortably close by me. I abandoned my stately throne of cargo boxes and rapidly scrambled under the truck for protection from the flying shrapnel.

Directly, I was startled to feel a tugging on one of my combat boots. Out of the darkness a soft calm voice politely inquired of me, "What are you doing under the truck?" It was a real dumb question and a rather stupid time for the unsolicited inquiry. I caustically replied, "Just trying to avoid the damned shrapnel." The persistent interrogator very slowly and precisely again asked, "Do-you-know-what-this-truck-is-carrying?" I started to say, "high explosives" but by this time we both were running a fast hundred yard dash away from the truck for a safer haven. I have absolutely no clue as to who the unknown noncom buck sergeant was who risked his life to get me away from the military vehicle loaded with its deadly cargo.

The shelling abruptly ended with no trucks hit. The convoy commander most likely was aware the road juncture was under artillery "time fire" and this was the reason the ammo trucks stopped short of the crossroads. I had the uneasy feeling the convoy officer cut the "safe" distance a little too short.

Climbing on top of my ammunition-case perch, the trucks moved through the shell pockmarked intersection. I was uncommonly angry at myself for my brief spell of embarrassing stupidity when I sought shelter under the ammunition-laden truck. This was worse than Lockwood running back upstairs to add more wood to the fire at our OP.

The ammunition carrying convoy continued into the periphery of the village away from the crossroad and came to a halt. Incoming German artillery fire could be once again be heard at the crossroads we had just passed. It was "time fire", indicating German artillery observers most likely did not have the important convoy spotted.

A solitary rifle shot suddenly shattered the late night calm. An enemy sniper in a nearby dwelling had fatally shot one of the convoy's commissioned officers in the head. We again scattered away from the vicinity of the ammo trucks. The order came to "Shoot at anything that moves". This order implies, "The slightest movement coming from any building should be answered by our immediate gunfire on the source of the activity." The houses along both sides of the cobblestone road were mostly two stories high. All of the structures had wooden shutters over the windows. Positioning myself against a house on the side of the street shaded from the light of the moon, I nervously fidgeted with the carbine's trigger guard. I was desperately wishing to "dig in", but the concrete and stone street made this impossible. It was a very uncomfortable feeling being in the open and exposed to possible sniper fire. I also wondered if an enemy soldier would drop a "potato masher" (German hand grenade) from the window above me. My eyes strained for any tell-tale signs of movement. Every so often rifle shots would fracture the stillness of the night.

A brief moment later, my heart began to rapidly pound when I noticed an ever-so-slight movement of a second story window shutter on the opposite side of the street. I thought perhaps my eyes were tired from straining and were "feeding" me wrong information. Once again movement of the wooden shutter edged slightly more. This was not my imagination – it was for real! I aimed my carbine at the point of motion and placed my finger on the weapon's trigger. I had been extremely stupid once this night when seeking shelter under the ammo truck during the incoming artillery barrage. Silently vowing it would not happen again, I began to apply pressure on the trigger. My mind told me, "Fire." My intuition said, "Wait!" I was gambling with my life since I was the only U.S. soldier in the immediate area. I certainly could become a casualty just as easily as the dead lieutenant shot by the sniper. I also was disobeying the order, "Shoot at anything that moves". If only I could just catch a glimpse of a gun barrel I would not have the slightest hesitation to open fire. The shutter slowly closed and my trigger finger relaxed.

More anxious waiting and watching for signs of any motion. The street door on the same building was now being nudged open. Pressure was again being applied on the trigger of the carbine. Again, my "sixth sense" was screamed at me, "Hold your fire." Stepping out of the open doorway, in full view, was an elderly man, bent with age and dressed in a light-colored night cap and gown. He trudged toward the street and relieved himself in the gutter. The old timer turned around and shuffled slowly back into the building, closing the door behind him. My pulse rate gradually returned to near normal and the elderly Alsation's longevity continued.

Word soon arrived announcing the sniper who killed the lieutenant had also become a fatality of the war. With the approach of dawn, residents of the Alsation village slowly emerged from the buildings to welcome us with black bread, wine and lots of smiles.

The critically needed supply of artillery ammunition was safely delivered to nearby gun crews. Arranged transportation soon delivered me back to my battery howitzers. It had been a long stressful night.

Once again, I found myself among the black 614th Tank Destroyers. This was the same group which had provided me with my new winter trousers earlier in the campaign. Whenever near the vicinity of the 614th, I knew tough combat fighting would not be too far behind.

The 614th TD Battalion used a three-inch (bore measurement) antitank gun, towed by what is known as a half-track conveyance. The vehicle had tire wheels on the front end and treads somewhat similar to a tank on the rear. The platoon also had some lightly armed reconnaissance vehicles. The 614th Tank Destroyers were given some real difficult battle assignments. I often wondered if my new winter trousers had been intended for one of their men who had become a casualty of the war before having a chance to wear them.

Whenever our FO unit dropped in on the 614th, they would always ask if we wanted something to eat or drink and if we had a place to stay for the night. On this occasion we were both hungry and in need of sleeping space. The night we spent with these black soldiers was a memorable interlude in the war – one which I would never forget. For perhaps an hour or so, a group of them sang negro spirituals and popular tunes of the time. During the singing they would walk around the room, keeping rhythm with clapping hands and swaying body movements. I was delighted when they sang the song, *Paper Doll*. It was a joy to be with these men, and for a brief moment of time – the war was far away and we all were comrades, joined by the songs of home.

Twelve-hours later many of the black soldiers would be dead or wounded. The black 614th Tank Destroyer Battalion was one of the premier battle units of World War II. I know the Nazis hated them for their tenacious fighting ability. The Nazis undoubtedly were resentful that it was a military unit of black soldiers that was besting the white German super-race of the Third Reich. At times, I also had the feeling another conflict was taking place between black soldiers and some of the white soldiers of the then segregated United States military. Many white soldiers still referred to black soldiers as "niggers"; however, I never once heard a 103rd Division combat soldier remark negatively about the fighting ability of these black soldiers.

The 614th TD's departed early in the morning. They informed us they were presenting a "minstrel show" near the town of Climbach, France. It was their usual, unusual way of saying, "We have a combat mission assigned to us near the town of Climbach." We left soon after their departure and also headed toward the same village. The "minstrel show" the 614th put on, was one hell of a performance in devotion, courage and sacrifice. The division task force, made up of the 411th Infantry, division engineers, tanks and the 614th TD's was going to attempt the crossing of the German border near Climbach, France. The black tank destroyers were assigned to keep German gun positions occupied with the platoon's three-inch (seventy-five milimeters) antitank guns while the 411th Infantry Regiment infiltrated the flanks of the enemy gun emplacements.

The TD platoon would be sitting ducks for the Germans protecting their homeland.

Platoon casualties for the 614th were heavy. The one remaining gun and its crew kept firing – silencing two enemy tanks and a pillbox fortification camouflaged as a house. When they ran out of ammunition for their remaining three-inch guns, one of the surviving crew members drove a truck of needed ammunition almost to the antitank weapon before it bogged down in the mud. The black soldier than broke open the ammo boxes, carried the needed explosives over to the gun and continued firing the only operating anti-tank weapon.

The 614th TD Platoon lost over half of their men, three antitank weapons, two half-tracks, an armored car, and two Jeeps to enemy action. I came by the carnage moments later and noticed a black soldier seated in the top of the gun turret of the armored vehicle. It was obvious the armored car had taken a direct hit. The occupant was calmly smoking a cigarette. He nonchalantly waved to us as our FO group passed by. Later an infantryman informed me the armored car's driver had lost both legs and was waiting for medical assistance. The infantryman also told me the severely injured man had stemmed the flow of blood from his wounds by using the electric cord from his radio headset as tourniquets.

As far as I can determine, 103rd Infantry Division soldiers were the first Allied troops to fight their way onto soil of the German homeland during the war. Our stay was very brief. It was December and we were ordered to withdraw from the area without any explanation. It made me wonder why we occupied the area at such a cost in lives only to hand it back to the Nazis.

Mid-December was approaching and we soon would learn the reason our division units withdrew from that part of Germany.

Postscript

If any reader is fortunate enough to have a recording of *Coming in on a Wing and a Prayer* (McHugh/Adamson, 5-19-1943) as sung by The Golden Gate Quartet, you will have a very good likeness of the type of singing performed by some members of the 614th Tank Destroyer Battalion the night we stayed with them. One of the Negro spirituals the black soldiers sang was most likely the best known of the spirituals. It was – *Swing Low, Sweet Chariot*. Most Negro spirituals began with singing the refrain first, followed by the verse. All the songs were perfomed with a feeling of enormous exaltation and genuineness.

****

For the support the 614th Tank Destroyers gave in the battle of Climbach, the Third Platoon, C Company, was presented the prestigious Presidential Unit Citation.

The Third Platoon, Company C, 614ᵗʰ Tank Destroyer Battalion, is cited for outstanding performance of duty in action against the enemy on 14 December 1944 in the vicinity of Climbach, France…Its valorous conduct in the face of overwhelming odds enabled the task force to capture its objective. The grim determination, the indomitable fighting spirit and the esprit de corp displayed by all member of the Third Platoon reflect the highest tradition of the armed forces of the Untied States.

****

On April 30, 1996, seven African-American veterans of World War II were nominated to receive the Medal of Honor. The list of names was forwarded to Congress which must waive the time limit for the World War II medals. The nominees to receive the medal were identified by military historians.

The nominees on the list were: First Lieutenant Vernon Baker, 76, of St. Maries, Idaho, the only one of the seven men still alive; Private George Watson of Birmingham, Alabama; Staff Sergeant Edward Carter Jr. of Los Angeles; First Lieutenant John Fox of Boston; Private First Class Willy James Jr. of Kansas City, Kansas; and Staff Sergeant Ruben Rivers of Tecumseh, Oklahoma.

If no member of the 614ᵗʰ Tank Destroyer Battalion is on this list, then in the opinion of a veteran of the conflict, the list of nominees should be made longer.

****

It is highly conceivable the border of Germany had been previously crossed by U.S. Army patrols before units of the 103ʳᵈ Division crossed in force near Climbach.

****

I never worried my parents by telling them about any combat related incidents. Most letters home only mentioned geographical sights or trivial happenings. The following is an article given to me by my older brother, Donald, about two years ago (1995). The clipping appeared (1945) in the *Emporia Gazette*. The article contains several non-important inaccuracies mostly due to delays in news reports sent to the states or slowness in writing letters on my part. I was a sergeant and the event took place earlier in Alsace, France.

> *Cpl. Kenneth L. Lenke, who is with the Seventh Army in Austria, looked up from his jeep to see Georges Kieffer, self-styled "worlds tallest man", who is 8 ½ feet tall, standing near. After Corporal Lenke visited with Mr. Kieffer, FFI district leader, he went to camp and found a box of cookies sent him by his parents, Mr. and Mrs. George F. Lenke, 128 South Congress. In one of the papers in which the cookies were packed he found a picture of Mr. Kieffer which now hangs on his barracks wall.*

****

Radio transmissions involving forward observers went to a specially trained group of artillery men in a Fire Control Center where information was processed and then relayed to battery weapons crews. Fire Control personnel could see the "big picture" of what was taking place. They would determine altitude and azimuths for howitzers for the gun crews, choose the type of shells to be used, number of powder bags to propel the missiles and determine the number of howitzers required for the mission. The howitzer crews could devote their full attention to gun settings, counting powder bags and picking the correct type of artillery shell or fuse detonators to be used.

****

Radio or phone communication language had to be precise to avoid short rounds or other dangerous situations. The word "repeat" to an artilleryman, means: "Fire another salvo just like the last one fired". We would always state, "Say again your last transmission" and never use the word "repeat" in conveying this request – unless we desired another salvo of artillery directed on the last requested objective.

Chapter Fifteen

The Ardennes Offensive

The foot soldier understands it is academy generals who ultimately make the tactical decisions for front line combat fighters. Infantrymen were always last in line to know the selected military strategy authored by top "brass". The German Ardennes (Battle of the Bulge) surprise offensive was an exception to the established chain of command.

—37531447

With the Vosges Mountain campaign now behind, 103rd Division troops began moving north in France. The division was paralleling the west side of the north flowing Rhine River. It had become a part of a military setup which placed the 103rd Infantry Division under the command of General George S. Patton. Such military groupings were often structured to increase both manpower and firepower for a given sector of the front.

Once again we would learn additional names of French and German cities – both large and small. Forbach, Sessenheim, Sarreguemines, Klingenmunster, Landau, Speyer, Worms, Mannheim, and Metz would be our new battle ground. It would provide 37531447 with many memories – mostly discomforting.

We discovered more "hills" to climb. They were called the Haardt Mountains. These mountains were not as formidable as the Vosges. They were, however, in close proximity to the extensive German Siegfried Line of fortifications.

American troops were presently in a region where local residents were mostly bilingual – speaking both French and German languages. It was often impossible to ascertain their true political allegiances. It was only natural for U.S. soldiers to be more suspicious of anyone communicating in German instead of verbalizing in French. We were provided with German phrase booklets to assist with the language uncertainty.

Much of the division's new mission would be devoted to defensive tactics to minimize the effect of Nazi probing counterattacks. We were performing more night time missions than usual.

To help us see the frontal area (no man's land) on dark cloudy nights, U.S. rear-positioned searchlight units would direct powerful beams of light on the low-hanging cloud layer. The light would diffuse back to the ground, providing artificial "moon light". The simulated moonlight made it far more difficult for enemy patrols to penetrate battle lines without being spotted. This unusual night lighting system was a tactical strategy which seemed to work to our advantage.

Dates and sequences of events taking place are usually not important to the average foot soldier. What was taking place in the immediate vicinity was far more meaningful. Most troops did not possess the slightest insight concerning tactical formats. For the combat soldier other worries were far more weighty.

One concern – "How much longer might the good fortune of staying healthy or alive continue?" The average battle life of an infantry company rifleman was approximately 28 days. I am not certain about the battle life expectancy for a forward observer. We often moved with the infantry and on some occasions we would locate observation positions ahead of infantry lines. Forward observers were; however, rotated to rear positions more frequently than the full time warrior – the infantryman.

Throughout the hard-fought campaign for the Vosges Mountains, the German Air Force (Luftwaffe) was conspicuously absent. We were presently positioned closer to industrial centers in Germany and Luftwaffe air activity was noticeably on the increase. It was essential for Nazis to maintain high industrial output for the war effort. It was just as vital to our air force to eliminate the German industrial output. "Dog fights" in the overhead sky would often be observed with great interest. Most of the United States' fighter planes were P-51 "Mustangs" or P-38 twinboom Lockheed "Lightnings." The Nazis usually countered with ME-109's ("Messerschmitts"). It was extremely sad to observe any of our fighter planes being shot down by the enemy. It was especially disheartening to not view any life-saving parachute open.

It was awesome to witness large daytime formations of Allied bombers, escorted by the P-51's, on their way to strike German industrial centers. Allied planes were continuing the bombing of German military production sites during the night. We were close enough to the on-going activity to observe the light flashes from the exploding bombs, hear the rumble of the explosions and feel the ground beneath us shaking. The unfolding scene was reminiscent of a fast approaching old-fashioned summer thunderstorm in the Flint Hills of eastern Kansas.

It had to be a worrisome concern for the bomber crews passing through the thick curtain of Nazi antiaircraft or having their B-17's or B-24's trapped by the probing beams coming from German search lights. German antiaircraft artillery took its toll on the big bombers. I did not have any desire to trade military occupations with air force crew members who both day and night would face constant danger. I was small enough in size to qualify as a B-17 bomber ball turret gunner.

I recalled the earlier personal disappointment at Fort Leavenworth when not assigned to the air force. I wondered if Private Torres, who was inducted into the army with me at Fort Leavenworth, was the underside B-17 turret gunner. His small wiry size could have well-qualified him for this dangerous assignment.

Division soldiers were being "put to bed" more often now by a small German spotter plane dubbed "Bedcheck Charlie". We had to be extremely cautious using any lights which could possibly be noticed by this lone enemy aircraft. This was especially true for the use of cigarette lighters. Most of us were utilizing a small tubular type of catalytic device that did not emit light when firing up a cigarette. The cigarette was inserted into the end of the lighter and puffing on the cigarette activated the lighter. This small lone plane bothered me to the point of downright displeasure. Perhaps it was gathering information which could possibly determine the ultimate fate of so many soldiers, including my kismet.

In the morning we took up a new OP overlooking a village held by the enemy. We had not been in position very long when two low-flying United States P-47 aircraft approached in single file over the snow-covered village. Each aircraft released a 500 pound bomb on a target not visible to us. It was alarming to notice the bomb the first plane dropped had evidently grazed the frozen ground or possibly the roadway. The bomb was now ricocheting back up into the sky, positioning itself very close to the direct flight path of the tailing P-47. The pilot of the trailing plane also released a 500-pounder and suddenly became aware of the serious menacing problem in front of him. With adrenaline flowing, he powered the P-47's engine to a thunderous noise level. The extra needed acceleration made it possible for the pilot to avoid the errant bomb. The first plane's bomb exploded harmlessly in mid-air approximately fifty yards behind the second P-47. The concussion from both explosions cleared most of the snow from the village housetops, changing the color of the white snowy rooftops almost instantly to tile-red. It reminded me of placards participants of a football half-time show would use to create different scenes in the seating section of the stadium. For a moment it seemed as if the snowy winter had changed instantaneously into spring.

The Republic-built Thunderbolts returned several more times, strafing the area with their eight "wing-mounted" .50-caliber machine guns. We were not certain the nature of the intended target. Often our tactical air force went out searching for enemy military activities without being specifically requested by land-based observers. Many ground troops owe their longevity to the close support provided by these heroic air force pilots.

Darkness had arrived by the time our weary FO contingent returned to the location of our gun batteries. During periods of low activity, a canvas pyramid squad tent would occasionally be raised to shelter some of the noncoms of Battery A. Arriving at a late hour, I entered the tent, threw down my bedroll and optimistically hoped to obtain some well-needed rest. I no longer bothered the mess sergeant for a cup of coffee or a sandwich. The bastard had already made it clear the request for something to eat or drink would inconvenience him too damned much.

Perhaps the most monumental barrier standing in the way of obtaining a good night of sleep inside the tent was First Sergeant Trish. The sergeant had a terrific snoring problem. As exhausted as I was, the top kick's hog-like sounds kept me from falling asleep. If it had not been inclement weather, I would have opted to repose outside.

Not to be denied my sleep, I decided to try a novel approach to this bothersome acoustical issue. I had been around our commander, Captain Hanlon, long enough to do a pretty fair imitation of the captain's voice. My scheme was worth a try. With an authoritarian tone to my voice, I loudly shouted, "Sergeant Trish, this is Captain Hanlon! Have you ordered those vehicles I requested?"

The sergeant was definitely programed to respond to the captain's name or voice frequency. The top kick's reaction far exceeded my wildest expectation. The blaring atrocious snoring immediately ceased. Trish sat straight up, displaying both alarm and bewilderment and commenced to wonder what in hell had just happened. He began to fret about what trucks he was supposed to have ordered for the commanding officer. It would be a prolonged duration before the sergeant would be able to resume his sleep. I felt somewhat certain the exemplary top kick was starting to question the status of his mental health.

Several days later I again returned from a stint of observation duty. It was well into the dark side of the night when I entered the pyramidal-shaped squad tent. To my dismay the fabric structure was completely lacking its usual wall-to-wall "carpet" of soldiers. The empty tent brought back memories of my first night at Camp Howze, Texas. I briefly wondered about the strangeness of this highly unexpected vacancy. This time no one advised me against sleeping in the make-shift barracks. Rather than seeking an explanation for my seemingly good fortune, I rolled out my sleeping bag and quickly dropped off to an unbroken slumber.

Sounds of activity awakened me at daybreak and I slowly nudged my eyelids to the almost open position. I became quite interested when my eyes, now fully open, began to slowly study the canvas walls and ceiling of the tent. A wide fiendish smile slowly spread across my face. The shelter resembled a planetarium full of resplendent stars, highlighted by the brilliant morning sunshine. The tent closely resembled the one Bud and I almost burned down from our creosote bush fire while on maneuvers at Fort Bliss, Texas. I rolled up the bedroll, placed my boots on my feet and slowly emerged from the canvas tent. I felt rather confident what had created the new "ventilation system" in the olive-drab fabric shelter.

Once outside, other battery soldiers were dumfounded to witness my lone exit from the tent. They were in a semi-state of disbelief when realizing I had spent the better part of the night inside the fabric edifice. An explanation for their unusual reaction was fast in coming. It confirmed my theory of what caused the round holes in the canvas. The previous day the tent had been strafed by enemy aircraft. Thankfully nobody had been injured in the daytime incident. I secretly hoped both the mess sergeant and supply sergeant had to make a desperate departure from the shelter. A real "taste" of flying bullets might possibly help improve their attitude towards me.

One of the more strange decisions handed down from "higher ups" was the one made to collect all of our gas masks. We were never given the reasons for this unprecedented decree. I considered the edict rather anomalous since German soldiers invariably always carried their gas masks. Perhaps it was more of a psychological move made by upper echelon commanders, conveying the warning message to the Nazis, "Don't you sons-of-bitches even think about using poison gas." I was harboring the gnawing notion we were being used as chips for this bizarre military poker game.

Once more our FO group was given the assignment to shell German fortifications along the Siegfried Line. During the artillery bombardment we were greatly disappointed to observe the 105mm missiles bouncing off of the concrete and steel enemy fortifications. Our tactical air force was also striking these well-constructed defensive positions with their bombs. Our battery artillery marked the location of the strong points with white phosphorous shells. Some damage was inflicted on the fortifications by the tactical planes; however, the enemy positions continued to fire on our own troops.

Unexpectedly one of the Nazi artillery shells landed ten yards to my right. Fortunately the projectile was a dud (a shell failing to explode). It was totally uncanny to observe the malfunctioning projectile charting a zig-zag course, ricocheting off of tree trunks in its path until completely expending its kinetic energy. I was extremely appreciative of being "given" an opportunity to sentinel this ghostly "one-of-a-kind" event. Shortly, a unit of United States self-propelled eight-inch artillery arrived. The maximum range of this weapon was close to 18,000 yards (approximately ten miles). On this occasion they would be firing a 200 pound explosive shell directly at the enemy fortifications from a distance of 400 yards. Some of the concrete and steel fortifications were neutralized by these SP guns.

Later that night I heard one of our big tanks slowly move to possibly take up a better firing position. The tank apparently ran over a stacked group of enemy "Teller" anti-tank mines and became a disabled burning inferno. I began to hear the appalling screams of the tank crew as they attempted to escape from inside the blazing inferno. Those making it out of the tank became instant victims of a nearby German machine gun. A sudden silence along the battle line became so intense it actually seemed to possess a nauseating harsh discordant buzzing aura. Everyone knew there were no survivors from the U.S. tank.

In the morning our units stopped the probing attack and withdrew from the Siegfried Line.

A heavy snow began to fall. German activity was on the increase and the weather had become extremely foul. Our howitzers were moved to a new location close to a small village. Instead of staying in the town, Captain Hanlon ordered us to pitch tents and dig in for the duration of the cold snowy night. The not too distant buildings of the village appeared so warm and inviting. Almost everyone in the battery did their share of bitching over the seemingly poor decision the captain made placing us outdoors in the harsh inclement weather.

During the night the village was "hammered" by a very intense and lengthy enemy artillery barrage. The captain deserved much credit for his seemingly unpopular decision – one which had undoubtedly spared Battery A from certain casualties and loss of equipment.

Enemy pressure dramatically tapered off in our sector after the shelling of the village. It was more of an ominous type of silence. While tinkering with the dial on a recently "unearthed" German wet battery operated radio, I heard an English-speaking broadcast highly upsetting to me. The broadcast was informing listeners, "The Nazis have launched a major offensive near the city of Ardennes." The radio broadcast continued, "Teams of well-trained English-speaking Germans dressed in United States Army uniforms are infiltrating Allied lines and conducting acts of sabotage." It was rather late at night, but I thought it best to inform Captain Hanlon about the information just heard on the radio. The captain politely thanked me for the information but passed it off as more German propaganda. I did not question the captain's reply since an enemy counter attack appeared so unlikely – even to me.

Later in the night an excited and concerned Captain Hanlon placed our artillery unit on the highest alert status. He had received upper echelon information about a large unexpected German offensive just north of our defensive sector. The information given to the captain corroborated the report I had given him a few hours earlier.

A Jeep pulling a trailer made an unexpected appearance at our battery site. The trailer contained our gas masks. The

Ken Lenke Photograph (January 1945)
"37531447" at a winter artillery observation bunker during the Alsace-Ardennes Campaign

masks were suddenly being "resurrected" based on reports German military was resorting to the use of poison gas. We picked out our own gas masks as identified by the last four digits of our army serial number. We were ordered to place the gas masks on our face to determine if they sealed properly. It was fortunate for us no gas attack had been made by the enemy. The masks would not fit. The rubber protective seals had hardened and would no longer conform to facial features. The devices were absolutely worthless for the protective purpose intended. A day or so later new masks arrived that correctly sealed to the face.

The weather was becoming worse and a heavy snowfall was making movement difficult. We had been supplied with better water proof boots that helped keep our feet warm and supposedly dry. Our socks became damp from perspiration and it was necessary to change them often. Soldiers neglecting to do so would run the risk of getting "trench foot". Most of us carried an extra pair of socks under the webbing inside our molded helmet liner. All socks would be rotated from the feet to the helmet liner and back to the feet again. No one worried about the aroma coming from the unclean socks in the liner. It wasn't high on the list of priorities.

Our FO contingent spent much effort and ammunition trying to destroy an enemy observation post in the Siegfried chain of German defenses. This particular fortification had a fairly large periscope that would come up from the ground every now and then. It was the only visible part of the fortification. I was not completely satisfied the obnoxious periscope was destroyed; however, it ceased for the time being the spooky ritual of peeking up at us and then disappearing back into the ground.

Everyone had the German offensive on their minds. Our intelligence section needed information about what was taking place with the enemy in our sector. The best way to obtain this information was to take some prisoners. The task was given to the Black 761st Tank Battalion. They, like the 614th Tank Destroyers, were always close by when needed.

Earlier in the campaign, I noticed one of the 761st tanks had a bushel basket secured to the tank near the rear of the gun turret. Whenever the tank "wound up" its big engine, a chicken having a short cord tied to one leg and the other end of the cordage secured to the basket, would stand up and loudly squawk its objection. When the tank began to move the chicken would settle back down into the basket as if it enjoyed the ride. Up to this time, the appearance of the tank with the basket and chicken was the object of much good-natured joking and interesting black/white commentary. It was definitely a morale booster for all who witnessed the uncommon decoration adorning the Sherman tank driven by the black tankers.

When attached to General Patton's Third Army, the chicken and the basket suddenly vanished. General Patton did not "cotton" to such antics from soldiers under his command. As for the fate of the fowl – I can only surmise it became genuine

Ken Lenke Photograph (1945)
928th Forward Observers during Ardennes fighting
L to R; Diamond, Richardson and Greene

"chicken-in-the-basket".

In the attempt to take a few prisoners for interrogation, a solitary tank from the 761st made a slow cautious journey into no-mans-land where a small village was located. I had a front row seat at our OP for this happening. While our artillery made certain the German periscope from the nearby fortification would not come up, the tank made its way into the village. The driver parked the tank and idled the engine. To my great surprise I noticed two German soldiers nonchalantly coming down the village street, walking as if they didn't have a worry in the world. Each was carrying a pair of hobnail boots. They most likely were taking the boots to a local shoe cobbler for repair. When rounding the corner of the street, they unexpectedly came face to face with the dreadful reality of the moment. The two enemy soldiers immediately became aware the tank was not German as they gazed into the faces of *black* tankers and the business end of the tank's machine gun. Both "shoppers" obediently dropped their weaponry and clambered onto the front of the tank – still clutching their spare boots. It was hilarious to see the facial expressions on the new captives that seemed to express the notion, "This just isn't our day". The widely grinning leather-helmeted black tankers, with goggles positioned high on their tanker headgear, triumphantly returned to deliver their "catch-of-the-day" to the awaiting intelligence section.

Christmas Eve was an event having extra importance for our artillery battalion. Word had reached us of the massacre by the Nazis, of a United States artillery unit in the Ardennes sector near the town of Malmedy. The news of the massacre made us angry. The rapid advance of German units was stalling, thanks in part to the heroic efforts of the 101st Airborne Division holding the key city of Bastogne. We also were buoyed knowing that the temporary commander of the 101st Airborne Division, General Anthony C. McAuliffe, had basically told the krauts, "Go to hell" when they demanded the surrender of the 101st Airborne and the highly strategic city, Bastogne.

Even though the military situation was improving north of us, everyone was still pretty much on edge. The weather was cold and heavy snow continued to fall. Bad weather was grounding flights of our tactical air force. The manpower in our sector appeared to be thinly stretched to a critical danger point. Christmas Eve was going to be observed by all of the battery FO's in spite of the rather questionable outlook for our longevity. We were in a potato growing region, in out of the cold weather and our back mail from home had just arrived. Among the letters were special Christmas packages full of goodies. My mother had sent me oatmeal cookies and peanuts in the shell. One of our group pilfered cooking oil from the mess sergeant's supplies. It would be used to make "french fries". The captain's Jeep driver, Corporal Chipman, came over to join our cozy little group of forward observers.

What we still needed was firewood for the small stove and a Christmas tree. With no apparent enemy action in the vicinity, it was decided a fire would be safe after dark. A warm fire would lend itself to the occasion of our celebration and I definitely wanted this Christmas Eve to be better than my last one at Fort Bliss. On that occasion, I missed most of Christmas Eve as well as Christmas day while engaged in a uneven contest with a full bottle of gin.

Chipman and 37531447 departed in the captain's Jeep to search for firewood and a Christmas tree. In the darkness a barn was spotted having a large shell hole on the street side of the structure. Firewood was usually stored in barns attached to the living quarters. It was snowing very hard and all sounds seemed to be muffled.

Chipman stayed with the Jeep parked outside by the barn while I stealthy entered the barn to scrounge for firewood. A large supply of split wood was fortuitously positioned close to the shell hole. I promptly began pitching the short sticks of firewood through the shell hole where it would silently fall into the deep snow close to the Jeep. I could see the Tennessee rebel placing the wood in the back of the captain's Jeep. I calculated we had a sufficient amount of stove wood and was leaving the barn carrying a couple of extra pieces under one arm. I was suddenly confronted by the angry owner of the wood.

The German-speaking Alsation man insisted I place the firewood I was carrying back on the stack. I became both stubborn and annoyed at the son-of-bitch for begrudging me two small pieces of firewood on this Christmas Eve. I was certain he was not aware of the Jeep-full of wood outside.

Dropping the wood on the barn floor by my feet, removing my ever present carbine from my shoulder and using defiant and understandable body language, I was strongly hinting his damned wood was going with me one way or the other. The tone of my voice, the waving carbine and a small packet of K-ration cigarettes conveyed the certainty this would be the bottom-line offer he could expect for the firewood. The former owner of the wood reluctantly retrieved the cigarettes tossed by his feet and moved out of my way. I "one-handed" the pieces of the wood from the floor, backed out of the barn and headed for the Jeep.

We made one additional stop. Chipman removed the sharp axe from its carrier mount located just below the Jeeps's driver-side. Similar to a true Tennessee mountain man, the captains's chauffeur, using several brisk powerful blows, hastily downed one of the small evergreen trees growing in front of a modest Alsation house. Chipman tossed the tree on top of the snow-covered firewood and we headed back to our friends. The snow-covered Jeep with its cargo of firewood, evergreen tree and two laughing artillery soldiers could well have qualified as a subject for a wartime Christmas greeting card.

We enjoyed a traditional Christmas Eve. Our purloined tree was draped with ribbons from the Christmas packages. Even one of our Silver Star medal (award given for battlefield valor) recipients enjoyed the warmth of the evening in the basement of our temporary home. He had missed the formal observance of Hanukkah earlier. He placed his Silver Star Medal on the top of the tree. I remained completely sober for the night. Our "father image", Sergeant Keane, of the Fort Bliss training days, would have been extremely proud of me.

The following morning Corporal Chipman informed us our Christmas tree had once been growing in the yard of the town's mayor. Discovering his tree missing, the local politician had gone to the captain to protest the huge loss his "spread" had suffered. The captain never found out who committed the "evil" deed. I suspect Captain Hanlon really didn't give a shit who had cut down the local hack's tree. The mayor's loss of his tree and the loss of the angry Alsation's firewood would not begin to collate with the toll of the dead and wounded men from the Cactus Division. I never felt compunctious over either the firewood or the small tree. Both "victims" of our Christmas Eve raid had done real well under Nazi occupation. They also may have believed the current Nazi offensive at Ardennes would succeed in changing the tide of the war – back in their favor.

Postscript

Many years later I read an article (most likely some science magazine?) that the kinetic (moving energy) delivered on the hardened fortifications of the Siegfried Line by each projectile coming from the eight-inch self propelled weapons was equivalent to the energy delivered by a speeding express train traveling ninety miles an hour striking the fortifications head on. The concussion wave created by the eight-inch two hundred pound shells hitting the German forts would cause severe bleeding from the eyes, ears and noses of the soldiers inside.

****

The P-47 Thunderbolt fighter aircraft was a real "workhorse" in both the European and Pacific areas of combat. It was the heaviest fighter plane in the world and could reach speeds slightly greater than 400 miles per hour. P-47 pilots were credited with shooting down 3,315 German planes and destroying over 3,000 Nazi aircraft on the ground. In addition, the Thunderbolt was involved in the destruction of 9,000 railroad locomotives, 86,000 railroad cars, 6,000 armored vehicles and 86,000 trucks.

The P-47 served for a time escorting bombers in the European Theatre of Operations. When the fast P-51 Mustangs became operational, they took over the escort duty from the P-47's. While in Fort Bliss learning aircraft identification, we dubbed the P-47 "the flying beer bottle" because the craft resembled a beer bottle with a propeller and wings.

****

The ball turret of the B-17 bomber was so small that few gunners could even wear a parachute. The turret could be rotated in almost every direction. The space was very tiny and often the gunner would have to curl his body like a somersaulting gymnast in order to fire the big machine guns utilizing hand and foot pedals. The ball turret gunner was in a dangerous location as well as a cold lonely place.

****

The P-47's flying the bombing mission that dropped the 500 pound bombs in front of us, undoubtedly were using bombs having timing fuses which caused the bomb to explode in the air and not on making primary contact with the ground. The intended target could well have been some type of building housing a military objective or German vehicles on the street.

****

"Colorful Germanic celebrations are a deep-rooted tradition in Alsace. Once a part of Germany, it held its first *Christkindelsmarkt* more than 500 years ago. The first written record of a Christmas tree anywhere was in Selestat, on December 21, 1521: Officials budgeted two schillings for the city forester to cut holiday trees."

The 103rd Infantry Division's 409th Infantry Regiment participated in some hard fighting in and around the walled city of Selestat. We were not too distant from this city when Corporal Chipman "axed" the Mayor's tree for our own *Christkindelsmarkt.*

****

The name "Bedcheck Charlie" given to the meddlesome German aircraft out gathering data carried over into the Korean War. During the Korean conflict the enemy was using a fabric covered plane known as a PO-2. It was extremely light weight and so slow – advanced U.S. aircraft had trouble shooting them down. Radar went through the plane's fuselage instead of bouncing back. One American F-94 was going so fast it flew through the PO-2's whereupon both crafts were destroyed. The Korean war came on the heels of World War II and many U.S. soldiers served in both of the conflicts.

195

Bedcheck Charlie was a name most likely carried over from soldiers of World War II.

****

I have never been able to rid myself of the terrifying screams coming from the men attempting to escape the fiery tank disabled by German mines. The complete scenario of this event often capriciously returns to haunt me.

****

Following is a partial history of the War in Europe involving the United States' Third and Seventh Armies as presented in the descriptive folder of the Lorraine (France) American Cemetery.

> *The U.S. Third Army resumed its pursuit of the enemy across France early in September 1944, after a brief halt because of a shortage of fuel. Except at Metz, where extremely heavy fortifications and resistance were encountered, the U.S. Third Army advanced rapidly and crossed the Moselle River. By late September, Nancy was liberated and juncture with the U.S. Seventh Army, which was advancing northward from the beaches of southern France, was made near Epinal. Upon the joining of these two Armies, a solid allied front was established that extended to the Swiss border.*
>
> *Throughout October, the two Armies pushed aggressively eastward against increasingly strong resistance. The U.S. Third Army drove toward the Saar River and the U.S. Seventh Army into the Vosges Mountains, as the enemy fortress at Metz was encircled and it capitulated on 22 November (103rd U.S. Army Infantry Division entered combat on 11 November). Its outer forts, however, did not surrender until 13 December. Bypassing this resistance, the U.S. Third Army continued to advance, capturing Saarguemines*

on 6 December 1944. By mid-December, several bridgeheads had been established across the Saar River and the Third Army began preparations for breaching the Siegfried Line. Meanwhile on 11 November, the U.S. Seventh Army to the south launched an attack eastward capturing Saarebourg on 20 November 1944. Moving rapidly, it outflanked, then penetrated the vital Saverne Gap in the Vosges Mountains. Sending the French 2nd Armored Division to liberate Strasbourg on the Rhine River, The U.S. Seventh Army turned northward advancing along the west bank of the Rhine against the defenses of the Siegfried Line, simultaneously aiding the U.S. Third Army operations to the north.

Throughout these operations, the U.S. Ninth Air Force and the U.S. First Tactical Air Force rendered vital air support to the U.S. Third and Seventh Armies, respectively, despite severe rainstorms and cold weather.

The progress of the two U.S. Armies was halted temporarily by the enemy's final major counter offensive of the war, which began in the Ardennes Forest on 16 December 1944. Officially designated the Ardennes-Alsace Campaign, it became known as the "Battle of the Bulge." The U.S. Third Army moved quickly northward to counter this threat, as the U.S. Seventh Army and the French First Army to the south extended their lines northward to cover more front. The second phase of the enemy's final counteroffensive was launched on New Year's eve against the U.S. Seventh Army and the French First Army. The assault began a drive for the Saverne Gap followed by an attack across the Rhine toward Strasbourg. After furious fighting on all fronts in bitterly cold weather, the last major enemy offensive was halted and the U.S. Third and Seventh Armies resumed their assault on the Siegfried Line. The line was soon broken and all enemy units were cleared from the west bank of the Rhine. In March 1945 the two

> *U.S. armies crossed the Rhine River and began their drive into Germany.*

****

Buried in the Lorraine American Cemetery are 10,489 of our military dead. One of those was Victor Brecht from Chase County, Kansas. Victor Brecht was a member of bomber crew from the 384th Bomb Group whose plane (Boeing B-17) was shot down over Munich (Munchen), Germany. He was on his last required flight mission before being rotated back to the United States when he lost his life. The highly decorated airman had first been buried in Germany and after the war, re-buried in the Lorraine American Cemetery.

Chapter Sixteen

Attacking the Siegfried Line

Fatalism suggests all happenings are predetermined by fate and the course of events, can not be deviated by human beings. I occasionally ruminate over this exegesis. If not human beings, what divinity would condone such hellish mass death and destruction?

—37531447

The German Ardennes thrust beginning shortly before Christmas was slowly grinding to a standstill. The stormy chilling winter weather was now being replaced with mostly fair skies. This allowed planes from our tactical air force and heavy bombers to rain destruction upon the enemy forces. Artillery forward observers were kept very busy with their usual wartime occupation – the destruction of enemy forces.

Staff Sergeant Richardson, ranking noncom in charge of one of the forward observer teams, was missing a thumb from his left hand. I always wondered how he wangled his way into the army with this disability. The absent appendage certainly did not interfere with his outstanding ability as an FO. When the sergeant held field glasses to his eyes to search for artillery targets the missing part of his hand was quite evident. He was a terrific noncom and it was a great experience whenever 37531447 was assigned the radio operator position for Sergeant Richardson's FO group.

Richardson was somewhat older than the rest of us. The Dinuba, Californian was also another father image for us youngsters. Whenever we appeared "down in the dumps", the

199

Staff Sergeant Richardson from Dinuba, California, utilizing an Alsation (France) vineyard for an artillery observation position.

sergeant would gather us around him, reach into his pocket and carefully fish out a dilapidated vintage billfold. He would slowly and methodically fumble through his cache of assorted items with his thumb hand until he eventually "rediscovered" a very officious-appearing document resembling a U.S. wartime ration card. The card displayed a number of places along each edge that could be punched out. One of the dozen or so places along the border of the card apparently had already been punched. Lettering at the top indicated it was an "Official Wartime 'Nooky" Ration Card". The remaining space was taken up with a photograph of a stunning nude woman. For a short moment the war vanished and we youngsters were behaving more like high school freshmen having just learned sexes were usually both male and female in gender and – what some of those differences were. The crafty "old sarge" never would reveal any specifics about the one missing number already punched. I suspicioned it was lacking when he obtained the "racy" item.

Often the miniscule things – such as the staff sergeant's "ration card", mail from home or a hot meal – would provide a much needed boost in morale.

Richardson was a legend to infantrymen. On one occasion an infantry officer requested artillery assistance to eliminate a problem causing difficulties for his platoon. The staff sergeant did not waste any time as he inquired of the officer, "Sir, what is the nature of the target and where is it located?" The officer pointed his finger at a specific building and replied, "It is the basement window…the second window from the right." The platoon officer emphasized one additional point when he added, "It's a machine gun nest." The staff sergeant causally replied, "Well,…let's just see what we can do about that."

In most target situations, the first artillery round is simply a reference marker and was used in adjusting following artillery rounds. In this instance, the primary round of artillery entered the small basement window exactly where the infantry officer had requested. The enemy machine gun position no longer existed.

The "old" staff sergeant took the infantry officer's verbal accolades right in stride when, with eyes twinkling and a smile on his face, he routinely inquired, "Anything else we can do for you, sir?" Our FO contingent knew the destruction of the nettlesome machine gun nest with the first artillery round was nothing but exceptional luck. Conceivably every forward observer group at one time or another achieved such a fortuitous episode.

Later on in the war, Staff Sergeant Richardson turned down a battlefield commission – awarding him the rank of a second lieutenant. Richardson felt as if he was just a Californian doing the job of cardinal forward observer and in this case, rank didn't mean a damn thing to him. I am not aware of anyone from our artillery unit accepting an offered "battlefield" commission.

It was an especially heavyhearted occasion when orders came to pull back from some of the Alsation territory we previously had taken. The Nazis were mounting a strong offensive in our sector which would likely cut us off from our main forces. Division forces were being sent to occupy positions formerly held by Patton's Third Army units. With German forces stalled with their "Operation Northwind" (Ardennes Offensive/Battle of the Bulge), the Nazi forces chose our defensive sector to launch an all-out attack.

The issued order to withdraw (retreat) from our positions came none too soon. German tanks were beginning to shell our location with their 88mm guns in an effort to outflank us on both sides. Nonessential equipment was abandoned and we barely managed to escape the Nazi "Gordian" knot. I was extremely delighted the captain never remembered the damned bazooka. German tanks were rather well constructed and the bazooka was not too effective unless it disabled the tank tracks. Harsh winter conditions and slick icy roads were an additional enemy we had to fight. Since the Nazis also faced the same appalling weather conditions it may have been the key factor allowing us to escape. The massacre occurring earlier at Malmedy was still very fresh in our minds.

While pulling back through some of the Alsation villages previously liberated, we were pelted by snowballs hurled by the townspeople. We were thankful it was just balls of snow and not something more lethal. The Nazis would undoubtedly seek out villagers who had helped us earlier and sentence them to death or send them to prison camps. We felt deeply saddened over a retreat allowing Nazis back into the Alsation cities we so bitterly fought to retake.

I especially thought about an Alsation man, who a few days earlier, had warned me of German land mines when we were looking for a suitable site for our howitzers. I had asked the man if the Germans had mined the area where we desired to place the battery guns. The Alsation looked squarely at me, dropped his pants and displayed his genital area. His genitalia was completely missing – showing only scar tissue. He had stepped on one of the mines earlier. He displayed much anger as he repeated over and over, "*Les Boche, les Boche*" (offensive slang meaning "the Germans") while pointing to the area we were planning to initially place the howitzers. I swept a different area with the mine detector for an alternate battery gun site.

The rapid retreat ended when our forces took up better defensive positions. The division began rotating infantry regiments and their support groups. Two infantry regiments were on the front line while the remaining regiment was getting some R and R in the Bouxwiller area of Alsace. With the Nazi advance into France halted, we had some time to prepare for the upcoming spring offensive.

I began investigating an abandoned two-story German school house in Bouxwiller. The building had numerous huge narrow tall glass windows. While searching the second floor of the building, I came across some German school text books. Most printed material was extolling the virtues of Adolph Hitler and the glorious future of the "Third Reich."

Without warning, the entire building began to tremble as if a high magnitude earthquake were taking place. Subsequently, I heard a tremendous explosion mixed with the sound of shattering window glass of the schoolhouse. My initial thought suggested the building had become the victim of an errant Nazi "buzz bomb". I cautiously moved through broken glass toward the now windowless area of the building to obtain a better view.

The street was rapidly filling with panic-stricken civilians, most of the terror-stricken townspeople were running and pushing perambulators containing children as well as pulling small wagons of cherished belongings. Somehow, the scene I was gazing upon just did not appear courtly; however, nobody ever informed me that war is civilized.

Noticing a huge cloud of smoke and dust mushrooming into the sky a short distance away, I ran down the stairway and exited the damaged school building. I was running in the direction of the blast area to determine if I could be of possible help.

When speeding to the location of the blast, a horrendous thought descended upon me. In my haste to reach the explosion site, I had left my carbine in the schoolhouse. I returned to the school house but the gun was nowhere to be found. I vacated the building empty handed without my faithful companion. It bothered me considerably to lose the gun. The fact I did not have a weapon gave me an unsoldierly feeling. It was just as bothersome to my self-esteem, to think I would have to tell the invidious supply sergeant, "I lost my carbine and I need a replacement weapon."

Returning to the disaster scene, I glanced at something on the ground bringing me to an abrupt halt. It was the lower portion of a human leg still encased in the remains of a tattered combat boot belonging to an American soldier. The tract close by contained many other fragmented body parts, pieces of a military vehicle, as well as numerous unexploded U.S. Army anti-tank mines.

I unexpectedly noticed another object. It was a carbine similar to the one I carelessly lost and it was in perfect condition. Only the weapon's serial number would be different. This would be my weapon of choice until the end of the war. I had a very realistic notion who might have been the benefactor of my "new" .30-caliber rifle.

The nearby area was serving as a storage depot for U.S. anti-tank mines. The few survivors, still walking about, surmised a military truck may have accidently backed over one of the powerful devices, thereby detonating a large portion of the mine dump. I had some doubts about this explanation. Combat engineers handling mines had to be extremely careful. It is unlikely they would be so careless as to back a truck over one of the lethal devices.

I still puzzled about what happened to my carbine in the school house. Perhaps I had not been alone in the building and perchance the deadly explosion had not been an accident.

"It's 'gonna' be "85, 86, 87,– –, 89, 90. That's how my kids is a 'gonna' learn their numbers if I ever 'gits' back home. They ain't gonna be no damned eighty-eight." I was listening to one of the black 614th Tank Destroyer soldiers carefully evaluating the ever closer proximity of arriving artillery shells from one of the most dreaded weapons in the German arsenal – the 88mm (three and a half inches) high velocity artillery piece. A short interval later, after the shelling ceased, I finished the previous brief conversation by telling the black tanker, "You know...you have one hell of a good idea about forgetting the number eighty-eight."

Our artillery unit was using a projectile having a new type of fuse on the front end. The new device was called a "proximity fuse" incorporating a midget-sized transceiver capable of emitting radio waves. When the projectile came close to an object its reflected radio waves would trigger the device and cause the shell to explode.

Division Artillery had a small spotter plane used to locate possible enemy targets for their artillery. Since Division Artillery was not directly a part of our battery artillery network, we did not perceive what was taking place with this completely separate artillery unit.

On one particular mission we were actively working, one of our proximity-fused projectiles exploded high overhead instead of above our selected target on the ground. Upon closer examination of the daytime sky, we saw the little spotter plane used by Division Artillery. Fortunately for the pilot of the plane, the shrapnel from the our 105 projectile did not strike the small aircraft. The little plane quickly vacated its former position. The German vehicles we had targeted made their escape. Without ever realizing the closeness of their demise, the good fortune blessing the enemy convoy was simply due to a military "snafu". Division Artillery and our battery in all likelihood were attempting to shell the same target. The pilot of the division's small plane possibly believed he had nearly become the victim of nearby German antiaircraft artillery.

Several days later Corporal Chipman and 37531447 were looking for a place to bed down for the night. Noticing a large barn located just off of a cobblestone courtyard, the Tennessee rebel wheeled the Jeep into the plaza. While promenading to the barn, a German "eighty-eight" artillery shell landed almost at our feet. The vehicle evidently had been spotted by enemy forward observers. The incoming lethal projectile turned out to be another dud. The sparks caused by friction between the steel projectile and the cobble-stone left a fascinating meteor-like trail as it entered the courtyard house – expending its forward motion. This latest encounter with enemy artillery was far too close for comfort. Noting no additional shells were fired in our direction, we opted to remain in the barn.

Chipman opened a can of Vienna sausages which he shared with me. That night I became very ill. I most likely was still thinking about the close call with the dreaded German 88mm high velocity weapon. This had been the second time a dud artillery projectile had landed close by me. I upchucked on the hay several times during the night. It did not help my present discomfort to observe several large barn rats patiently waiting to move in for another course of partially-digested Vienna sausages.

The only German artillery rounds I never worried too much about were those discharging numerous propaganda leaflets. These leaflets were graphically suggesting draft-exempt American defense plant workers were "sleeping" with our wives and our girl friends. It was the same worn message "Axis Sally" delivered to us at the port city of Marseilles. I felt certain there was a measure of truth in the message. Perhaps the most beneficial component of the arriving leaflets would be the paper the message was printed on. The propaganda sheets made the best quality toilet paper readily available. Bursting with hilarity, I was witnessing my comrades-in-arms gathering the precious paper "gifts" and stuff them inside their plastic helmet liner webbing next to the spare socks which were more or less drying. It was just hoped we would have the good fortune to survive long enough to make use of the opportune paper.

Radio transmitter-receiver and the power unit carried on our backs, could draw enemy fire as quickly as the mere presence of the 614th Tank Destroyers. The bulky radio equipment could be likened to the waving of a brilliant-colored red cape in front of an angry bull. The "bulls" in this case were German forward observers and damned near everyone else we were fighting. We frequently wondered if anyone ever informed infantrymen to keep their distance from radio-carrying artillery forward observers. The Nazis knew the important role communications played in the outcome of battles and would bestow upon those carrying such communication equipment – considerable special attention.

It was just a matter of time until we would be making another all-out attack on the heavily fortified Siegfried Line. We were approaching portions of the sophisticated French fortifications known as the Maginot Line. The French had constructed these concrete and steel bunkers opposite the Siegfried Line to protect France from a possible German invasion. When the war started in Europe, the German Panzer units outflanked the Maginot Line by spearheading through Holland and Belgium. The Maginot Line was all but useless. Most guns guarding France faced Germany and could not be turned to the rear. In contrast, many big guns of the Siegfried Line were designed to fire in any direction.

My artillery unit had constructed log-covered bunkers offering a degree of protection from German counter-fire tree-bursts coming from the Siegfried Line. Communication field wire was hooked up to all required places. The occupants in one of these bunkers were Captain Hanlon, Corporal Chipman and myself.

With the sun finished with daylight, the pristine wooded area became hidden in darkness. I was almost asleep when the army field telephone commenced to ring. Captain Hanlon took the call. Having an uneasy feeling I was about to become involved with part of the reason for the phone call, I began the process of putting on my footwear. As I continued listening to "our" end of the conversation, I became aware something had happened to Lieutenant Whidden. I also realized a request was being made to the captain for an additional FO crew. The forward observers would take part in the early morning infantry and tank assault against the highly fortified *Siegfried Line.*

Captain Hanlon summoned Corporal James Safford and informed the soldier he would be in charge of the requested FO crew for the mission. Safford may have had some college training (ASTP) before entering the army. He also was a very capable and smart forward observer. The captain asked the corporal, "Who do you want for your primary radio operator?"

The answer to the captain's inquiry was, "I want 37531447."

Corporal Sanders (not to be confused with Corporal Safford) would be carrying half of our radio equipment. I had very definite misgiving concerning the upcoming assignment.

· Most previous OP set-ups were placed in stationary positions. This time we would be stepping out of a trench and becomes part of an assault force attacking the most sophisticated, deceptive, and seemingly impregnable network of defensive fortifications perhaps ever constructed by man. In my mind the effectiveness of the Siegfried Line ranked comparably with the Great Wall of China constructed centuries earlier.

We immediately departed to rendezvous with other battalion FO groups. Upon arriving at the designated place, the Jeeps were parked and we commenced walking to the assigned battlefield location.

The nighttime sky was just beginning to introduce daybreak when a small cluster of officers was observed huddled in front of one of the abandoned and now useless concrete and steel fortifications of the French Maginot Line. One of the officers was holding a bazooka. Some unknown infantryman remarked, "The guy holding the bazooka is General McAuliffe!" Another 411th infantryman quipped, "Up this close to the front, he must be buckin' for another damn star."

Brigadier General Anthony McAuliffe had just become the new 103rd Division commander. The general previously had been temporary commander and Executive Officer of the 101st Airborne at Bastogne.

Arriving at the designated location for the impending all-out assault on the Siegfried Line, we were positioned just out of view of the enemy and close to the village, Nieder Schlettenbach.

The assault on the Siegfried Line would be launched with a withering barrage from all artillery assigned to the division. The target area was approximately a half-mile distant from our location.

While awaiting the artillery barrage to be initiated, I began to ponder the nature of this rather strange and unusual assignment. Corporal Safford had the vital area maps, Sanders the radio power pack and I had the transmitter-receiver. Before we could use the radio for transmitting purposes, it was necessary to remove the radio units from our backs in order to mate the radio system. Another mucky thought raced through my mind. If any one of us became separated or knocked out of action, our mission, whatever it was, would be almost impossible to carry out.

The above thoughts were quickly dismissed as the artillery barrage on the area of enemy fortifications commenced. It was a lengthy shelling and I disrelished the termination. The last shells now being lofted by our artillery units were smoke shells. The dcnse smoke would help temporarily screen us from enemy view during the initial attack.

Ominous rumbling of the black 761st Tank Battalion's fighting machines could be heard as the tanks slowly moved out of concealed positions and onto the roadway leading into Nieder Schlettenbach.

The massive tanks began to fire their big guns at nearby enemy fortifications. In return, the black tanker unit received heavy counter-fire.

Word was now being passed along informing infantry troops they would launch the assault on enemy positions in one minute.

It is extremely difficult to remember any specific thoughts entertained as our group began to move out. I was scared and must have thought this would be the last moments of my life on this planet. I most likely thought of my parents and perhaps my former fiance. I could have been thinking about my old friend Bud Pitts. Perhaps I would have told him, "Bud, I think we made it out of Texas." I do not recollect entertaining in any so-called "fox-hole" religious compromises.

Moving toward the end of the wide trench, a voice coming from the vicinity of my feet caught my attention. I do not recall what he first said; however, his parting remark registered on my memory bank. Gazing down on the ground I saw the face of a wounded black tanker. With his eyes firmly focusing on mine, admonished, "Soldier, give 'em hell." I responded, "We will", knowing damned well I had some serious doubts about fulfilling his earnest and passionate request.

When it came my turn to leave the protective trench I did not hesitate. Perhaps the moment suggested I was correct in not wanting to become married and leave a widow of the war. It is very difficult to describe the rapid series of thoughts cascading through my mind at an uncomprehensible accelerating velocity. It is not that I cannot remember the event – it is just difficult to elucidate the emotions of that moment. I once more was having the feeling of being in a state of protective custody. Perhaps I was realizing anything destined to take place was completely out of my "hands" and I was simply submissive to whatever "card" fate would deal.

Before long, I was racing into the open and moving along the roadway being utilized by the big American tanks. I was slightly ahead and to the right of one of the tanks when its 76mm gun fired a round. The muzzle blast of hot compressed gasses from the powder charge propelling the projectile promptly blew the steel helmet and helmet liner off of my head. I felt completely naked without the mostly psychological protection of the headgear. Bullets, unless their kinetic energy is almost spent, can penetrate steel helmets with little difficulty. I swiftly scooped up the headgear from the roadway and positioned it back on my head. They never taught us about the dangers of a tank's muzzle blast in basic training.

The protective smoke cover from our shells was thinning. Looking to my right I noticed a group of soldiers wearing what appeared to be enemy uniforms, running towards us carrying white flags of surrender. As I briefly gazed at this scene I noticed some of them beginning to limply fall to the ground. The sound of machine gun fire coming behind them suggest they were being shot by their own troops. It appeared as if most made it safely to our lines.

The small hamlet of Nieder Schlettenback, located in no-man's land was mostly shell-shattered debris. The roadway we were using began to make a sharp swing to the right. We now would be paralleling the enemy fortifications located on the left flank of the hilly terrain.

Corporal Safford was no longer in sight. He could move at a faster pace without the burden of the heavy tube-type radio and its power pack. What I feared would happen came to pass. The missing Safford carried the area maps most likely vital to the successful use of our artillery battery. It was still possible to locate an infantry officer having maps of the battle site.

Glancing backward I could see my laboring radio partner, Sanders, still following me. The tanks were widening the distance between each other as their threatening gun turrets continued to menacingly rotate toward machine gun emplacements located in concrete bunkers on the high terrain and fire.

My eyes became fixated on something hardly recognizable on the roadway. I eventually realized it was the remains of possibly two or three bodies that had been run over by the wide treads of one or more of the heavy tanks. It was of small comfort to notice they had been wearing the uniforms of our foes. There was a momentary wrenching of my stomach. This discomfort became quickly truncated as I began to notice numerous enemy bullets dancing briskly on the ground in front of me. Their numbers appeared to dramatically increase while approaching a recently enlarged widow opening in an almost completely destroyed building. The radio equipment on our backs had drawn the attention of one or more German machine gunners. In desperation I hurled myself through the open area of the building and Corporal Sanders quickly followed. We had jumped through the window not knowing the ground-level first floor was completely missing. We fell directly into the basement. It was a surprisingly soft landing right on top of a huge pile of very rotten potatoes. I had the weird sensation of being unceremoniously swallowed by some type of gooey quicksand.

Both of us managed to extricate our bodies from the sticky, rotting pile of cushioning misery and exit the building. The German machine gunners apparently chose another target when we disappeared. Sanders and I continued our journey along the road with the infantrymen. We both smelled like hell and looked the same way. It really didn't matter since neither one of us were in a style show.

The tankers were constantly raking the hillside with their turret guns as well as their machine guns. The noise of the battle was awesome, but not loud enough to mask the impacting sound of a bullet striking the soldier behind me. Turning my head, fully expecting to find my radio partner on the ground, I noticed the victim was a infantryman who had passed up the laboring corporal. A quick glance at the fallen Cactus soldier told me a medic would not be of any help. A large portion of his head was missing. Before turning back around I again heard the sickening thump of an enemy bullet striking the infantryman just ahead of me. When struck, he uttered one small sound and fell on the roadside. I could see blood spurting from a bullet wound in the man's back near the heart area. He, too, would not require medical attention.

Enemy machine gunners were a short distance up the hillside firing the deadly weapon from a concrete bunker. It would be just a matter of moments before we too, would become victims of enemy bullets. They definitely wanted the communication radio silenced. Little did the enemy gunners realize the radio was already practically useless.

I did something we were cautioned against doing. We had been warned to never use an enemy foxhole because the vast majority of them were heavily booby-trapped. To remain on the open road meant almost certain death. Similar to the open window we had earlier jumped through, here, inviting to be used, was a rather large enemy foxhole having a wicker lining. In a way it was just making a choice between almost certain death from the machine gun bullets or death by an explosive charge. I dived headfirst into the abandoned sanctuary and Sanders fell right on top of me. We both had taken an enormous gamble and temporarily won. The foxhole had not been booby-trapped with explosives.

The enemy machine gunners noticing us disappear into the foxhole, would periodically fire a burst at us. The gunner's lethal bullets just cleared our heads and were impacting on the opposite side, chewing up portions of the shelter's wicker lining. Every now and then a German would shout down to us to come out and surrender. We knew damn well what his real intent was.

Compounding our current problem, the foxhole came under attack from enemy mortars. Mortar rounds do not make any serious sounds announcing their arrival. Incoming mortar rounds reminded me of the line in Carl Sandburg's poem *Fog*, "The fog comes on little cat feet". So do the fuckin' mortar rounds.

It was rather weird how enemy mortar fire could bracket our commandeered foxhole but was seemingly unable to split the bracket to eliminate us. During our current predicament we pondered how time can whimsically stand motionless and move rapidly ahead simultaneously.

Sanders and I were very much cognizant we would have to vacate our protective temporary shelter or risk a German hand grenade finishing us off. Bullets periodically continued serenading our "guest" quarters as well as numerous nearby mortar rounds.

With the day now approaching sunset, our bodies cramped and no other friendly troops using the road, the moment to leave our shelter was fast approaching. All we needed to do was to move across the road to the safety of a protecting berm and the nearby forest. The length of the pathway to the other side of the road was providing me with the allusion of a unit of distance unreasonably expanding.

Another unexpected problem developed upon detecting the sound of a distant artillery weapon. We had noted the sound earlier but it just didn't seem too important at the time. We could hear the projectile pass over us and strike a building a quarter of a mile distant. Two sounds were noted when the shell landed. First, the shell exploding and the second sound was that of the entire building crashing down. This definitely was not an eighty-eight, but something far larger than anything the Germans had used on us previously. This huge enemy artillery piece may have been the reason for the absence of friendly troops using the roadway.

Eventually the firing pattern of this big gun was determined. The huge shell would pass over us every ten minutes. The first hit had been on the right side of the road leading back into Nieder Schlettenbach. The next missile was on the left side of the road closer to town. Ten minutes later, back on the right side; once again moving closer to the town. There was no variation in the firing pattern.

Corporal Sanders and I knew it was imperative to abandon the foxhole since darkness was rapidly approaching. It would just be a matter of time before an enemy grenade would be tossed or fired our way. Eyeing the road, we decided to leave the foxhole for the dash to the opposite roadside. After making certain our cramped legs worked and we had all our radio gear, we took one final glance across the roadway just after the machine gun fired another burst into the side of the foxhole. What we saw next was downright unexpected. A full moon was just coming up over the forested ridge. The moon's appearance was near the top off our "unwanted occurrences" list. It would light up the area like a searchlight.

Perhaps Moon Grandmother (Native American term for the moon) was telling us, "Move it!" At that moment a fire-fight broke out in the proximity of the enemy machine guns. The bright full moon evidently spotlighted the machine gun nest. We both completed the rapid sprint across the road to the relative safety of the berm. Not one bullet came flying our way, thanks to the infantrymen from a 411th Company Platoon who brought sudden silence to the pillbox causing our drawn-out ordeal of being pinned down. The full moon had been a blessing – not a curse. We felt badly knowing we were not able to keep up with Corporal Safford. This feeling, however, was tempered by the reality of knowing the two of us had kept the attention of both an enemy machine gun emplacement and mortar crew for the better part of a day. While the enemy was occupied firing at us, they were not killing other Cactus Division soldiers.

After crossing the road we hugged the ground and waited for the next projectile from the mammoth gun. It passed over us on our side of the road just as we predicted. The following round should be on the opposite side of the road, giving us almost twenty minutes to start our journey back to the vicinity of Nieder Schlettenbach. Once back to the town we could find friendly troops and the location of the battery howitzers.

Our good fortune was still with us. The German projectile was right on schedule as another big round struck the right side of the road. Each shell was moving ever closer to Nieder Schlettenbach.

Cautiously walking for five minutes more, we halted to await the arrival of the next anticipated explosive missile. If all went as we were predicting, the shell should strike a short distance ahead of us. Each step we took through the forested area was a big concern. A large portion of the land area had been laced with anti-personnel mines.

We were contemplating what the vocal password and the countersigns were. It was quite likely we would be stopped and challenged by friendly guards. By the time we agreed the password might possibly be "pianissimo", the sound of the big siege gun firing once again reached our ears. The next ado was the arriving missile passing very closely overhead. It fell on our side of the road a short distance in front of us.

Resuming the moonlight hike, we began to smell the putrid acrid odor of a recently exploded enemy shell. German high explosives had a definite nauseating pungent smell that was somewhat different than our explosives. We knew we were close to where the last big shell had just landed.

Neither one of us were prepared for what we observed at the site of the freshly-made shell crater. My trigger finger immediately went inside the trigger guard of the carbine. Grotesquely strewn around the crater were the badly mangled bodies of German soldiers who had just been killed by "friendly fire" from the big German gun. In all likelihood the freshly killed troops had been a squad of Nazi soldiers bypassed during the original attack. Our immediate concern some had survived the blast proved groundless. Had they not been struck by their own artillery, we most likely would have walked headlong into an enemy ambush. This was the last shell coming from the unknown weapon. I pondered the irony of this episode.

Eventually we reached the vicinity where the Jeeps were parked. Sure enough, we were given the order to halt and give the password. I am not certain of what I replied helped as much as my slight southern accent. Anyway we were greeted by black tanker guards. We were directed to a building now being used as the military command post where we would spend the remainder of the night.

Corporal Sanders and I most likely dispensed the vivid impression we both had just arrived from far inside the Gates of Hell.

Removing the burdensome radio pack and dropping to the floor, 37531447 was physically, mentally and emotionally drained. He fell asleep not completely certain if he were alive or deceased or…if even mattered.

Awakening sometime the next morning, I noticed the black soldiers were gone. Observing a blanket covering me and remembering I did not have a blanket, I asked one of the white soldiers pulling duty in the command post, "Where did this blanket come from?"

His reply, "One of the black tankers from the 761st Tank Battalion covered you with his blanket as he was leaving."

Postscript

McAuliffe told the Germans demanding the surrender of the 101st Airborne during the battle for the city of Bastogne, a four-letter word which became quite well known: "Nuts". The Nazis did not understand the meaning of the idiom and asked for clarification. An American officer informed the Germans that it meant, "Go to Hell."

****

Corporal Safford was a line corporal and I was a sergeant technician. In the army, a line corporal was in a leadership position while I was a sergeant in the technical role. This is why Captain Hanlon called for Corporal Safford to be in charge of the FO group assaulting the Siegfried instead of me. I had worked with Safford on other occasions and knew he was very capable of commanding the mission.

****

The German counter-offensive that almost had us trapped was a phase of "Operation North Wind" initiated by the Germans. American and French troops were greatly over-extended. We had taken up positions that were vacated by the American Third Army of Patton. The bulk of Patton's troops had been moved further north and were involved in halting the surprise German Ardennes offensive.

The American Seventh Army and the French Sixth Army Group were precariously holding on to a 120-mile front. When the Germans realized the Ardennes Offensive was not going to be successful they threw their remaining forces at our long thin line extending from Colmar, France to north of the large French city of Strasbourg located west of the Rhine river.

General Eisenhower was willing to give up Strasbourg to the Germans; however, French General de Gaul informed Eisenhower he would withdraw his troops from the Allied Command if Strasbourg was to be sacrificed back to the Nazis while Seventh Army units (including the 103rd Division) were falling back. Eisenhower relented on his plan to allow Strasbourg to fall into German control but did inform General de Gaul that it was up to the French to defend the city.

The Germans established a bridgehead over the Rhine River and were heading for Strasbourg when tough French soldiers put a stop to the threatening drive at the last bridge before advancing enemy troops would enter Strasbourg.

****

When our artillery unit was almost trapped in Alsace by the counter-attacking Germans, the Nazi commander for the attack was none other than the much-hated Heinrich Himmler who earlier in the war was appointed by Hitler to oversee all "racial" matters. In August of 1943 he was appointed Minister of the Interior, in which post he oversaw the "Final Solution" and authorized the medical experiments of the dreaded SS doctors. Himmler who was commanding the "Army Group Upper Rhine" (the Nazi military unit attacking our positions) was no general and was soon replaced.

Heinrich Himmler was an extremely devious individual. Toward the end of the war he desperately attempted to improve his simulacrum by ordering a halt to the Final Solution. The reality of the situation suggested most extermination sites were already in Allied hands, thereby denying Himmler a place to continue carrying out the Final Solution. Considering his sinuous characteristics, he most likely was attempting to cut a deal that hopefully would save his butt.

After Germany surrendered, Himmler tried to escape in disguise; however, he was captured on May 23, 1945 and shortly afterward committed suicide by taking poison.

****

It was a large German railroad gun shelling Nieder Schlettenbach and most likely was a 274 millimeter weapon using an explosive projectile close to 11 inches in diameter.

Both Russell Pitts and I had heard stories that the big railroad weapon was hidden from view in a railroad tunnel. After the weapon fired it "retreated" into the underground shelter until it was ready to fire the next round. U.S. Tactical Air Force bombed both ends of the tunnel ending the usefulness of the huge artillery piece. The full moon may well have exposed the railroad tracks leading to the tunnel entrances for our tactical airforce.

****

To this day I have absolutely no craving for canned Vienna sausages.

****

When the anti-tank mine storage facility in Bouxwiller was destroyed it was being operated by the 328th Combat Engineer Battalion. Records in my possession indicate the explosion occurred on the 28th of January 1945. Four U.S. Soldiers were killed in the "accident'. No mention is made of the number of injured. The 328th Combat Engineer Battalion was a supporting member of the 103rd Infantry Division.

****

While exploring the German schoolhouse and discovering what type of reading material German youth were subjected to for their long term indoctrination for the achieving of Third Reich goals, I learned a valuable lesson. If one cherishes freedom of a democracy, it comes with a price tag for its citizens.

****

The German Army arsenal had more than forty types of anti-vehicle mines for use during the war. Most were buried in the ground and detonated by pressure of either man or vehicle. I have often wondered how close I came to stepping on one of these devices during the episode of attacking the Siegfried Line.

****

Due to the often long distances involved in communication between forward observers and their fire control centers, they did not have the luxury of using the so-called "walkie-talkie" FM voice radio weighing only a few pounds. The hand-held lighter walkie-talkie used by U.S. Infantry had an approximate range of two miles.

****

The Maginot Line "protecting" France was equipped with guns, a scaled down railroad, hospital, electric power and could house almost 60 French military divisions (300,000 troops). The Nazis used only 19 divisions to keep the huge number of French divisions at bay and therefore could use the great difference in manpower needs to sweep around the Belgium end of the Maginot zone of fortifications. The Maginot Line was a very expensive mistake for France. It did little to stop the Nazi invasion of that country.

****

Although I cannot recall making any "foxhole" religious compromises, I did carry a small copy of the *New Testament of the Holy Bible* in one of my shirt pockets. I am not certain if I ever read anything from the book; nevertheless, the book did provide me with a measure of comfort – knowing it might stop an almost spent bullet if it struck that particular spot. My comments are not intended to show disrespect for the *Holy Bible* but are offered more to help the reader understand my emense problem wrestling with the paradox of a loving Christ and the cruel reality of a hellish war.

Chapter Seventeen

The Siegfried Line Crumbles

"Could it be that existence and death are only illusions?"
—37531447

I would never know how my physical appearance manifested itself to the black tanker when covering me with his own blanket. My clothing reeked with the stench of rotten potatoes and the smell probably rivaled or surpassed my body odor when I debarked from the *Monticello* in Marseilles. Perhaps he just looked at my face and sensed I had spent an arduous period of time in Gehenna. Combat soldiers always had different facial expression than rear echelon "paper pushers".

Corporal Sanders and 37531447 began to inquire the whereabouts of the artillery battery. Most of the day was spent waiting or watching reserve battle units move forward. It most likely would be nightfall before we would succeed in finding the new location of our howitzers. Meanwhile, three other members out of the nine forward observers beginning the mission, returned to pick up their Jeeps.

As darkness settled in, sporadic military action was still occurring in the vicinity. The military term for such activity was called "mopping up". This phrase when used in news releases by rear positioned war correspondents always seemed to have a diminutive tone to the danger factor. In reality "mopping up" meant shooting, being shot at, removing mines, bobby traps, body recovery and encountering other dangerous potentially deadly perils.

The fragmented FO contingents were finally given verbal instructions to follow the tail-end of an arriving convoy. We were apprised it would be going into the general vicinity of our battalion guns. The new instructions did not seem to convey any definitive location of our artillery units.

Corporal Sanders and I were travelling in the hindmost vehicle in the convoy. Safford, who had maps of the area had not returned from the fighting still going on in the Siegfried Line and we were highly concerned about his fate. Portions of other battalion FO crews were riding in the two Jeeps ahead of us. We had traveled for several hours on a dark forested road when we began to observe magnesium flares in the sky just ahead of the lengthy motor convoy. Forward progress came to a standstill. We were needlessly informed the crossroad just ahead was receiving German artillery fire. The shelling ceased as abruptly as it had started.

Even after the artillery shells ahead of us had stopped falling and the absence of other flares indicated it might be safe to resume the movement of the convoy, the Jeep ahead remained motionless. I became increasingly annoyed over the lengthy delay. The longer the wait, the more impatient I became. Instructing Sanders to remain with our vehicle, I walked forward to the preceding Jeep to ascertain if the occupants could determine any logical reason for the nettlesome dawdling. An observer from their Jeep walked with me to the leading Jeep. Upon arriving at the first Jeep, we uncovered the shocking reason for our period of non-movement. The solitary driver in the vehicle was sound asleep! Gazing ahead, we could only discern the vast empty darkness of the forested road. The large convoy we were tailing had completely vanished into the blackness of the night.

Once more we were on our own and in uncertain territory. None of our group had area maps. Without maps we didn't have the slightest clue as to where in hell we should be or where we should be going. Even if we had maps it was doubtful we could determine the new position of battalion guns. We couldn't use the radio to ask for the location of battery gun positions. The enemy would most likely learn the whereabouts of our battalion if its position were transmitted to us.

A brief strategy session led to the decision to continue down the lonely road. We soon reached the crossroads which had been the object of the earlier enemy shelling. It was definitely not a location or time frame to have another pow-wow. All three vehicles continued straight through the crossroad area until it was relatively safe to stop. We conferred and agreed to continue in the same direction. Moments later my intuition alarm was loudly screaming, "You have screwed up!" Before I could sort out anything positive, the shadowy hulk of a pack animal, carrying supplies to infantrymen, blocked the way of our jeep. A deep, definitely southern voice coming from an unseen location softly cautioned, "Jus' bump 'er lightly and she'll move over so y'all can get by." We followed the given instructions and continued in the same direction down the road. My intuition must have been wrong. We evidently were still in friendly territory.

Upon arriving at the outskirts of a relatively small hamlet, I once more retrieved the nagging feeling something was definitely amiss and perhaps my previous perspicacity had correctly diagnosed our current situation. We most certainly should not be where we now were. Parking all of the vehicles in the enclosed courtyard of the first building we reached, we began removing each vehicle's engine coil wire from under the hood and concealing them. The five of us were now ready to make the next incalculable move. The small collection of completely adrift artillery forward observers made a path leading to the entry of the dwelling. After knocking several times, the door slowly opened and a middle-aged man, along with his wife, laid eyes on United States soldiers.

From their undisguised facial expressions we knew beyond the slightest allusion of a doubt, they were not expecting any Allied soldiers. They did not panic but both appeared to be exceptionally ill at ease and were displaying a high level of nervous discomfort with our sudden appearance. Our cozy little FO group was not exactly at ease either. It fell my lot to be silently elected the spokesperson for the forward observers. I did have a Germanic last name, spoke poor, but passable German and was the ranking noncom. Probably the real reason for my speaking part was everyone was looking my direction urging me to say something – soon!

Up to this moment the disturbed couple was not exactly displaying any friendly characteristics. Almost instantly, I became transformed into the Mark Twain character of Tom Sawyer, an unequalled mast of "bending" the truth. Looking directly at the couple and in a matter of fact style, I quickly informed the apprehensive pair, "We are the advance group of a large column of American panzer units, accompanied by numerous divisions of infantry." The now frightened couple looked at each other in alarm as I continued, "These fighting units will soon be entering this very village." Other FO's in our small assemblage nodded their helmeted heads in unison, adding animated emphasis to reinforce my strongly worded "truthful" statements of fabrication.

After a momentary pause to reflect on my spoken words, the couple hastily brought us wine and black bread. Tensions eased slightly; nevertheless, we still had a cautious mistrust about our "hosts". We kept our carbines on standby while we treated ourselves to the much undeserved bread and wine. The ongoing scene reminded me of the Biblical painting of *The Last Supper*. We had bread and wine but all I wanted was…to hear the cock crow and get the hell out of there.

The entire assemblage remained in the same room until the beginning of daybreak. Thanking our "hosts" for the bread and wine, I informed the couple, "It would be best for your well-being if you would remain inside the house when the United States' panzer units arrive." We returned to the Jeeps, replaced the coil wires and sped out of the courtyard, heading back in the direction we had previously come.

Three kilometers later we met an approaching 103rd Division infantry company ready to wrestle the town we had just vacated from enemy control. They were just foot soldiers without any tanks, heavy artillery or large numbers of men. The officer in charge, noting our Jeeps, flagged us down and inquired, "Are you guys with the engineers?"

It was not unusual for engineers to precede infantry. Engineers would often be involved with mine removal, barbed wire removal, eliminating road blocks and other hazardous duties. Army Engineers were often unsung heroes during combat.

I replied, "No sir. We are field artillery forward observers."

Infantrymen in the battle formation began to grin and shake their heads in disbelief. They must have figured artillery FO's are crazy bastards for being so far ahead of infantry units.

I volunteered additional information to the company officer by adding, "We did not observe any German outposts or defensive positions at the edge of the village." The infantry lieutenant received additional information suggesting the Nazis may have departed from the opposite end of the village under the cover of darkness. The piddling-sized infantry unit was happy to hear the report. I knew these veterans of the 103rd Division would, nevertheless, use a judicial military approach upon approaching their objective.

A large portion of the day was utilized in the attempt to locate our artillery battalion position. The convoy we were following the night before, undoubtedly had taken a different route at the crossroads.

When finally locating the howitzers darkness was once again rapidly replacing the remaining daylight. It was a great comfort to notice Corporal Safford standing among the artillery soldiers. He too, never fully understood the nature of our mission near Nieder Schlettenbach a couple of days earlier.

I did perceive hot food being served by the kitchen crew. For once, I had fortuitously arrived in time to partake of the hot chow. Although quite hungry, the longing to have a warm meal was secondary to what I really wanted at the moment. 37531447 did not bother to pass through the chow line.

A small mountain brook was close by and my desire to change filthy clothes and wash off several days of road muck became the primary priority. Completing washing my hands and face in the small nearby brook, I noticed something definitely out of place slightly upstream. Upon further investigation, I came upon the body of an enemy soldier lying face up in the shallow flowing water. I slowly made my way closer and gazed down upon the unfortunate victim. He was still wearing his eye glasses. The left lens of his eyepiece had been shot out by the bullet ending his life. The dead soldier had an unusually peaceful expression on his face. Most of the physical damage, to the deceased soldier, was in the area where the bullet made its exit. Draped around the neck of the former adversary was a large garland of garlic bulbs. The smell of the garlic was very pronounced. I once had been informed wearing garlands of garlic would bring the wearer good luck. I now had serious reservations about the relationship between garlic garlands and good fortune. I also had the uneasy perception I was invading the privacy of the dead soldier by my presence. His remaining eye had not closed and appeared to be staring back at me. I slowly turned around, walked away and mulled over the cruelty of war.

Finding my duffel, I replaced my begrimed clothing and snuggled into my sleeping bag. I was still thinking about the dead enemy soldier "asleep" in the stream. He looked too damned young to be in the German military. The thought occurred to me that I was not a hell of a lot older than the dead German youth.

Before falling asleep, I also had time to reflect about a rifleman with the 411th Infantry Regiment. Earlier in the fighting I noticed the soldier seated under a tree leaning back on the tree trunk. It was during a time when enemy numerous rounds of artillery were incoming and the rest of us were seeking shelter from flying shrapnel. After the shelling ceased, I searched for the tree where I had last seen the infantryman. He was still in the same position and the only change I noticed was he now was reading a comic book. Somewhat intrigued by his seemingly eccentric behavior, I ambled over to where he was and inquired, "Why did you sit against this tree and not take cover from the shelling?" When his eyes shifted upward from the comic book, the cactus division soldier calmly replied, "If your 'number' is up, it doesn't matter what you do." He paused momentarily to study the puzzled expression spreading across my face and then added, "I lost a good friend during a shelling early in the campaign. He had constructed a damned good foxhole covered with logs and dirt. A German '88' landed right in the small opening to his foxhole blowing him to bits." The infantryman reiterated, "Yep, if it has your number on it, it will get you no matter what you do." I slowly nodded my head slightly up and down and walked away. I was recalling the two 88's – both duds – that landed close to me and my close brush with a sniper.

Following a somewhat restful sleep, the morning sun awakened me and the aroma of cooked food drifted my way. It would be the first hot meal I had eaten for quite some time.

During the day our entire artillery battalion became part of a task force which would muscle its way through the badly crippled Siegfried Line. This time I would be riding in the captain's Jeep serving as the radio operator. The 409th Infantry Regiment would be part of the task force continuing the pursuit of the Germans. I kept wondering if Sergeant Pitts had survived the battle of the Siegfried Line.

It was rather ironic to meet a 411th Infantryman who had participated in the assault on the troublesome machine gun position that had Corporal Sanders and me pinned down. In the darkness of night it is not unusual for combat soldiers of either side to become separated. The 411th Infantry rifleman recounted an adventure with his German speaking platoon leader. During the darkness in the heavily forested area of the Siegfried fortifications, the American platoon sergeant heard an anxious soft voice of an enemy soldier pleadingly ask, *"Adolph, wo bist du?"* ("Adolph, where are you?"). The platoon leader speaking in a low muffled voice replied, *"Kom mal her"* ("Come over here"). The German's voice, now sounding much closer, once again whispered, *"Wo bist du, Adolph?"* The 103rd Infantry platoon leader again quietly softly uttered the same reply, *"Kom mal her."* The U.S. infantryman soon captured one completely surprised enemy prisoner of war.

The motorized task group heading for the Rhine River would consist of 103rd Division infantrymen, division artillery, the 761st Tankers and other units.

Near the Klingenmuenster Valley, the task force caught up with a retreating – mostly horse-drawn German convoy. The Nazi convoy was attempting to reach the safety of the Rhine River. The use of horses strongly hinted the German war machine was deteriorating rapidly. The horse-drawn convoy was badly out-gunned by the task force and our Tactical Air Force planes. The beautiful mountain valley road was littered with wreckage along with the corpses of German military dead. In addition, numerous horses had become innocent victims of the war. Many of the horses of the convoy were badly wounded while others were peacefully grazing in the meadow. We did not destroy the badly injured horses for fear of drawing either enemy or friendly fire. Small arms fire had a tendency to make soldiers nervous and trigger happy.

While the road ahead was being cleared of debris we had a lunch break. I was becoming so conditioned to seeing dead soldiers – the mangled human enemy bodies lying close by did not greatly disturb me while eating K-rations. I began to realize *I was not the same naïve person who started basic training* at Fort Bliss. My earlier period of innocence had vaporized. I had now become quite calloused to the sights and sounds of war and death, although it still hurt to see Cactus men or other American soldiers who were KIA (killed in action).

The "Task Force Rhine" was breaking through the final portion of the Siegfried Line. We were crossing the Rhine River on a pontoon bridge constructed by American engineers to replace the destroyed permanent bridge once spanning the river.

Major General Anthony C. McAuliffe, Commander of the 103rd Division, congratulated officers and soldiers of all military units attached to the 103rd Division's push through the Siegfried. The general let be known his praise for the task force.

> *The first stage of our operation has been completed. You broke through the famous Siegfried defenses and then boldly exploited your success. You have taken more than 4,700 prisoners. You have fought valiantly and intelligently, and you have led all the way. I congratulate you.*

Ken Lenke Photograph
German machine-gun nest in the Siegfried line disguised as a log house

Although the general was generous with the rightly deserved praise, my thoughts were on the large numbers of casualties of United States soldiers lost in the process.

The Germans were certain it would be impossible to break through the fortifications of the hellish Siegfried Line. At times, I thought their erroneous assessment was correct.

The black wounded tanker near Nieder Schlettenbach who told me to "Give them hell" got his wish. Hell is exactly what the enemy received.

As for the unknown black tanker who placed his own blanket over me at the command post, I would liked to have been given the opportunity to express my gratitude to him in person.

There would be more fighting at a new "there" all too soon.

Postscript

The reason the coil wire was removed from each Jeep was to prevent the theft of the vehicles. Military vehicles did not have keys; instead, each had an "off-on" type ignition starting switch.

****

The smell of garlic brings back the unsolicited war memory of the dead enemy soldier in the shallow brook. I still have difficulty eating any food containing garlic.

****

Sergeant Russell Pitts remembers pack animals being used to bring supplies into the rugged terrain. Bud was with Company G of the 409th Infantry Regiment and helped unload the critical combat necessities brought in by the mules and their "mule skinners". I was never certain what made up the cargo on the back of the almost invisible pack animal when I was advised, "Jus' bump 'er lightly and she'll move over." Critical supplies usually meant ammunition for infantry use, food and medical previsions. On the return trip the mules, shepherded by mule skinners, would be transporting bodies of 103rd Infantry Division soldiers killed in action.

It would be within logical reasoning to believe Bud Pitts and I were in the same area at the same time without either of us knowing it.

In the book, *The Trail of the Cactus,* Sergeant James "Mule Skinner" Holmes relates:

> *On the return from the harsh terrain of the front lines, the mules were reluctant to carry their new burdens (KIAs). They began to buck, kick and snort. A lively commotion got underway that attracted the Germans. They (the Germans) added to the melee with a fair artillery barrage. The teamsters forgot about their mules, seeking instead a place for personal cover. Unattended, the mules got completely out of control and started running through the underbrush. After an hour the mules were caught, calmed down, reloaded and sent on their way.*

****

The unofficial equipment toll exacted on the German vehicle and horse-drawn convoy by our task force and tactical air units was:

twenty-five trucks	five 75mm cannons
ten autos	twelve 37mm weapons
five tracked vehicles	one 170mm weapon
? – kitchen vehicles	116 horse-drawn carriages

Judging from the equipment toll it is feasible that 200 German soldiers may have lost their lives in this action.

Chapter Eighteen

The Rhine River Occupation

"I wished he could have witnessed the cessation of the long bitter world conflict. He was our Commander in Chief."

—37531447

The 103rd Division was relieved from combat duty after breaching the fortifications of the Siegfried Line. Other military units were assigned the task of pursuing Nazi soldiers. There were two clear reasons for our new operational task. We had taken considerable German territory that must be maintained in a controlled status. Perhaps the greater concern was the need for human replacements for the division's extensive battlefield casualties.

The insensitive term *"replacements"* was eventually phased out of the military dictionary by the sweet-tempered word *"reinforcements"*. With high losses of United States military personnel in both the Pacific and European Theatre of the war, the euphemism may well have reflected the need to use a more palatable word for home front consumption. Hardened front line soldiers definitely comprehended the expression "reinforcements" still implied "replacement" troops.

Moderating springtime brought an end to the miserable unsettled April weather. Division units were stationed east of the Rhine River, slightly north of Mannheim in southern Germany. They were positioned close to the rugged mountainous country of Austria. My misgivings about the day we would be forced to fight our way across the Rhine River proved to be unfounded.

The open river territory had been abandoned by the soldiers of the Third Reich in favor of new defensive positions in the lofty Alpine terrain farther to the south.

To make us feel more at ease following the bitter brutal battle for the Vosges Mountains and the breaching of the Siegfried Line, division soldiers were entertained by groups sponsored by the United Service Organization (USO). One of the entertainers was the legendary German-born American actress Marlene Dietrich. It was a

231

tremendous emancipation of uptightness to have our minds and eyes occupied on something else besides the multitudinous dangers of combat. Marlene delivered her gravel-voiced rendition of *Lili Marlene*. This song was popular in Germany as well as in the United States. Some of the combat soldiers seated close to Miss Dietrich observed she was wearing a Cactus Division shoulder patch on the garter of her leg. I must have missed seeing the identifying divisional patch; besides, I already knew what the division shoulder patch looked like.

We were briefed by our commanding officer concerning the rules of fraternization with German civilians. Special orders came down from Lieutenant-General Jacob L. Devers, Commanding Officer of the Sixth Army. The lengthy memorandum listed seven items dealing with German-American relations for now and the near future. The main points of the proclamation were:

1. *To remember always that Germany, though "conquered", is still a dangerous enemy nation.*
2. *Never to trust Germans, collectively or individually.*
3. *To defeat German efforts to poison my thoughts or influence my attitude.*
4. *To avoid acts of violence, except when required by military necessity.*
5. *To conduct myself at all times so as to command the respect of the German people for myself, for the United States, and for the Allied cause.*
6. *Never to associate with Germans.*
7. *To be fair but firm with the Germans.*

The usage of the word "conquered" in item "one" of General Dever's memorandum was slightly premature.

Cactus Division soldiers had just experienced some rather strenuous times. Item number "six" in the lieutenant-general's memo would become the first of the seven edicts to be disregarded. It was kind of a "Fraulein on the Rhine" thing.

During occupational duty I was approached by a rather young and joyfully smiling German frau. She appeared to take great delight in informing me, in almost flawless English, "You Americans are now going to lose the war." Momentarily mulling her quixotic remark, I became somewhat mystified over the woman's gleeful demeanor in uttering such a surprising statement – words seemingly manifesting a high level of bona fide conviction. Brimming with curiosity I prompted the query, "What makes you think so?"

Speaking in a dulcet tone of voice, she enthusiastically proclaimed, "Your President Roosevelt is dead!"

I was utterly dumbfounded over the woman's pronunciamento. It was not so much about hearing my first news of the death of President Roosevelt, but more by the apparent honest conviction the woman embraced concerning the permutation of the outcome of the conflict in Europe.

"President Roosevelt's death would in no way alter the direction of the war for Germany." I retorted. Her smile dwindled somewhat as I continued, "The United States already has a new president. His name is Harry Truman." Apparently not interested in my words, she turned away and departed. I felt confident my most worthy scholarly lecture fell on closed ears.

The 928th Field Artillery was assigned a sector of German territory to control. I was placed in charge of a group manning a road block on the edge of a small village. We busied ourselves with constructing a protective emplacement for one of the battery's .30-caliber machine guns. It was the same type of weapon the platoon staff sergeant at Camp Howze, Texas had so dramatically instructed me how to operate. I felt unusually self-confident how to manipulate the weapon if need be.

Assigned duties would include checking civilian passes and stopping vehicles for inspection. PFC Sanders, my radio partner during the Siegfried line battle, would be working with me. The manner in which he handled the situation while being pinned down by enemy fire gave me much confidence in his ability to handle any unwanted problems.

One dark evening while manning the outpost, a structure ablaze in the next community was observed. We suddenly began to hear a chorus of unidentifiable garbled sounds flowing outward from our little village. In striving to sort out the strange approaching clamor, I definitely believed I was hearing the sound of running horses. Perchance my mind was playing a mischievous prank with my "memory bank". Stepping out of our fortified position and onto the roadway, 37531447 made ready to intercept whatever was now rapidly approaching. Sanders remained with the machine gun, turning the gun's meaningful end in the direction of the oncoming hullabaloo.

Out of the darkness of the night appeared a team of horses pulling an old-fashioned pumper fire wagon. Immediately behind the vintage pumper unit was another horse drawn flat-bed wagon loaded with members of the village fire brigade.

I could hardly believe what my eyes were seeing. All of the men appeared to be elderly and wearing a most unusual colorful assortment of headgear. Some wore the spiked steel helmets of World War I, others were adorned with French military helmets, some wore Nazi helmets and other were adorned with head covering – conceivably dating back to the beginning of the Roman Empire. The unfolding scenario, currently appearing before my eyes, reminded me of the old *Keystone Cops* cartoon movies I had viewed as a lad at the Uptown Theater in Strong City, Kansas.

The drivers of the wagons reluctantly reined their galloping horses to a halt. The machine gun Sanders was now pointing at the group had persuaded them it was a prudent decision on their part. The fire brigade impressed me with their urgent desire to help extinguish the burning blaze in the neighboring town. I forthwith remembered edict number "five" recently given to us by General Devers covering rules of fraternization. It stated, "To conduct myself at all times so as to command the respect of the German people, for myself, for the United States and for the Allied cause." I saw nothing out of the ordinary with villagers from one community helping others in neighboring towns with fire problems. It was done the same way in the rural communities of Kansas. Besides – I wanted to "Command the respect of the German people."

Stepping aside, I waved the entire colorful entourage through the military checkpoint.

Requesting another soldier to remain with PFC Sanders, I began hoofing it to the location of the burning edifice. My intent was to make certain all the men were indeed members of the local fire brigade and not German military.

Approaching the blazing structure, I was just in time to witness the pumper wagon drop a fire hose into the town's water well, some distance from the conflagration. I commenced observing the resplendent helmeted crew we had earlier allowed to pass our checkpoint, unwind their fire hose and drag the coupling end toward the direction of the blaze. Those remaining with the antiquated pumper were beginning to energetically raise and lower the pump's handles, sending a surge of water rushing through the fire hose even as it was being dragged toward the direction of the burning building.

Tracking the large serpent-like "catheter" until it had reached its fullest possible length, I became a spectator to one of the more hilarious episodes I had experienced during my military career. My timing was flawless to now perceive the rushing water from the end of the hose falling harmlessly onto the ground. The fire brigade from the village of the burning structure had positioned their fire hose from the burning dwelling toward the general direction of the town's water well. Both hoses by themselves were not long enough to reach the fire. All that remained was to connect the two water conduits belonging to each fire brigade. Shaking my head in total disbelief, I noted the couplings on the ends of both hoses embraced different fittings, making it impossible to "mate" the fire hoses. The would-be fire fighters' chagrined facial expressions, body language, confused excited guttural voices and the continuing flow of water from the hose, abundantly watering only the ground, made me once again mentally evaluate Adolph Hitler's super race concept for the intended 1,000 year reign of the Third Reich. The two-story building was completely reduced to a pile of blackened rubble.

A few days later First Sergeant Trish, along with other battery soldiers, improperly requisitioned a Dodge weapons carrier to visit a neighboring town. 37531447 was a member of the group. It was rumored a contingent of Polish refugees was quartered in a not-to-distant village and most of the occupants were women. If the refugees were not German, we could not be accused of breaking the rules of fraternization recently imposed upon us by General Devers.

While departing under the cover of darkness to check out this Polish connection, the heavy military vehicle rounded a sharp turn on the supposedly deserted road way and collided with a small Volkswagon "bug" driven by a German civilian. Sergeant Trish irately shouted at the uninjured driver, "You should not be out driving at this time of night!" Our driver backed up from the now restructured

Volkswagen and our capricious assemblage sped on toward our planned destination some ten kilometers distant.

I was beginning to receive "bad vibes" strongly suggesting the evening would not turn out to be a buoyant party night. We were using an unauthorized military vehicle, driving in a reckless manner and had just left the scene of a accident involving a military vehicle. Each violation would be "just cause" for stockade time or reduction in rank.

Upon reaching our destination we discovered the refugees were indeed from Poland. They were extremely delighted to see soldiers from the United States. Most Polish men had been forced into Nazi labor camps elsewhere. We conversed briefly for a short time before my ears were alerting me of the unmistakable engine sound of a Jeep speeding ever closer to our location. I took immediate evasive action and split from the group.

As the approaching vehicle neared, I could recognize Captain Hanlon seated on the passenger side and Corporal Chipman doing the chauffeuring. Upon spotting the weapons carrier the Jeep unceremoniously slid to a halt. Everyone else was nervously standing around the vehicle which had transported the battery revelers to the refugee camp, including some of the young women. From my hidden vantage point I could ascertain great displeasure in Captain Hanlon's voice as he ordered the exploring expeditionary force to return without delay and report to him. The captain's Jeep turned around and returned in the direction it had come.

Sergeant Trish promptly gathered up the would-be "goodwill ambassadors" for the return trip. When they could not find me, they departed. I commenced the six-mile trek back by myself on foot. Someone had advised the captain that I had been an associate member of the gang of wayward culprits. Captain Hanlon did not give up searching for me and his vehicle made several night-time forays along the deserted road in a diligent attempt to find me. Each time I heard the approaching vehicle I would vanish into the nearby forest until it was out of sight. I would then continue on my trek back. Even with my ever-present carbine I still had sniper concerns and some well-deserved worries about stepping on possible mines still positioned along the roadside.

My bid for a safe return was successful. I immediately slipped into my bed at the house assigned to Corporal Chipman and myself. First Sergeant Trish and Corporal Chipman, the captain's Jeep driver for the night, were ordered to determine if I was in my sleeping quarters. If I were in my bed I certainly could not have been with the group at the Polish refuge camp. The searching duo discovered I was on my roost and soundly "sleeping". Sergeant Trish informed the captain he (the top kick) possibly had been mistaken in believing I was part of the mischievous group. When the captain's Jeep driver returned from reporting to the captain, he was grinning like a Cheshire cat while he questioned, "O.K. Yankee, how did 'yawl' manage to pull it off?" I replied, "I considered it a challenge."

I felt rather certain the captain suspicioned I had been with the gang. He either lacked direct proof to pursue the issue further or he just might have appreciated my infantry training tactics used to avoid his dragnet. I placed far more creedence with the idea that he was lacking proof.

The driver of the wrecked Volkswagen claimed to be a medical doctor making house calls on patients at night. He had complained to the captain about the problem he had encountered with the captain's soldiers and their military vehicle. I felt strongly that our battery commander had definitely violated numbers "one" and "three" of General Dever's edicts; namely, "Never trust Germans collectively and individually", and "Defeat German efforts to poison my thoughts or influence my attitude".

For punishment the captain demoted the entire group of non-coms, including Sergeant Trish. Almost everyone liked the old top kick and believed his chastisement was excessive. The former first sergeant was a good soldier and most of us believed his reduction in rank was the only known mistake our battery commander ever made during his captaincy.

It was return to the "spit and polish" of garrison life. The captain wanted our artillery battery to appear impressive for the German civilian population. We were part of the so-called "crack troops" that had been so effectively pulverizing the mighty Nazi military war machine.

Captain Hanlon promoted a short stocky staff sergeant to be the new first sergeant. In military language, the new top kick was considered by some as a "brown nose" and not too well-liked by some of the artillerymen.

The newly promoted first sergeant placed small black communication wire (W-130) on the parade ground where our formations for report would take place. The wire was tightly secured at each end with steel pins driven into the ground. The almost invisible wire was so positioned that if the end of our boots just touched the wire, the ranks making up the formation, theoretically – should be straight. This procedure; however, did not take into account the differing length of the individual soldier's feet. The straight ranks of the artillerymen would really impress the "conquered" German civilians who in all likelihood would be eyeing the formation proceedings. The neophyte first sergeant also positioned the black wire at the exact spot where he would stop, do a quick right-face, salute the captain and dish out his required message, "All present and accounted for, Sir!" The battery soldiers were briefed ahead of time about the wire and instructed to place the toes of their combat boots just touching the earth-colored insulated metallic communications wire.

The appointed time arrived when the call to formation sounded. A surprisingly large assemblage of German civilians were indeed showing up to observe the "goings on". Up to this point all had gone as planned. Soldiers were in adjusted straight lines and everything appeared to be military "spit and polish" at its peak garrison achievement.

Possibly the fledgling first sergeant was thinking about his newly-sprung position of. importance. Then again, he may have been concentrating on the delivery of his would-be classy and impressive military salute to the captain. It is even possible the captain was slightly too far to the left of the middle of the formation he was now facing. In any eventuality, the first sergeant completely forgot about the secured small black wire marking his spot to stop, do a right face and salute the captain while giving the "Battery Report". Impressively double-timing to make his report, the first sergeant's feet became hopelessly snared in the wire he had aforetime positioned. The top-ranking battery noncom promptly gravitated face downward onto German homeland turf, smack-dab in front of the now thoroughly embarrassed and militarily disgraced leader of Battery "A" United States' Army's 928th Field Artillery.

The entire artillery battery valiantly fought off the tremendous urge of uncontrollable laughter. German civilians gazing on the disastrous scene could only shake their heads in utter disbelief. The astonished German civilians were most likely wondering, "How in hell could such a group of fucked-up United States soldiers possibly defeat our invincible and glorious Nazi military?" I did a nimble side glance in the direction of former First Sergeant Trish. Trish was displaying an extremely satisfying sly "Bud Pitts" type of smile on his countenance. A highly annoyed Captain Hanlon never waited for the chagrined top kick to stand up to make the report of, "All present and accounted for, Sir." Instead, the captain promptly dismissed the formation and stalked rapidly back to the security of his quarters. To put it mildly, the captain appeared extremely pissed about his choice for the new first sergeant.

Such was our stint at garrison duty.

During the brief interlude of occupational duty, we were witness to huge waves of Allied bombers coming to put the finishing touches on the Third Reich's industrial output. There would be many civilian casualties along with the German factories.

The bombers were seldom challenged by the Luftwaffe. Earlier in the war, bombers would release long strips of metal foil strips called "window" or "chaff". The foil would remain floating in the atmosphere for quite some time before reaching the ground. Its purpose was to confuse enemy radar. New advances in German radar now made the procedure mostly ineffective.

It was absolutely awesome to hear deafening thunderous noise emanating from the piston-driven aircraft engines as countless waves of Allied heavy bombers, perhaps numbering up to a thousand or more, were flying overhead. Many bombing sorties were also carried out in broad daylight. Some of the planes on the night raids would appear sinisterly silhouetted in front of a near full moon while on their mission of destruction to the heartland of Germany.

Two new weapons had been recently introduced by the Nazis. One, the "buzz bomb", usually was heading toward England. Buzz bombs derived such a name due to their pulsating jet engines that noisily propelled the weapon towards the target area. The other weapon was referred to as a "Screaming Meemie". The meemies were eight inch diameter rocket shells. They sounded very similar to a pack of coyotes howling in concert. I felt the meemies were more psychological than damaging. It exploded after burying itself well into the ground. Most of the damage from them was usually miniscule. It also was the time when V-2 rocket missiles were being launched, the Allies were lacking weaponry capable of destroying the high flying missile.

Following two weeks of garrison life, the 928th Field Artillery's "A" battery returned to active combat duty. Some artillery soldiers believed our commanding officer may have requested the sudden restoration to combat status.

Postscript

I was very much aware of the consequences of using military property without proper authorization as well as leaving the scene of an accident with the military vehicle. I also knew Captain Hanlon well enough to know he would take strong disciplinary measures over the episode. Another truthful incentive would be – just the challenge. As far as I can recall, all of the other men were from gun batteries and I was the only FO with the group. It was a matter of pride with me to successfully escape without being caught. The newly promoted top kick for the battery soon took his responsibilities in stride and did a professional job of running the battery.

****

I still ruminate about what thoughts must have passed through the mind of the German woman who first informed me about the death of President Roosevelt. Especially when President Truman eventually would order the use of the atomic bomb on the Empirical Land of Japan. I also wonder if the German woman ever realized the Nazis had almost succeeded in their efforts in constructing their own atomic bomb.

I have no reservations whatsoever in believing if the Nazis had succeeded in making the first atomic bomb, the German Fuhrer would have happily used it on the countries of France, England, Russia, and the United States. I felt in time, even the Japanese would not be spared the use of a German atomic bomb. Japanese facial appearances just did not correlate very well with the Aryan image.

****

Some Germans were quite apprehensive over the unexpected death of the American President. Many Germans felt it would eventually leave them the probable reduced clemency of Joseph Stalin and Winston Churchill.

****

The recruitment of "boy soldiers" by Germany was indicative of the last-resort efforts of a desperate country. Perhaps the sudden heavy recruitment and training of black men from the United States, men formerly believed to be genetically unfit for military combat service, was suggesting a manpower problem was also manifesting itself in the United States.

****

I lack any meaningful explanation for my continuous unflagging apprehension over accosting the Rhine River.

Chapter Nineteen

The Fighting in Europe Ends

Grass

Pile the bodies high at Austerlitz and Waterloo
Shovel them under and let me work –
    I am the grass; I cover all.

And pile them high at Gettysburg
And pile them high at Ypres and Verdun.
Shovel them under and let me work.
Two years, ten years, and passengers ask the conductor:
    What place is this?
    Where are we now?

    I am the grass.
    Let me work.

—Carl Sandburg

Our next combat operation would differ in many characteristics than previous missions. When not engaged in sporadic firefights, infantry personnel would be riding on top of the Sherman tanks. It would be a classic unrelenting pursuit of the retreating German forces. Even though Nazi troops were weary and becoming demoralized, they were fighting on their homeland soil and still posed a dangerous threat. The German Ardennes offensive had taught us not to be complacent with our adversary.

Occasionally the rapid advance would run into pockets of heavy rear-guard resistance from German combat groups. Most of these annoying last ditch enemy efforts were quickly neutralized by tanks, tank destroyers, engineers and infantry units.

The Neckar River would be crossed twice – once at Heidelberg, and a short time later, twenty miles north of Stuttgart.

Taking enemy territory was much faster due to the lighter resistance and fewer fortifications. There were times when German soldiers would have to wait their turn to find someone qualified to accept their surrender. Ages of the prisoners were older or younger than those taken earlier in the campaign. The age extremes suggested the end was drawing near for the lengthy agonizing struggle to crush Nazi oppression.

Our motorized convoy was more exposed than usual as it proceeded south toward the Austrian border. The German Air Force began to make its presence known as ME-109's prowled the area looking for a worthy target such as our huge convoy. The 534th antiaircraft battalion traveling with us was using quadruple-mounted .50-caliber machine guns. One of these lethal weapons had been named "The Devil's Typewriter" by its crew. I thought the name to extremely apropos.

All three of the 103rd Division infantry regiments were now working very closely with each other on the swift drive toward the towering Alps Mountains. The military convoy also appeared to be gathering an unusually large number of antiaircraft artillery, engineers, armored units and special vehicles that could operate on solid land as well as in the water. These amphibious trucks, known as "ducks" (DUKW's), gave hint of possible water crossings lurking somewhere ahead.

Comprehending the war in Europe might soon reach a point of conclusion, suddenly became a double-edged sword. The realization we might still be alive when fighting ceased was greatly tempered by reality of the "other war". There still was the troublesome and nagging assumption we would be shipped to the Pacific Theatre of Operations as part of an invasion force launched against the Japanese homeland. Each of us were toying with the unlikely fantasy of being granted furloughs home prior to being ordered to the Pacific war zone.

The Germans in their hasty retreat toward the south were placing numerous satchel charges on the big trees along the roadway. The resulting explosions would drop the trees on the road and slow our progress. The convoy would come to a halt as engineers cleared the area of the fallen trees, enemy mines and bobby traps. Other sections of the Alpine highway would be blocked by rocks blasted loose by the withdrawing enemy.

Whenever our convoy stopped for what appeared to be a lengthy wait, the soldiers would take the time to dig protective foxholes along the roadside. The enemy still had planes flying.

During one of these waiting periods the first jet aircraft I had ever heard about or observed, came flying low over our lengthy convoy. The enemy plane approached our convoy so silently and swiftly, the antiaircraft crew from "The Devil's Typewriter" was unable to target the swift low-flying jet powered fighter. The aircraft's pilot did not strafe our part of the convoy. Perhaps he was out of ammunition. The Luftwaffe pilot began the plane's steep climb as it neared our vehicle. The noise from the jet's engine was thunderous as the enemy aircraft rapidly accelerated straight up into the sky until it was hardly discernible. The appearance of this new type of enemy jet-propelled aircraft was both majestic and alarming. After the jet plane vanished from view and the engine noise abated, I became aware of the shouting angry voice of a member of one of Battery A's howitzer gun crew. During the excitement of the enemy jet aircraft, Private Wojner had jumped into the vacant one-man foxhole Private Miller had just completed. Both oldsters, highly fearing the enemy jet aircraft would reappear, were engaged in a heated dispute. The terrified Miller was hysterically shouting, "Wojner, get into your own foxhole." Whereas Private Wojner just hunkered down deeper – completely disregarding Miller's fervent plea to vacate the premise. Wojner's muffled voice, again coming from near the bottom of the shelter, yelled, "Use my fox hole, Miller!" The nearly identical constructed foxholes had been dug almost side by side. The episode generated much laughter from those close at hand, greatly abating the anxiety for almost everyone – aside from Private Miller. The German jet did not return.

The removal of the enemy roadblocks signaled the continuence of the convoy's course south towards the Alps Mountains. We were approaching Kirchheim, Germany the third week in April. A few days later we crossed the Danube River east of Ulm, Germany. I was thrilled at finally seeing the river that we had sung about in the Southside Grammar School, *The Blue Danube*. The river did not appear to be all that blue.

The convoy split up after crossing the Danube. Our Jeep was traveling with the division's 409th and 411th infantry regiments. We were approaching the foothills of the lofty Bavarian Alps.

The military land armada soon arrived at the edge of a city named "Landsberg", Germany.

None of us ever received any basic training or battlefield experience that would help us cope with the next sight. 103rd Division soldiers discovered a group of Nazi concentration "work camps" used as holding pens for political enemies of the Third Reich. How many Jews, Poles, Russians, French and non-conforming Germans had perished from beatings, starvation, heinous torture, human medical experiments, filth and exposure to winter weather – most likely would never be known. The camps were part of the "Final Solution" to exterminate human beings considered to be inferior to the "superior" people of the Third Reich.

Photographs taken by 103rd Division cameraman, Bertram Sanders, from just one of the six concentration sites in the area can partially tell of the atrocities uncovered. Descriptive words fail me. It is nearly impossible to accurately describe this horrific arena of brutality unless one could include the piteous sounds emanating from the dying and the putrid smell of filth and decomposing bodies strewn about the barbed wire enclosed squalid prison camp.

As we waited, German soldiers and camp guards were given

Photos taken by 103rd Division cameraman, Pfc. Bertram Sanders, at one of the concentration camps in Landsberg. Photographed shortly following the capture of the city by the 411th Infantry Regiment

specific orders by infantrymen to place their hands on top of their helmets. The now German prisoners of war were tersely ordered to, "Run double time down the road. If you stop or leave the road you will be shot!" Military police would intern the group. These German "soldiers" would pass alongside our parked Jeep on their journey downhill. Facial expressions on these Nazis were filled with stark terror as they realized it was they who were now the prisoners and undoubtedly wondered what their ultimate fate might be. They knew exactly what type of place they operated and were definitely aware of the monstrosities taking place in the "labor" camps.

An exodus of the least feeble former camp prisoners commenced their piteous effort to walk along the same downhill road. Their emaciated physical appearance made me wonder if they were really human beings from this planet or aliens from another world having some resemblances of androids.

Every time a German soldier ran by, these "walking skeletons" – still brimful of intense resolve and hatred, would attempt to swing their walking stick to strike their former keepers. The inmates were far too frail to be successful. Most of the walking "living" could not have weighed much more than sixty or seventy pounds. I had never witnessed such intense hatred and fervid resolve to seek *immediate* retribution. Frustration was graphically imprinted in each pair of the former inmates' hollow sunken eyes. I observed this macabre scene for well over an hour. Not one German soldier was ever struck a blow from a walking stick. Ironically, *Wehrmacht* soldier's belt buckles were embossed with the words *GOTT MIT UNS* (God Is With Us). I wondered how in hell God could possibly be with these Nazis sons-of-bitches after viewing these abject "work" camps.

Nearing the border between Germany and Austria our convoy began to enter the snow-covered Austrian Alps. We were approaching the beautiful city of Oberammergau. Many buildings in this historic city had colorful murals painted on their walls. Corporal Chipman and I were informed by the scholarly Captain Hanlon, "This particular city was the site of the world renowned *Passion Play*." The captain added, "This religious event is held every ten years." At first, I did not fully understand how the word "passion" was being used by the captain I had never heard of the happening; in addition, the word "passion" meant something entirely different to me. Apparently some of the

409th Infantry Regiment soldiers were in a similar thinking mode. One of the crusty GI's jokingly remarked, "Hey, did you hear that the military police has some guy who says he's Jesus in jail?" The response was, "No, but did you know the 'old man' (military slang term meaning "the captain") is sleeping with the Virgin Mary?" Undoubtedly Cactus Division soldiers were beginning to feel happy that the war in Europe was winding down to a victorious conclusion for our troops.

I continued thinking about the prison camps and quietly wondered, "How in hell could it be possible to have such an insidious, vile and inhumane site located such a short distance from a village completely dedicated and devoted to the remembrance of Jesus Christ?" I did not receive a satisfactory reply to my silent query.

While traveling in the vicinity of Oberammergau we received news informing us...Adolph Hitler was dead. Many doubted the report even though it conceivably might be true. I recalled past conversations with other division soldiers as to the best way the Nazi Fuhrer should be put to death if he were captured. Apparently no one wanted him to have an easy death. My thoughts turned once again to the woman who had abreasted me of President Roosevelt's death. I wondered what she might now be thinking.

After passing through Oberammergau, we next came to Garmisch-partenkirchen. Once again, the knowledgeable captain exclaimed, "This city was the site of the 1936 Winter Olympic games."

By this time there were even more motorized units joining the chase to link up with the United States Army units driving north in Italy.

We were approaching the city of Mittenwald and another village called Scharnitz. Scharnitz was being defended by members of a Nazi SS Officers Candidate College. The convoy was once again held up on any forward progress until the 409th Infantry cleared the fierce pocket of resistance from the would-be Nazi officers. Though Hitler was dead, the war was still not over. The 409th Infantry Regiment took unwanted casualties in this last bloody action. The Alpine terrain at Scharnitz was high enough in elevation to have winter snow still covering the ground.

In the vicinity of Scharnitz, I would receive some unwelcome and disquieting news. I was informed that my artillery friend, PFC

McDougall, the soldier who had his cigarette pilfered from his "FDR" cigarette holder in Marseilles, had been seriously wounded.

The next objective for the task force was to take the city of Innsbruck. It was a beautiful Tyrolean city snuggled in the Alps Mountains near the Brenner Pass leading to Italy.

Darkness was subtly decending as our huge armada of military might threaded its way slowly down the winding road of the Austrian Alps. All of the vehicles were still using the small, almost invisible, blackout lights. Our Jeep was quite close to the front end of the massive convoy. Captain Hanlon was seated in front and Corporal Chipman was the chauffeur. 37531447 was in the back seat monitoring the radio frequency of the huge task force.

The Alps Mountains were thunderously reverberating from the noise coming from the huge armada of United States Army tanks and other military vehicles. It could well have been the type of convoy Captain Hanson might have been envisioning when departing Fort Bliss, Texas with his momentary "armada" of one vehicle.

Ken Lenke Photograph
Corporal Artist P. Chipman
Captain Hanlon's Jeep Driver (Germany)

Every now and then the convoy would come to a halt. High-ranking American officers were negotiating with their Nazi counterparts in the city of Innsbruck. I believed it senseless to lose more lives or destroy this beautiful "queen city" nestled in the mountainous region of the winding Inn River. Many Austrians were also innocent victims of Nazi oppression. Our big bombers had run out of targets; however, Innsbruck could be quickly neutralized by these available aircraft.

More waiting. Word was now arriving over radio informing us we would be given orders to turn off the tiny blackout lights on all vehicles and make ready to *turn on the bright full-powered headlights*. The last time I had seen bright vehicle headlights was when leaving New York City. The order seemed to be imprudent as hell for a combat situation. The instructions to turn on vehicle headlights caused much well-deserved concern and need for clarification was justified. The order was stated once more, "Full vehicle headlights are to be turned on to the bright position on radio voice command!"

Not knowing what had transpired, it was somewhat troublesome being so close to the lead vehicles of the convoy. It would be informing Nazi gunners, "Here we are." The radio suddenly splintered the airwaves one more time with the order, "Activate all vehicle headlights."

Turning my head to the rear to spectacle the winding mountain road were multitudinous headlights as far as the eye could discern. I roughly estimated the length of the task force to be somewhere between twenty and twenty-five miles. The sight was absolutely awesome and equally incredible. My eyes were moist while witnessing this panorama of United States soldiers with their equipment moving ahead to continue the short journey into Innsbruck, Austria. I kept wondering if the decision to turn on the bright headlights was more for psychological purposes and was designed to convey a message to the garrison of enemy defenders suggesting the peaceful surrender of Innsbruck was an extremely wise choice.

For the first time 37531447 had the realistic feeling he would actually survive the war in Europe.

Once inside Innsbruck, Chipman was ordered by the captain to park the Jeep near the Innsbruck railroad station. We observed a small contingent of German soldiers detraining. We were not certain if they were aware Innsbruck was no longer under Nazi control.

It was an unusually delicate situation to have the Germans, still carrying their weapons, and walking by the driver side of our Jeep. I was imploring destiny, "This is not the time or place for either German or United States soldiers to do something stupid." My carbine was positioned on my lap with the loaded barrel pointing to the left side of the Jeep. I kept my trigger finger inside the trigger guard. My thought about not doing anything stupid was abruptly interrupted when one of the enemy soldiers came staggering by the Jeep holding a "burp gun"

Photograph courtesy of Bunnie Watts, 1998
LORRAINE AMERICAN MILITARY CEMETERY
Saint Avold, France (near Metz, France)

(a small rapid fire German machine pistol) in one hand and a partial bottle of cognac in the other. He muttered something unintelligible when he saw me. I returned the gaze and replied in German, "*Guten abend*" (Good evening). The inebriated enemy soldier moved on – taking the diminutive crisis along with him.

At daybreak we traveled in the Jeep up the snow-covered Brenner Pass to slightly beyond the village of Brenner and crossed the Austrian border into Italy. I do not know why I picked up a recently discarded red and black arm-band having the hated Nazi swastika emblem and stuffed it my combat jacket pocket. We left the Austrian-Italian border and returned to Innsbruck.

We were extremely proud to have completed the tasks given to the division of fighting men who wore the Arizona Sonoran Desert saguaro cactus emblem on their left shoulder sleeve. We were equally proud of ever other outfit helping make our objectives possible to accomplish.

Most of us were keenly aware we soon would be on our way to the Pacific war zone for the impending invasion of Japan. The very thought was highly distressing.

Postscript

On May 9, 1945, at 0001 hour (one minute after midnight) the conflict in Europe officially came to its conclusion. There were no celebrations, no laughter, no bragging and no drinks all the way around. Thoughts were on division soldiers who had fallen in battle. Division soldiers meeting untimely deaths, would be buried in United States' military cemeteries located at St. Die, Epinal, Lorraine and elsewhere. My artillery friend, McDougall, would be one of those eternally "resting" in a French cemetery.

****

Official records would indicate the 103rd Infantry Division had 720 men killed in action, 3,329 wounded in action and 101 who died from battle wounds (DOW). Of the three infantry regiments making up the 103rd Infantry Division, the 411th Infantry Regiment sustained the highest number of KIA's and DOW's.

****

In regard to my friend, PFC McDougall, I was later informed an officer, not from our artillery unit, ordered some from McDougall's howitzer crew to assist in removing rocks blocking a roadway. During the process, McDougall picked up a rock having a German pressure release type land mine underneath. The resulting explosion severed both of his arms. I was further told the medics got him to a field hospital and his condition was stabilized following the removal of both of the corporal's mangled legs. When McDougall awakened from the effects of the anesthesia, he realized both of his arms were missing. When he eventually looked down his hospital bed and noticed the bedding was flat where his legs should have been, his heart stopped beating and he crossed over into the "next world".

This incident was one of the rare times I ever expressed audible anger about an officer. While uttering curses aimed at the absent officer, I slammed my steel helmet to the ground in useless rage and despair and proclaimed, "Engineers were trained and equipped for this type of situation, God damn it! Not artillerymen." I felt there was neither need for the urgency nor reason for the stupidity on the part of the officer. I may well have not known the actual situation since I was neither present at the scene at the time of his injury nor at the aid station.

****

The German jet aircraft flying over our convoy was most likely a Me-163 or an Me-262.

****

Landsberg was the city where Adolph Hitler wrote his book *Mein Kampf* (My Struggle). It was written in a prison cell where he was incarcerated during the pre-Nazi political period of Germany.

In 1933, Adolph Hitler had been incarcerated in cell #7 at Landsberg. The jail confinement had been made into a shrine by the Nazis. A plaque above the cell door, when translated into English proclaimed:

"Here, a system that was dishonorable, imprisoned Germany's greatest son in November, 1923 until December of 1924."

37531447 was born January 7, 1924.

****

When our task force came across the concentration camps at Landsberg, we were not aware of even more notorious and larger extermination camps at Dachau, Auschwitz, and elsewhere.

****

I yet hold the belief engineer battalions, medics, doctors and nurses were never given enough credit or praise for the important role they performed during World War II. I believe this much over-looked approbation was similar to the men who served in the United States Merchant Marine whose bravery and losses in wartime have all but been forgotten.

****

I possess no additional knowledge about what happened to Lieutenant Whidden. The commissioned officer sent to replace him was a real "jerk". I can not recall any forward observer who wanted to be part of his FO team. I think we all felt he was an incompetent officer, more full of bullshit than brains. He couldn't read a map and led us through the same town twice before he got it figured out. He continuously kept babbling about his "Passing Clouds" cigarettes he obtained in England and the little "kick" he received after smoking them. Some German official once handed me two bottles of quality wine to give to the lieutenant – for whatever unknown reason. The artillery officer appeared to be quite content with his "Passing Clouds". The German's gift of excellent wine – somehow, never located the lieutenant.

****

To the present moment I possess the Nazi arm band picked up in Brenner Pass. At the time I did not understand the reason why I chose to pick up the hated Nazi emblem. After Germany's seizure of Austria in 1938, Brenner Pass became the boundary between Nazi Germany and Italy. Subsequently, many years after the war, I learned Adolph Hitler and Benito Mussolini met in Brenner on three different occasions. Not all of these meetings – perhaps none – were amicable between the two world dictators. Hitler did most of the talking and Mussolini did the listening. Perchance the arm band represents a partial closure of the conflict in Europe for 37531447.

****

The Rhine River flows northward to the North Sea; however, The Danube River has its beginning in the Black Forest Region of West Germany and flows eastward some 2,816 kilometers (1,750 miles) across much of Europe and enters the Black Sea. The Inn River, flowing through Innsbruck, Austria, has headwater beginnings in the mountains of Northern Italy. It merges with the Salzatch River north of Salzburg, Austria, and joins the Danube for the lengthy journey to the Black Sea. Salzburg was the setting for the highly popular postwar movie – *The Sound of Music*.

The well-known waltz music, *The Blue Danube*, was composed by Johann Strauss, who called Vienna, Austria, a city located on the Danube River, his home.

The United States Army's 103rd Infantry Division, when fighting along the Danube River, was in an area of previous warfare involving the early historic armies of Augustus – Roman Emperor (63 B.C. – A.D. 14), Charlemagne – "Charles the Great" (742 A.D. – 814 A.D.) and Napoleon. The Nazi Armies of Adolph Hitler also marched along the Danube.

****

After the conclusion of the war in Europe, I noticed a familiar face – one well etched in my memory. It was the comic book reading 103rd Infantry Division soldier, who earlier in the fighting, elucidated to me, "…if your number is up – it doesn't matter what you do." I congratulated the philosophical infantryman for surviving the bitter combat of the campaign.

The "covering of grass" would have to wait for him.

Chapter Twenty

Alpine Occupational Duties

Where there is much desire to learn, there of necessity will be much arguing, much writing, many opinions; for opinion in good men is but knowledge in the making.

—from Milton, 1644, Areopagitica

37531447 was elated to find out his friend, Sergeant Russell Pitts, had survived the last days of combat. It was a big boost to his morale, especially after the tragic loss of his artillery companion, PFC McDougall. He sensed there were many occasions when Bud and he wished they had spent a little more time in El Paso and less in Europe.

The artillery battery was assigned a sector in the Tyrolean Alps to carry out occupational duties. Spring was warmer than usual, fruit trees were in full bloom, and the Inn River – now visibly pregnant with melting mountain snow water – scurried through the alpine valley floor. With the lofty Bavarian Alps cradling the charming Alpine city of Innsbruck, the location bestowed an awesome backdrop of beauty and tranquillity.

It would be in this "picture-perfect" postcard setting, 103rd Division soldiers would relax and contemplate possible further combat action in the Pacific Theatre of Operations. Most of them believed they would be directly involved with the impending invasion of the Japanese homeland.

Corporal Chipman and I would be provided billet by ourselves in a typical Tyrolean house. Military decree stated:

"All buildings used to house U.S. troops must be vacated by their former occupants during the occupational duty of United States military personnel."

We would take extra good care of the appropriated Austrian chalet during our temporary stay.

Regular formations were once again established and it was back to the mostly hated "spit and polish" routine of military life.

In free moments of time I found myself walking the short distance from my billet to the banks of the meandering Inn River. The sound of the rushing water coursing its way to a distant sea helped me reflect on recent happenings occurring during combat. It was a time of partial healing – often instantaneously shattered into multitudinous bits and pieces by knowing I would soon be enduring the painful repetition of combat once again – in an entirely different global arena of battle.

Very few incidents took place requiring military force during the occupational duties. The Austrian people were very cordial and presented a genuine impression our military forces had unchained their country from the unwelcome soldiers of Hitler's short-lived Third Reich.

Local citizenry went about everyday pursuits as if everything had almost returned to normal. Traditional cultural activities consisting of festivals and parades were rather common. I know of no negative incidents marring the relationship between the men from our military artillery battery and the Austrian community.

Battery activities consisted mostly of military drills, inspections and divisional "pass in review" parades. Traditional American games of softball and baseball were initiated among U.S. troops occupying the surrounding area. I was informed one softball field for an artillery battalion had first base in Austria and the "home plate" in Italy.

FO's Bill Tyner, Melvin Green, and I took a journey to the top of Hafelekar Mountain on an enclosed cable car to the ski area overlooking the city of Innsbruck. Once on top of the mountain we lounged around at the Seegrube Resort and took in the magnificent beauty of the snow-capped Tyrolean Alps. A rather large advisory sign declared the resort – "OFF LIMITS TO COMMISSIONED OFFICERS." It certainly was the type of relaxation where enlisted men wouldn't have to jump to attention and salute. I am certain officers had a similar laid-back site and they too, would appreciate not having to return salutes to enlisted men.

During the brief stay at the Seegrube Resort I chanced my first attempt at the simple art of skiing. Clamping skis onto my combat boots (no ski boots at this time) and mustering courage for the start of my slight down hill run, I promptly fell on my butt. Getting back on my feet with the wooden contraptions was an extremely difficult task for me. Turning around was something similar to a discriminating obstacle course which caused one ski to be hopelessly entrenched firmly on top of the other ski – thereby impeding all movement in any direction. I made the prudent decision to remove the capricious devices from my feet and returned to the protective safety of a lounge chair. At least I would always be able to honestly verbalize, "I have been on skis in the Tyrolean Alps Mountains of Austria."

Hiking was usually an enjoyable pastime for me. One afternoon I began a walk up a forested mountain valley on the edge of the village where we were staying. I was hiking alone without any baggage on my back. I did, however, continue to carry my carbine and some extra ammo clips. I was really enjoying the solitude of my solo excursion – especially since no one was attempting to use my body for target practice. All during my hike I was musing over the possible reasons for the complete lack of mountain songbirds. Their cheerful sounds would have added even more pleasure to my outing.

It was always a strange perception for me to be alerted to possible peril before the realization of the actual crisis. This gifted phenomenon had served me well during combat. I once again was receiving a forewarning of impending danger. This special ability was something I could never explain. Perhaps it was some genre of cellular memory from a different past life.

While absorbing the tremendous natural beauty of the nearby mountains, I had carelessly approached uncomfortably close to a rather spacious Austrian mountain chalet. Seated on the balcony railing of the large outer deck of the building was a group of men in civilian clothing. They had every appearance conforming to the profile of the Nazi Waffen SS soldier. A Waffen SS member was supposed to be the upper crust of the Nazi dogma of professional soldiers. All were about the same age and appeared to be in superb physical condition. It was obvious they were not *Volkssturmers* (Germans who were part of the home guard forces) straight from the farm. The way they were eyeing me gave me the hair-tingling feeling I was about to become a post-war trophy. I continued my unhesitating stroll toward the group whose members were so intensely studying my unexpected arrival.

Looking up at them – I greeted them in German. *"Guten tag"* (Good day/afternoon).

One of the men answered back in flawless English, "Good afternoon."

Replying in English I continued the dialogue, "Where are all the birds?"

The reply, once more in English, "What birds are you referring to?"

I instantly was alerted that the man seated on the deck railing understood American idioms. "The kind that fly" was my repartee.

His next query, "Are you by yourself?"

I answered back in German, "*Ja, ich bin alleine*" (yes, I am alone").

The group spokesman, apparently desiring confirmation to his previous inquiry, again questioned, "No one else is with you?"

Speaking once more in German I replied, "*Nein! Ich bin alleine*" (No! I am alone").

At this point I indifferently turned my back on the group and began to nonchalantly amble back in the direction of my approach. Had I guessed wrong with my answers to the spokesperson's questions, I posibly would soon feel a bullet strike me. I was less confident inside of me than my outer sureness indicated. I slowly disappeared from view of the Alpine mountain chalet and hastily picked up the pace. Nothing had happened to me; however, I felt certain these men were former SS troops in hiding. I also had the strong inclination they did not "buy" my truthful answers and believed I was lying when I told them I was by myself. Not once did their acting prolocutor ever use the German language during the verbal exchanges.

Upon returning to the battery area I reported the incident to the officer in charge. He assured me the mountain chalet would soon be checked. A few days later United States Army soldiers made a sweep of the entire Austrian occupational zone, taking some eighty thousand hiding SS troops. Some were from the isolated chalet I had accidently stumbled onto earlier.

The following week, a widely grinning Corporal Chipman flagged me down and informed me Captain Hanlon had granted each of us a two-week pass to visit the United Kingdom and Scotland.

Our trip and tour of England most likely would be very pleasant. On the "down-side", I knew the two-week furlough was in lieu of a journey back to the United States. Japan undoubtedly would be my next military combat destination.

Much similar to the train trip from Camp Howze, Texas to New York City, I remember very little about our stay in England. I do recall visiting St Paul's Cathedral and making a trip to Brighton, located on the southern coast of England. I sat on the seawall of this coastal city for a very long time listening to the surf gently make contact with the beach. I had a tremendous feeling of loneliness – mixed with thoughts of the Red River, the fighting I had been through, not being able to go back home and the impending dangerous invasion of Japan.

Chipman and I did not use our passes to visit Scotland. Neither did we chase any girls, visit very many bars nor take in any movies.

It was the middle of June when the two of us returned to our unit still located in the Bavarian Alps Mountains. I had not been back with the outfit very long before I managed to find myself in trouble with Captain Hanlon.

Early one morning Chipman determined to get the vintage Mercedes parked at our quarters started. Much to our surprise, the blamed vehicle coughed, sputtered and sprang to life with all engine cylinders purring. Chipman jumped in behind the steering wheel and hollered, "Hop in for a test drive."

Both of us were quite aware the morning formation would soon be called. In spite of this meaningful key information, the captain's chauffeur headed out of town some five kilometers in distance. I suggested to my driver friend, "Let's get this thing turned around and get back so we will not miss the formation." The corporal agreed and herded the sleek-looking Mercedes around and streaking in the direction from which we had come. Suddenly the old car had "chronic cardiac failure" and coasted to an untimely standstill.

Ten minutes later, Chipman had the cantankerous engine running perfectly. If the blamed engine kept working there still might be a slim outside chance to be on time for the formation, providing we did not stop at our quarters. The corporal floored the rehabilitated chimera and soon we were back in the vicinity of the town.

Some two hundred yards from the formation gathering area was a small narrow wooden bridge having a noticeable hump. As our classic vehicle crossed the bridge the planking timbers loudly rattled like a huge washboard and we momentarily became airborne. The fired up Mercedes once more touched the roadway and slithered to a stop in a cloud of mountain dust – now unmistakably drifting slowly over Captain Hanlon and the formation already in progress.

Exiting the old German auto we were greeted with the chortle of uncontrollable laughter coming from the formation of artillerymen and the highly amused Austrian civilians. Chipman was grinning as if he had just won a Tennessee catfish dinner complete with hush puppies and grits.

Captain Hanlon was definitely not amused by our antics. He commenced berating his own driver with a genuine military tongue lashing and then, after fully warming up on the corporal, heaped the pinnacle of his stinging articulational fury upon me. I was the recipient of a lengthy lecture from the commanding officer, eventually concluding with a demotion of two ranks – to that of Private First Class. I suspect Captain Hanlon got even with me for the earlier episode occurring at the Polish refugee camp. I certainly did not hold any malice toward him for his seemingly harsh action. I had no one to blame but myself. I rationalized the demotion would not inconvenience me all that much. I still would be a forward observer. I also couldn't see how I was going to use the money I lost by reduction in rank in the Pacific war zone.

With little activity going on, I got caught up on my letter writing and eventually penned a note to my parents telling them about the newspaper picture of Georges Kieffer and stated I had placed the photo of "the Alsation giant" on the "barracks" wall.

The interesting decision concering how the 103rd Division was to be managed as a combat army infantry unit came to pass. The good news, the 103rd Infantry Division would be transported to the United States to be deactivated. The bad part, many of us would not be making the return trip to the United States with the division.

A system of credit points (85 points required) was created by "higher ups" to determine the eligibility of each soldier making the return trip stateside. I cannot recall all the ways credit points could be amassed. Points were given for: the length of military service, overseas service, combat duty,

Ken Lenke Photograph
Berchtesgaden – Hitler's mountain retreat in the Alps of southern Bavaria near Salzburg. The telephone handset 37531447 is holding came from Hitler's guesthouse at his mountaintop fortress.

Ken Lenke Photograph
Corporal Chipman and 37531447 at
Camp St. Louis (Near Rheims, France)

medals such as bronze and silver stars etc., battle wounds, and campaign battle stars. I was ten points shy to qualify for the required necessary number of points for the trip home. The majority of Cactus Division soldiers did not have sufficient points and most would be transferred to the United States Army's 45th (Thunderbird) Infantry Division. 45th Division men having sufficient number of points would fill the ranks of the 103rd Division for the journey back to the United States.

I still would be with trusted soldiers familiar to me in the new divisional assignment.

Even though disappointed over the lack of sufficient points to return home, I was highly pleased Corporal Ellsworth Lockwood, the Hayward, Californian, would be returning to the United States. With his five points received for his battle wound (for which I felt responsible) and the five for the cluster to his Purple Heart for getting his tooth broken in the Alsation wine cellar (for which I too, was blamable), he had amassed the required number of points to qualify for return to the United States. The happily smiling Californian thanked me for the trouble I had caused him. Still grinning and unusually relaxed in appearance, he remarked, "I guess you will be going to Japan." I answered his facetious remark with a genuine smile and a kidding finger expression. We shook hands for the last time. I was very happy for him as well as relieved to know I would never have a third opportunity to cause him an unwanted problem in Japan.

Eventually we would depart from the magnificent Alps of Austria and be transported by army trucks to a staging area in western France.

The journey from Innsbruck, Austria, was very long in both distance and time. The top speed of the convoy was close to twenty-two miles per hour. This gait was just slightly faster than the top speed of the navy's *Monticello* which transported us from the harbor at New York City to Marseilles, France. The reason given for the slow pace was: "Hard use of the vehicles during our military campaign made the trucks unreliable and the slower speed will decrease the likelihood of equipment failure."

The snail-like pace appeared to be even more noticeable while the convoy was traveling on the wide autobahn. This super highway was constructed by the Germans to handle their military vehicles as well as serve for aircraft runways.

We stayed one night bivouacked in the historic German university city of Hiedelburg. I was denied permission to visit my brother, Ralph, who was stationed with the 94th Signal Battalion in the city. I still was not in very good "standing" with the captain.

The convoy entered France and a few days later arrived at our new staging destination. I was assigned to Camp St. Louis while other units were sent to nearby Camp Lucky Strike. We were located fairly close to Paris.

Following the first few days of my stay at Camp St. Louis, I was promoted to the rank of Corporal. The promotion came as a complete surprise. I believe Captain Hanlon must have had some good chuckles over our classy style of showing up at one of his Austrian formations in the Mercedes touring car. He also may have figured he had been a little harsh with his order for my reduction of two ranks and no reduction in rank for his driver, Corporal Chipman. As mentioned before, Captain Hanlon was a sharp officer and an outstanding artillery battery commander.

It was the month of July. To break up the boredom of camp life we were given numerous opportunities to visit Paris. We would use the same trucks which had transported us so slowly from the Alps Mountains to our present location. The trucks were now seemingly operated by a brotherhood of maniacal drivers who forgot all about the hard battle usage of the trucks. Each driver appeared to take tremendous delight in establishing new and exciting speed records for each trip into Paris and return.

During most of my battle tenure in France and Germany, I would periodically jot a letter to a soldier serving in a field hospital in France. We had been good chums before the beginning of my military service. He kept asking me in each of his letters to help him get transferred to combat status so he could be with me. Each time I wrote back to him I avoided mentioning anything about his petition to join ranks with me. I had not been in Camp St. Louis very long when in strolled my Kansas friend, Donald Smith. Don was the only known prewar acquaintance I ever met during training or wartime duty. We had a great visit along with a wonderful trip into Paris. The thing most remembered at this reunion was Don's unsolicited statement, "I know why you never would mention the subject of helping me obtain a transfer to your outfit." Pausing momentarily, he thoughtfully reflected, "We received a large number of battle wounded from the 103rd Infantry Division." I replied, "Your analysis of my reasoning for not wanting you with me – is correct. You were trained for working with a battlefield hospital, and I was trained for my combat occupation." I did not want to mention battlefield replacements sustained unusually high rates of casualties.

What a thrill it was to actually be in Paris visiting many of the tourist sights I had read about in school, such as the *Arc D'Triomphe, La Tour Eiffel,* and the River Seine.

On another occasion while visiting the huge city of Paris, I was accompanied by Corporal Chipman. We decided to make a visit to the Paris Opera House. After walking up the steps we entered the foyer and discovered an opera was actually being presented on stage. We were stopped by an attendant who informed us some rather pricey admission tickets would be required for entry. I was not brought up on opera music and my Tennessee friend was only raised with the music of the "Grand Old Opry" coming from Nashville's – Ryman Auditorium. All we wanted to do was view the stage and leave. Other late arriving paying opera patrons arrived and during this timely distraction, we bolted out of view into one of the mezzanines followed by angry shouts from the attendant. After briefly (and quietly) viewing the performing stage, we made a circuitous path to avoid the attendant on the lower level. Without notice, a young U.S. soldier, wearing one stripe and a "SHAEF" (Supreme Headquarters Allied Expeditionary Force) patch on his finely tailored neat uniform, began to scold us for not wearing neckties, proclaiming, "You both have committed a very serious breach of opera etiquette!" The sandy-haired blue-eyed Chipman promptly moved very close to the neatly uniformed "soldier" and muttered a soft-toned "eloquent sermon" – nose to nose – directed at the garrison soldier attached to General Eisenhower's headquarters. With blazing blue eyes firmly glaring at the PFC, the corporal proclaimed, "Son, where we all have been you don't wear a fuckin' necktie." He added, "I don't think y'all have served one damned day in combat, have yuh?" The bewildered garrison soldier replied, "No, sir!" With Chipman almost seemingly satisfied, we departed from the Paris Opera House with the leathery-faced soldier from Tennessee still incoherently grumbling something about a necktie, the opera house, SHAEF and a pip-squeek PFC.

I had never witnessed the Tennessean this disturbed all through the rigors of combat. I expect the rebel was just releasing some stored up anger and the PFC from SHAEF was the momentary innocent victim of the Jeep driver's wrath.

At other times, Sergeant Bill Tyner would usually make the trip with me into Paris. Bill was one of the nicest clean-cut gentlemen you would ever expect in the military. He had received both the Purple Heart and the Bronze Star medals. The Iowan from Shenandoh was a terrific FO for our old Battery A of the 928th Field Artillery. He was the type of guy you would want your own daughter to wed.

To avoid most possibilities of contacting venereal disease, we were issued required condoms before being granted passes to visit the capital city of France. I doubted if the issued condoms encouraged or discouraged promiscuous activity by the soldiers. If a soldier came down with a serious case of VD, he could be granted a dishonorable discharge from the military. I have no idea what incident led up to the military edict stating:

"If you do not return on the scheduled time to the trucks returning you from Paris to Camp St. Louis, you will be required to 'visit' an aid station for a *prophylatic cleansing.*"

The announcement of this decree was the only time I ever heard Sergeant Tyner utter the sexual naughty word so commonly used by most soldiers. His usage of the word was as a noun, not an adjective. The highly agitated Iowan felt if he were inadvertently delayed by something other than sexual activity, he should not be subjected to a highly embarrassing and humiliating mandatory "prophylatic cleansing".

The piqued Sergeant clumsily and unconvincingly commented, "If I have to take a 'pro' and I haven't done anything, I'm going to start to do a little fucking." Similar to Corporal Chipman's outburst at the Paris Opera House, Tyner found the opportunity to release some of his frustration. It did, however, bring forth a riotous round of laughter from the gathering of dubious artillerymen. We knew beyond a shadow of doubt, the Iowa farm boy would not have engaged in any sexual activity even if a gorgeous and overly ambitious Paris prostitute attempted to force herself onto the forward observer. He undoubtedly would have told her, "*Mon Dieu, laissez-moi tranquille. Allez-vousen! Zut allors!*" ("Oh my God leave me alone darn it!"). It was sort of a relief for all of us just to know the Iowan even knew the meaning of the "f" word.

My final trip into Paris was extremely memorable. It was either August the sixth or the seventh of 1945. It was nearing the hour to head for the trucks to return to Camp St Louis. Upon hearing a loud commotion at a street corner newspaper stand, I decided to go to the crowded place to determine for myself why so many excited Frenchmen were wildly waving newspapers in the air and joyously shouting French words meaning, "Long live France!" and "Long live the Untied States of America!" Glancing at the newspaper's bold-printed headlines were the words, *"BOMB de L'ATOMIC."*

I was not very proficient in the French language, written or spoken; however, upon viewing the newspaper headline, I understood the reason for their animated intense excitement. The newspapers reported the United States had dropped a new type of bomb on the Japanese city – Hiroshima. The new weapon was an atomic bomb.

37531447 knew nothing about such a device creating the equivalent of 20,000 tons of TNT in just one bomb. The result to the city of Hiroshima was disastrous. As a new member of the 45th Infantry Division, soon to be fighting Japanese soldiers in the Pacific battle zone – it was damn good news for him.

I hastened to the loading area where the big open trucks were awaiting to transport us back to Camp St. Louis. We were still in the downtown part of Paris. Other combat soldiers boarding the truck were also quite delighted over the use of this new powerful bomb dropped upon the Japanese city. I do not recall any soldier mentioning the word "vengeance". It was more of a matter of giving us some optimism Japan would call it "quits" and we would not have to participate in the likely high casualty invasion of their homeland.

As our convoy began the return trip to Camp St. Louis, soldiers aboard the vehicles celebrated the news of the atomic bomb. Some unknown GI took out one of his issued condoms, blew it up and turned it loose in the air. Before long the night sky was full of the jetting devices making their erratic Anacreontic flights toward the sidewalks of Paris. They were quickly gathered by *"Les femmes"*. It was undoubtedly best we were returning to camp. I feel certain the *mademoiselles* of Paris were also in a celebrating demeanor.

After two more days of waiting, Japan still had not surrendered. Perhaps it was wishful thinking on our part to believe the Japanese would surrender and the years of world-wide conflict would come to a benignant termination.

Three days following the bombing of Hiroshima, a second atomic bomb was dropped on the city of Nagasaki. On August 16th, Japan did capitulate and the terrible war ended. On September 2, 1945, the official signing took place aboard the United States battleship *Missouri*.

A few days later it was announced that a contingent of 45th Division soldiers would be transported to the French coastal city of Le Havre, located on the English Channel. 37531447 would be among the group to be transported back to the United States.

Passes were issued to visit the city of Le Havre. We were cautioned to walk in pairs if we elected to visit the French port city. We were told the reason for this precaution was due to some residual hard feelings toward the United States. Many citizens of Le Havre felt as if the port city had suffered unusually excessive damage before the D-Day invasion. Apparently German fortifications of the city had been shelled rather heavily by the U.S. Navy, giving the Nazis the impression the city was the intended landing point on "D" Day. Resentment directed to the United States over the war damage was still present in the minds of some of the French people of Le Havre. It was the only time I ever refused a pass while in military service. Unlike the citizens of the city, I couldn't forget the soldiers who had given so much during the invasion of Normandy.

On September 12, 1945, our contingent of troops came aboard the small S.S. *Marine Panther* for the return trip to New York City.

The ocean voyage was quite smooth and relatively uneventful. I volunteered to work in the ship's commissary, carrying mess supplies from the cargo hold to the ship's kitchen. The work helped pass the time. My crew boss was a black Merchant Marine officer. During slack times our small work detail was treated to the best of food and fruit juices by the officer.

Each morning while at sea, the official ship bugler would awaken the army men with his own version of reveille played over the ship's intercom. He would begin his diurnal morning ritual by playing the first few bars of the melodious tune, *Beautiful Dreamer* (Beautiful dreamer, awaken to me). He then would promptly "shift gears" and go directly into a shrill diabolical rendition of the military call, *Reveille*. It took us from the soft, dreamy and heavenly sounds – back to the reality we were still army soldiers. I was informed the sailor playing the bugle had been a trumpet player with one of the pre-war era Big Bands.

The return trip to New York city took almost eight days on

S.S. MARINE PANTHER ARRIVING NEW YORK SEPT. 12, 1945 WITH 2940 TROOPS.

S.S. Marine Panther Arriving at New York City on September 12, 1945. "37531447", a member of the 45th U.S. Infantry Division, was among those returning from the European Theatre of Operations.

the lone traveling S.S. *Marine Panther* (The *Monticello* took fifteen days in convoy going to Marseilles.) No one aboard complained about the shorter time period for our voyage back to the United States.

On September 12, 1945, the S.S. *Marine Panther*, carrying 2,940 United States Army troops, passed by Ambrose Lighthouse and entered the harbor channel of New York City.

Postscript

37531447 has had many discussions concerning the use of the atomic bomb on Japan by the United States. He has written the following commentary concerning the wartime usage of this horrendous new weapon:

The Emperor of Japan, along with others in high empirical positions, sought spiritual assistance from their Gods as they performed Shinto ceremonies at various shrines located throughout the Japanese Empire. Prayers were requested enlisting aid for the emperor's army to turn back an impending invasion fleet and landing force.

These powerful military units were postured to strike a decisive blow at the very homeland of the Japanese people.

The enemy would begin the massive invasion on Japan's southernmost island of Kyushu. The defending soldiers, inspired by their ceremonies and prayers directed at the deities, would enable the brave defenders to fight with great ferocity to protect the land from the enemy!

As the battle reached a critical phase, their prayers and ceremonies were answered. The Kamakazi appeared.

This would mark the second attempt by the *Mongols* to conquer the Japanese people. It was the year 1281 A.D. It marked the second time the Kamakazi (Divine Wind) had come to turn back the fierce invading barbaric forces of Kublai (there are other spellings of this first name) Khan, grandson of the notorious Genghis Khan.

After the battle, casualties for the would-be Mongol invaders were estimated to be as high as seventy percent of the attacking force. It definitely was spiritually proper the "Divine Wind" (typhoon) would arrive to drive the Mongol hordes of Kublai Khan away for the second time in seven years. After all, the Japanese having such reverent spiritual fervor, had done nothing improper to instigate the invasion attempt by Kublai Khan.

Japanese histories offer reliable accounts of these invasions by the atrocity-minded Mongols.

Nearly 670 years later, both Shinto and Buddhist prayers were being uttered by the Japanese beseeching assistance of the Divine Wind, the "Kamakazi". This time; however, something was drastically different!

Japanese warlords were believing it was they who held the virtiousness of divine power. Instead of obtaining help from the true Kamakazi, soon-to-die Japanese "suicide pilots" were made to believe their human sacrifice was the Divine Wind.

A Japanese Shintoist historically was required to give unqualified loyalty to the Emperor. Hirohito was the Emperor and was considered to be the descendent of the Sun-Goddess of the Shinto religion. The Emperor may well have only been a peripheral leader of Japan. If so, it did not help his image with the people of the United States to observe him, dressed in a military uniform and seated astride his prancing white horse, exhorting his military to prevail in battle.

Another major disparity was noted with the Japanese military. Many Japanese warlords were committing and/or condoning atrocities far more nefarious than the thirteenth century Mongols of Kublai Khan. Korean women were enslaved for gratification "pleasures" for Japanese officers and soldiers during the invasion of the old lands of their ancient enemy, the Mongols!

In China, thousands of Chinese citizens were raped, tortured and slaughtered by the Japanese military when they invaded the city of Nanking. Perhaps as many as one million Chinese perished at the hands of the Japanese during the ten-year war against China.

Not satisfied with aggression and barbarous atrocities in eastern Asia, The Harvard educated Isoroku Yamamoto masterminded a cowardly devastating attack on the United States' naval and army facilities located at Pearl Harbor, Hawaii. Coinciding with the sneak air attack at Hawaii, so-called Japanese "peace envoys" were engaging in sham talks in Washington, D.C.

The flow of blood of U.S. service men began the stream of tears shed by "gold star mothers" and other loved ones. The bombing of Pearl Harbor by the Japanese instantaneously united a country which was not officially at war and whose people were quite divided on the political issues of the time.

Following the raid on Pearl Harbor by Admiral Yamamoto's naval and air force, came the infamous and inhumane "Bataan Death March" of captured United States and Filipino servicemen. With almost 30,000 civilian captives, 12,000 American soldiers and a large number of Filipino troops, the entire group was forced to march from Corregidor on the Bataan Peninsula to distant transportation that would take them to Camp O'Donnell. The combined march and train trip took twelve days for those surviving.

During the forced march prisoners were shot, buried alive, stabbed repeatedly with bayonets, smacked in the face with belt buckles and sword scabbards, and struck slashing blows from samuri swords (one U.S. soldier was beheaded). Water and food was withheld from the prisoners. The stronger prisoners were not allowed to help the weaker. Stragglers were shot. A U.S. War Department report estimated over 5,000 American service men met death on the Bataan Death March. Hundreds of others, weakened and sick, died in the prison camp.

For many of the Shinto Japanese soldiers, their cruel behavior was a shameful dishonor to themselves, as well as to the *Shinto Code of Ethics* – condemning bestiality.

The list of atrocities is far from complete. One should not forget the Japanese Tartainian rape of the Philippines.

On May 25, 1945, The United States' Chiefs of Staff convened and made the decision to launch a "Normandy" type invasion similar to the one initiated against the shores of Nazi conquered western France. The United States Sixth Army was assigned the task for the initial invasion of the Japanese homeland. The 45th Infantry Division (37531447 was now a member of this division) may well have been part of this American invasion force.

The area marked for the contemplated invasion was none other than the island of Kyushu, where centuries before, Kublai Khan had twice met defeat.

Historically – *there has never been a successful invasion of the Japanese homeland!*

The Japanese defenders were, for the most part, well-trained infantrymen and home guard forces of men, women and children. All had been taught necessary skills in the use of rifles, anti-tank weapons, grenades, mortars, automatic weapons and other assorted types of deathware.

In addition, Japanese school children had been instructed in the use of bamboo spears and lengthy poles having bayonets mounted on the end.

As had been the case in the invasion of Normandy, the casualty toll for both sides would most likely be enormous – including the children "soldiers."

On August 6, 1945, the Kamakazi did arrive to the homeland of Japan. The Divine Wind came in the form of an atomic device released over the city of Hiroshima by a lone U.S. Air Force bomber that had been named by the plane's pilot, *Enola Gay*.

Not all of the crude atomic bomb's potential energy was activated by the detonation; however, the bomb did answer the prayers of the Japanese for the return of the Kamakazi!

One-half of the energy released from the atomic device was in the form of a devastating supersonic wind blast (300-600 mph) that destroyed reinforced buildings several kilometers (about two miles) distant. Approximately one-third of the energy was heat, and the remaining energy released was deadly radiation.

Even after the return of this new type of "Divine Wind", Japanese warlords desired further bloodshed. A military faction led by the Japanese General Korechika Anami, still desired to fight one more battle on Japan's home islands, regardless of the almost certain high level loss in lives for both the defenders and those making the land assault.

Three days later, on August 9, 1945, the city of Nagasaki also received a visit from the new type of Kamakazi. A second atomic bomb was released over the city. Most of the city was destroyed and again there was a high number of civilian casualties.

Could it be the Japanese warlords had lost much of their spirituality during the ten long years of aggression and shameful atrocities against mankind? Had their actions offended the true Kamakazi which on two other previous occasions had turned back the Mongols invasion attempts of Kublai Kahn?

One might, with some degree of logic, argue that the new type "Divine Wind" did favor the Japanese people. It brought about an end to a terrible conflict initiated by Japanese warlords, who in turn, had received reluctant approval for the bombing of Pearl Harbor from Emperor Hirohito.

The Emperor was perhaps among the first to rediscover spirituality when he suggested a termination to the long bitter conflict. Hirohito proclaimed, "I am a mortal…not a god." In an imperial doctrine broadcast he urged the nation to "Endure the unendurable of defeat."

To this day there are no exact figures indicating the number of deaths of civilians or military personnel occurring during World War II. Neither can anyone ever know what the casualty toll might have been had an invasion of Japan been initiated.

The civilians, who so tragically lost their lives at Hiroshima and Nagisaki, represented only a small fraction of the total civilian deaths occurring during the long bitter period of world-wide warfare. The victims of the atomic bomb were no more or no less important than the millions of other civilians who so tragically perished during the lengthy world-wide conflict – ignited by opportunistic hyenas and ideological charlatans.

The only viable difference between the victims of the atomic bomb and other civilian casualties of World War II, would be – the deaths of the Japanese civilians of Hiroshima and Nagisaki were caused by a new and horrendous device. A weapon both the Japanese and Germans were attempting to construct. *How would they have used the new weapon had they been the first to succeed in making the atomic bomb?*

In fairness, it should be noted many Japanese opposed the conflict with the United States but were stifled by their country's warlords. Even Japanese Admiral Yamamoto, believed the attack on Pearl Harbor would eventually be a military strategic blunder; however, he was overruled by the controlling warlords. Many Japanese soldiers firmly believing in the *Shinto Code of Ethics* refused to be associated with those committing atrocities.

****

One should keep in mind – most United States history books make little or no mention of atrocities committed against Native Americans (first Americans) by the U.S. Military. History books ignore to tell the story of the "Long Walk" of the Navajo and "The Trail of Tears" of the Cherokee people. Neither do the history books tell about the "Sand Creek Massacre" of Chief Black Kettle's Cheyenne people nor the slaughter of the Sioux at Wounded Knee. These events suggest the United States Military of those times, perpetrated their own versions of the "Bataan Death March".

****

Near the end of the war the Japanese Army had fifty-three infantry division and twenty-five brigades with a total of 2,350,000 troops in the homeland. ready for the suicidal defense against the Allied invasion. hese troops were to be backed up by almost 4,000,000 civilian army and navy workers and a civilian militia of 28,000,000 – the last armed mostly with sharpened poles, mines, and grenades.

The above quoted words are from noted military historians Thomas B. Allen and Norman Polmar taken from their book *World War II*, (The Encyclopedia of the War Years, 1941-1945).

Readers can make up their own mind regarding the cost in number of casualties for both sides during an invasion of the Japanese homeland.

****

Another sobering fact for the people living on the Japanese homeland – a reality often overlooked – was coastal waters of Japan were heavily laced with mines by the United States Navy and the small Japanese boat traffic bringing food and other needed supplies came to a halt. Countless Japanese people – perhaps millions, would have needlessly perished by freezing or starving to death, if the war had continued into the winter.

****

I was not aware of Japanese invasion plans presented to President Truman on June 29, 1945. President Truman approved of the plans for landings on southern *Kyushu* on November 1, 1945 by United States forces already in the Pacific. He also approved plans to invade Honshu near Tokyo on March 1, 1946 by using forces brought from Europe.

Looking at the two invasion dates, it appears the two invasions were four months apart. I can only surmise this would indicate some heavy fighting to throw back the Japanese on Kyushu. The Forty-fifth Infantry Division evidently was scheduled to be part of the attacking forces for the later invasion of Honshu.

The use of the atomic bomb must not have been seriously considered at the meeting with the President Truman on June 29, 1945. The first atomic bomb was used on Hiroshima on August 6, 1945, about 39 days after the meeting to approve the invasion of Kyushu by U.S. military forces already in the Pacific.

****

My monthly pay as a Sergeant Technician (T-4) with combat pay added was $98.28. When reduced to the rank of Private First Class my monthly pay became $68.04. The net difference in monthly pay was $30.24. There are 720 hours in a 30 day month. In the army you were technically on duty twenty-four hours of the day. The hourly pay as a T-4 Sergeant was thirteen and a half cents per hour. As a Private First Class the hourly pay was nine and a half cents per hour. In combat you often had to improvise the so-called "room and board".

****

I certainly was surprised to receive the promotion from Captain Hanlon so quickly when he elevated my rank from that of a PFC to the rank of a T-5 corporal. Fifty years later, I, again, reread the paper pass given to me to visit Paris when I was at Camp St. Louis. It had been signed by Captain S.J. Hanlon, Commanding Officer, *Battery A of 158th Field Artillery Battalion,* Forty-fifth Infantry Division. It was at this time I realized Captain Hanlon did not have the required number of points to return to the states and he would be my commanding officer with Battery A of the 158th Artillery Battalion serving with the Forty-fifth Infantry Division. I feel certain he wanted me to be his radio operator, infantry "specialist", mine sweeper for gun positions and forward observer. He knew I carried out military assignments professionally. He also was aware we both would be involved with the impending invasion of Japan.

****

At no time during the conflict in The European fighting did I ever recall the first sergeant or the captain ever visiting any of our forward observer positions.

****

Vokssturmers were home guard members made up of boys and older men. Although uniformed and participated in the fighting, they were not the professional well-trained German soldiers.

****

The Forty-fifth Infantry Division to which I had been assigned was originally a unit made up the combined Arizona, Colorado, New Mexico and Oklahoma National Guard. The division shoulder patch identifying the unit had changed several times. For a period of time the division had a design resembling a swastika. Although the design differed in orientation from the swastika used by the Nazi, it was an ancient good luck emblem most likely borrowed from the Hopi Indians of the Southwest. The shoulder patch was relinquished during the war due to its similar resemblance to the swastika and was replaced by the traditional Native American symbol representing the "bringer" of lightning, thunder and rain – the thunderbird.

The division was generally known as the Oklahoma National Guard. They participated in combat duty in Sicily, Naples-Foggia, Anzio, Rome-Arno, Southern France, Rhineland, Ardennes-Alsace and Central Europe. The division suffered 3,527 killed in action, 14,441 wounded and 553 died from wounds received. Had the division participated in the invasion of the homeland of Japan these numbers, beyond any doubt – would have been considerably higher.

****

The term "Gold Star Mother" was used to indicate a United States mother had lost one or more sons during the conflict.

****

Bud Pitts, rifleman from Company G of the 409th Infantry Regiment once told me, "I never liked to make friends with new replacements. They just didn't seem to 'last' too long." Bud believed the most dangerous occupation in an infantry regiment was held by that of a replacement. Many replacement soldiers were not trained infantrymen.

****

Perhaps the reason Captain Hanlon was so highly upset with Corporal Chipman and 37531447 over our late arrival in a Mercedes could have been – this was the second time one of his battery formations went awry. Perchance it brought back unwanted memories of the newly promoted top kick falling flat on his face during a called unit formation in occupied Germany. With Austrian civilians observing the formation, it may have been another highly embarrassing moment for the captain. I never understood why Corporal Chipman was not demoted. We both were guilty of the same thing. Perhaps the captain reasoned that the corporal's photographic memory might be "conveniently" lost.

****

The 103rd Infantry Division was awarded two campaign battle stars during the European campaign. One for the Rhineland and the other for the Central Europe campaign. There is fairly good evidence it should have been awarded another battle star for the role it performed in the Alsace-Ardennes fighting. General Jacob L. Devers wanted the division to be awarded the third star; however, even the military has their own brand of politics.

The book *World War II Order of Battle* (Shelby L. Stanton) lists three battle campaigns for the 103rd Infantry Division. Campaigns listed by Stanton were: Rhineland, Ardennes-Alsace and Central Europe.

Chapter Twenty-One

Final Army Days for 37531447

Right or wrong, to understand, one must try to understand circumstances existing at the time.
—Mary Ruth Blackburn

It is nearly impossible to describe the cascading amalgam of emotions as the slow-moving troop ship edged ever closer to the magnificent skyline of New York's harbor. We passed in full view of the "Grand Old Lady", better known as the *Statue of Liberty*. While viewing the prestigious historic gift from France, tears welled up in the tracing eyes of the hardened combat veterans, including those of 37531447. He knew many of the returning fighting men were reflecting about buddies who had fallen in battle and – not able to savor this special moment in time.

The sound of multitudinous discordant whistles from harbor ships filled the air as plumes of water, orchestrating from harbor fireboat hoses, artistically arced skyward welcoming troops back to the United States of America. The spray emanating from the fireboats created capricious colorful rainbows. It was awakening memories of my pre-war days in Chase County when rainbows would appear and mysteriously fade away in the misty river water dancing over the old mill dam.

While the small-sized *Marine Panther* was waiting for tug assistance in docking, the melodious sounds of familiar voices and nostalgic music reached my ears. It was coming from a rather small vessel positioned off starboard. On the deck of a neighboring vessel was a band of musicians and a trio of female voices harmonizing the familiar tunes of, *Beer Barrel Polka, I'll Be With In Apple Blossom Time, Rum and Cola* and *Boogie Woogie Bugle Boy*. Some one aboard the troop ship proclaimed the singing group of beauties to be the renowned Andrews Sisters (Patty. LaVerne and Maxene). It could well have been this famous trio. We knew they tirelessly performed countless concerts for American service men and women during the war.

The reality of being alive and back in the United States was beginning to penetrate my inner thoughts. It brought back a discomforting and pestering cerebration causing me to briefly mirror on the Red River forming the natural boundary separating Texas and Oklahoma.

Thoughts of the Red River temporarily evaporated when I noticed a uniformed soldier from our troop transport, remove his combat boots, climb onto the ships railing and while voicing a rather authentic Tarzan-like outcry, plunge feet first into the murky water of New York Harbor. The first U.S. soldier to debark prematurely from the *Marine Panther* commenced swimming toward the boat having the singing ladies. The veteran's impromptu exit was greeted with resounding boisterous cheers and much applause from the exhilarated arriving troops aboard the *Marine Panther*. The joyous sounds became even louder as the soldier was "fished" out of the water by the laughing crew of the smaller ship and the astonished threesome of ladies aboard the anchored entertainment center. I feel certain the exuberant soldier was reunited with us soon after we left the now docked troop transport.

It was absolutely fantastic taking the first steps back onto United States soil. The event was a happening this soldier often wondered if he would ever live long enough to experience. I recalled my earlier emotions when I took those last few uncertain footsteps to board the *Monticello* when departing for active duty from the very same harbor. This time I was experiencing incredible exhilaration – almost at its optimum.

Arriving troops were rapidly processed through the army facilities at Camp Kilmer, New Jersey and sent homeward bound. My military orders provided a two week furlough and rail transportation to Emporia, Kansas. The military papers presented me with one additional surprise. Following the two-week furlough home, I was instructed to report to Camp Joseph T. Robinson – not to the separation center at Fort Leavenworth. Camp Robinson was located just outside of Little Rock, Arkansas. I had come full circle with General Ben Lear when ordered to report to Camp Robinson. Not being immediately discharged from the army was not all that disappointing.

The reality of re-entry into civilian life and what changes could be in store for me were pesky concerns. I felt as if additional time in the military would be beneficial in helping me clear some of the storm clouds still permeating my life.

With an almost non-remembering furlough behind me, I reported to the duty officer at Camp Robinson. I soon discovered what my new military duties would embrace. I was assigned to a military police detachment in charge of guarding German prisoner-of-war camps situated in the vicinity of Little Rock, Arkansas. Apparently the facility was short-handed and soldiers eligible for discharge from the military had separation papers delayed in order to meet manpower requirements at the Little Rock POW camps. 37531447 puzzled over the irony of possibly ending his military career guarding some of the same German prisoners the 103rd Infantry Division had helped capture.

The majority of German prisoners in the various camps were *Volssturmers* and not the hard core Nazis. Their ages were from sixteen to sixty years. Many of the POW's worked at various jobs outside of the prison compound. Some labored in the camp laundry, many worked on neighboring cotton fields located in the vicinity. Others German prisoners were employed working in the large hotels of both Little Rock and the not too distant city of Hot Springs, Arkansas. The Germans were paid a small compensation for their work.

I was extremely fortunate to be assigned to a satellite prison camp situated on the shore of Lake Catherine near Hot Springs. A German father and his son were interned at the same time in the camp. Later, I had a conversation with the father and he related he had been captured by the British during World War One and placed in a prison camp in England for the duration of that conflict. I had some difficulty in deciding if the progenitor of his son had been lucky or unlucky.

When not pulling military police guard duty, I was deriving much pleasure observing the camp's inmates play soccer. The game of soccer was seldom played in the United States. Soccer appeared to be a highly spirited game. Often participants required medical attention requiring sutures installed at the camp infirmary for injuries received playing the contact sport.

The military duty at Lake Catherine was extremely pleasant. It was more like a paid vacation at some resort. A spiffy motorboat was placed at our disposal for recreational use on the lake. In addition, our small guard detachment was assigned a fantastic German POW cook who took great pride and delight in making certain we were well fed even at unusual hours. The cook's enthusiasm to please caused me to compare him with the cook of Battery A of the 928th Field Artillery during the campaign in Europe. After coming back from combat action at the front, even though I was fatigued, cold and hungry, the bastard told me to wait for the regular meal hour to even get a cup of hot coffee.

My stay at Lake Catherine was just what a "doctor" should have prescribed for my rehabilitation from combat duty. I treasured my moments of solitude by the serene lake where I could reflect about the past as well as consider the future. My tour of duty at the lake prison camp was an incredible blessing bestowed upon me by a caring and loving Spirit Guide.

The specific duty at the camp compound was to "man the front gate" during the night shift. The prisoners had repaired the small second-hand tube-type "superheterodyne" radio I had purchased and during the long night hours, I would wile away the time listening to country music and the melodious sounds of popular dance bands.

It was most comforting to realize I soon would be discharged from the army. I had an enormous feeling of independence to the point where I was not going to allow myself to be intimidated by anyone.

My combat experience against the German enemy never did interfere adversely with my attitude toward the prisoners in the camp. The prisoners seemed to sense my unbiased stance toward them. Inmates would often chat with me or want to tailor all of my dress uniforms. They took great delight in repairing any articles I had in my possession which were damaged or broken.

The German POW's were cognizant I was a combat veteran having served in Europe and especially in Germany. It was only natural they would ask me questions about the United States and their homeland. Most inquiries fell into two general categories. The first, "How did I feel about the complete destruction of New York City by the Luftwaffe?" The other often asked question, "What are the conditions inside Germany?"

Truthful answers to both questions appeared to fall on skeptical ears. They could neither envision the almost total destruction of large German cities, including Dresden and Cologne, nor could they fathom New York City was never bombed by the German Luftwaffe. I made no attempt to convince them I had voiced the truth. The *Volkssturmers* were soon to be repatriated and perchance later – would realize my spoken words had been declarations of truth.

Occasionally, I would wander over to the small USO club during my daylight off-duty hours. While visiting the club I would answer what little mail I received, consume a soft drink and just relax to the music of the jukebox. One of the ladies, a waitress, invited me to dance to one of the jukebox tunes with her. She did not "buy" my excuse, "I am a roller skater – not a dancer". I do not remember too much after she pulled me up out of the chair, except she held me so tightly I had to keep time to the music. The tune she "danced me to" was one having a definite Hawaiian beat. I also had the belief, that after the way she held me, I could swiftly master the beat of "honky-tonk" music. Perchance adapting back to civilian life would be less arduous than I previously envisioned.

It was the last time I visited the USO. It definitely was not by my choice. I had just become highly interested in enlisting for additional dancing lessons from my resolute "free-spirited" dancing mentor.

On proceeding to my quarters, I was given orders to return to the Little Rock POW camp. I would be the MP in charge of bringing back eight German prisoners to the facilities at Lake Catherine.

At Little Rock, eight *volkssturmers* climbed into the back of the olive-drab tarp-covered army vehicle. The driver and I commenced the late evening trek back to the Hot Springs prisoner camp on the shores of Lake Catherine. The weather was definitely in a cold nasty mood. Close to 2300 hours (11:00 PM), we arrived on the outskirts of a rather small Arkansas town. Noticing the lights still on inside a small dingy roadside café, the driver pulled the truck, and its cargo of overcoated prisoners, close to the front of the building and stopped. I walked to the rear of the military vehicle to inform the prisoners of our intent to leave them by themselves while the driver and I went inside the café for a sandwich and a cup of coffee. A promise was made to bring them hot coffee upon our return.

Leaving the small POW group to manage for themselves, the driver and I entered the dingy café. I felt quite at ease leaving the prisoners on their own. We all understood the war was over and the prisoners would soon be returning to Germany. Most of the prisoners from both camps knew me and appeared to respect my unbiased demeanor toward them.

Midway through our food and drink, a hysterical Arkansas civilian excitedly entered the café and loudly demanded, "Who is guarding the Germans in the army truck parked out front?"

Answering him in a polite reserved voice I replied, "I am the escort for the group. Why do you ask?"

"But they are Germans!", the still belligerent civilian snorted.

Becoming somewhat annoyed at his unwanted intrusion, I stiffly replied, "Sir, the war with Germany is over!"

The paranoid dick was still fuming and fearful for his "safety" as the driver and I picked up eight cups of coffee "to go" and eight candy bars, paid the bill and returned to our parked military vehicle. The number of cups of coffee and candy bars exactly matched the number of prisoners patiently huddled in the back of the cold tarp-covered stake truck. Each prisoner thanked us for our little gifts and we climbed up into the front seat of the vehicle to continue our odyssey toward Lake Catherine. I pondered what had occurred at the café and wondered how the confrontational local clod would have reacted had our human cargo been Negro soldiers of the United States Army. I disliked the answer to my previous thought.

Arriving safely at our destination the eight men were turned over to camp authorities and both the driver of the truck and I called it a night.

On the morning of the following day, I was informed I was being relieved of my Lake Catherine duties and would be immediately returning to the Little Rock POW camp. Since there was no mention of my discharge from the military, I felt quite certain the incident at the café with the prisoners had been reported to the camp commander at the Little Rock POW compound.

At Camp Robinson I was reassigned to be a guard in one of the towers surrounding the prison enclosure. In addition, I was placed on the night shift of guard duty. One of my chores would be to turn on the prison area lights at dusk and shut them off at daybreak.

The captain in charge of the prison camp immediately started the process of "hard-assing" me. His remarks and tone of voice suggested an unusual amount of aversion for 37531447.

Ken Lenke Photograph (January 7, 1945)
Ralph Lenke on the left with "37531447" at Emporia, Kansas—
"37531447" was AWOL from Camp Joseph T. Robinson at the time.

The commissioned officer's arrogant demeanor was not too dissimilar to that of the hated German Gestapo. I would soon be receiving my discharge papers for return to Fort Leavenworth, Kansas and his caustic remarks, although greatly annoying, had little outward effect on me.

Meanwhile, my brother, who had been last stationed in Heidelberg, Germany, with the United States Army Signal Corps, had arrived home from military duty. His birthday was on January sixth and mine – on the following day. I was downright certain the camp commander would nullify any thoughts I entertained granting me a weekend pass for a death in the family, let alone celebrating a birthday with my brother.

After making certain my army buddies would cover my camp obligations, I went AWOL (absent without leave), purchased a round-trip ticket on the Missouri Pacific Railroad Line. The nearest place to Emporia the train traveled was an obscure cattle loading station located near Yates Center, Kansas. The whistle stop was called Durrand. From there I hitchhiked the remainder of the distance to Emporia. My military police arm band emblazoned with the large letters "MP" (military police) offered me an extra measure of refuge for both the journey home and my subsequent return to Camp Joseph T. Robinson.

Following the birthday celebration with my brother, he drove me back to the whistle-stop of Durrand in a 1930 Model A Ford Sports Coupe. I boarded the "MOP" train for my return to Camp Robinson.

Everything had gone quite well during my two days of being absent without leave. I was, however, informed by my army buddies, "The captain has been searching all over the camp for you." My trusted comrades would inform the commander they thought they had just seen me at the USO, or possibly in the barracks area or in the latrine. The duty roster clerk had written in my name for guard duty while another buddy pulled the long night shift for me. I expect the captain might have been fearful to climb the guard tower in the dark of the night to determine if I was on duty. The vertical steps up the tower could be quite slippery.

Several more nights pulling tower duty passed. I was eagerly awaiting the moment when the military papers would arrive ordering me back to Fort Leavenworth. I was delighted when the duty clerk finally informed me, "The necessary paperwork for your return to Fort Leavenworth has arrived and you are scheduled to depart Camp Robinson in the morning." He added, "You ground transportation will be available at 0800 hours."

The last night at the POW facility found me pulling duty as usual in the prison guard tower. I had a gut-feeling the camp captain had everything to do with determining I was to work the shift. Inwardly, I was highly pissed at the nettlesome bastard; however, I also realized it would by my final night of duty under his military command.

Ken Lenke Photograph (1945)
Guard tower at the Little Rock, Arkansas Prisoner of War camp located at
Camp Joseph T. Robinson

In the pre-dawn darkness my replacement climbed into the guard tower to relieve me from duty. I had never seen the soldier before and was somewhat apprehensive over being "set up" by the camp commander. I asked for the passwords and he knew them. After more inquiries from me, I was convinced everything was legitimate. My replacement informed me he was new to the army and requested me to demonstrate how the .30-caliber carbine operated. On several recent occasions some fresh untrained guard replacements on night duty had accidently discharged their unfamiliar weapons, causing much apprehension among the veteran guards who had survived the riggers of combat. I went through the operational procedure several times with the neophyte soldier and eased his obvious fear over being a guard for "highly dangerous" prisoners of war. While turning over the unloaded weapon and a clip of ammunition to his possession, I made known to the visibly shaken soldier, "The prisoners are well-behaved and it is highly unlikely you will ever have to use your gun." I added this bit of advice, "If I were you, I wouldn't even place a live round of ammunition in the firing chamber of your gun." My calming words seemed to blunt a large portion of the fledgling soldier's obvious anxiety. I wished the new guard "well" and made my departure from the stilted observation tower.

Having been relieved from duty early in winter's morning darkness, I never entertained any thoughts about turning off compound floodlights when it became daylight. I felt as if it were no longer my responsibility to perform this routine diurnal task. Feeling extremely upbeat, I showered, put on my dress uniform, picked up my personal belongings and made my way in the direction of the command post. There I would retrieve my orders for departure to Fort Leavenworth for separation from the military.

Upon entering the CP, I was surprisingly puzzled to observe the camp captain staring at me from behind his desk, resembling a much-starved junkyard dog awaiting to pounce. He must have been impatiently awaiting my arrival. Before approving my egress from Camp Joseph T. Robinson, the son-of-bitch sarcastically asked, "Corporal, what time do they turn off the street lights in your hometown?" I understood full-well what the bastard had on his seemingly *prejudiced* mind.

In a greatly constrained tone of voice, I resplendently fibbed, "Sir, I live out in the country – and we do not have street lights."

The officer's flushed facial expression revealed an almost uncontrollable rage and a noticeable loathing of 37531447.

Before obtaining my awaiting orders, I slowly strolled over to the prison compound light switch and turned it to the "off" position. I was greeting the morning sun as I returned to the command post. After saluting the captain, I retrieved my discharge documents from the secretly amused duty clerk who was positioned close by. I turned once more to face the commissioned officer and presented him with a curt military salute (the salute is a military method that indicates mutual respect).

I did my last "about face" and expeditiously walked to the waiting Jeep taking me one small step closer to the termination of my military career. I do not recall if the captain returned my salute as required by an officer. It really did not matter because I honestly didn't give a shit.

I possibly could have been the last United States combat veteran "guarding" the German prisoner-of-war facilities at Camp Joseph T. Robinson.

Army serial number 37531447's last name was of Germanic origin. Coupled with facts he did not display any outward malice toward the German POW's, had left them unguarded at an Arkansas road-stop café and would often converse with them in both German and English – had apparently angered the *Jewish* camp captain who had never left the United States, never participated in a single moment of combat time during the entire war and never know how many lives had been saved at Landsberg, Germany and elsewhere by heroic action of the 103rd Infantry Division.

After witnessing so much hate in the war and observing Nazi atrocities at Landsberg, I was wondering how long the wounds caused by World War II would linger. Would it be a few decades, a few centuries or possibly – forever?

It was highly rib-tickling taking the same route on the Missouri Pacific Railroad Line that I had utilized just a few days earlier when I went AWOL. This time the United States Government was paying for the train ticket. I would be aboard for the full distance of 525 miles from Little Rock to Kansas City, Missouri. I had a pleasant "Bud Pitts smile" on my face as the train left Buffalo, Kansas. The next place would be the whistle stop (cattle loading pens) of Durrand. This time the train did not stop. It continued to speed through the small Kansas towns of Leroy, Westphalia, Garnett and eventually into Kansas City, Missouri.

One happening I did notice was the sound of the whistle coming from the Missouri Pacific steam engine. It was not shrill like most other steam locomotive sounds I had previously heard. The whistle was more of a low-pitched mournful reverent requiem. Perhaps it was a fitting tribute for all the people who had suffered or died as the result of the long bitter struggle during the recent war.

Arriving at Fort Leavenworth, I received a final medical examination, was presented the "Good Conduct" medal (Bud Pitts referred to this medal as the – "I never got caught medal") and a lapel button ("the ruptured duck") – indicating to the public I had served in the United States Military. In addition, I was given $100 of the $300 mustering-out pay (the rest to be paid later), $7.10 travel and meal allowance and a railroad ticket from Kansas City, Missouri to Emporia, Kansas.

Among the various documents I received during my honorable discharge from the United States Army was the *"Separation Qualification Record of Job Assignments"* while serving in the Army. It was furnished by the Army when a soldier leaves the military service. Included in my military specialties were the following: Antiaircraft Artillery Basic Training, Switchboard Operator, Radio Repairman, Ammunition Bearer, Messenger, Radio Operator and Military Policeman. Somehow I strongly suspicioned the printed list had left out some very fundamental combat specialties performed during my tour of combat duty. The piece of paper seemed impersonal and so damned platitudinous.

The length of 37531447's military duty had been two years, eight months and one day.

The reason and authority for separation from the military was: "Convenience of Government RR 1-1 (demobilization) AR (Army Regulation) 615-365."

The military personnel officer, presiding at my separation from the military, was First Lieutenant J.B. Rabinowitz of the Women's Army Corps serving as Assistant Adjutant.

Departing from Fort Leavenworth, I took a bus to Kansas City, Missouri, where I caught the first Atchison, Topeka, and Santa Fe Railroad train heading west to Emporia, Kansas.

When the steam engine pulled passenger train neared my final destination, I sauntered to the men's vestibule located at one end of the coach. I desired to "tidy a bit" and use the lavatory located adjacent to the vestibule. Upon entering the men's lounge, I noticed a middle-aged well-dressed individual standing on tiptoes, urinating in the drinking fountain. The crapulous businessman had erroneously mistaken the passenger coach drinking fountain for the men's urinal. Perhaps the chap was lamenting the conclusion of the war and regretting the "easy money" would no longer be coming his way. I felt as if he might have a more difficult time than I, adjusting to the termination of the long and bitter conflict known as World War II.

This incident would be the last memory for 37531447 while wearing the uniform of the United States Army.

Kenneth L. Lenke

Epilogue...

On June 21, 1946, Russell "Bud" Pitts and Joan Grove were united in marriage in Casper, Wyoming. 37531447 was honored to serve as "best man" at the wedding ceremony.

Bud was employed by the Standard Oil (AMOCO) refinery located in Casper.

Bud joined the Wyoming National Guard during the time he was employed at the refinery. The Wyoming National Guard unit was an artillery battalion. Bud eventually retired from both AMOCO and the Wyoming National Guard. While serving

Command Sergeant Major
Russell A. Pitts
Wyoming National Guard (1970)

Wedding Photograph of
Mr. and Mrs. Russell A. Pitts
Casper, Wyoming
L. to R.
Eileen Pringle
Joan Grove (Pitts)
Russell A. Pitts
Kenneth L. Lenke
(June 21, 1946)

with the Wyoming National Guard, Russell A. "Bud" Pits achieved the rank of Command Sergeant Major (an appointment awarded by the Pentagon).

After 37531447 received his Honorable Discharge from the military, he returned to Wyoming and worked one summer in Casper for the Chapman Construction Company. He returned to Emporia, Kansas and after much frustration in his life, enrolled at Kansas State Teachers College (Emporia State University) under the provision of the "United States Veterans' Bill of Rights".

Donald Smith, who visited 37531447 at Camp St. Louis in France, was highly instrumental in getting him enrolled in college after the cessation of hostilities following the author's discharge from the army. One late August summer evening, Donald, his twin brother Ronald and a younger brother James, made a surprise visit to the house of the former artilleryman's parents in Emporia, Kansas. Without a hint of what they wanted, the three young men escorted the artillery forward observer to their car and drove the twenty-miles west on old U.S. Highway 50 South, to Strong City, the place of his high school graduation. There, they located the local high school principal and requested a transcript of 37531447's high school record be sent to Kansas State Teachers College located in Emporia. The following morning, Don returned to the house and took his friend to the college to enroll as a member of the Freshman Class. He escorted 37531447 through the entire lengthy process until all necessary paper work had been completed. Perhaps this may have been an old war "debt" Don felt compelled to pay, a matter of friendship or perchance – both.

While attending Kansas State Teachers College, 37531447 was awarded both a Bachelor and Masters degree.

He also became married and eventually was the father of two children, Randal and Brian. His first marriage ended in failure.

Other colleges and universities 37531447 attended were: Michigan Tech of Houghton (geo-physics), University of Washington (oceanography), Arizona State University (geology) and Scottsdale Community College (cultural anthropology and Spanish).

After moving to Arizona he married a "Navy Brat" and they adopted a baby girl named – Kenja. His wife "Cindy" is a registered nurse.

The author often wonders who designed the saguaro (pronounced "sawh-war-oh") cactus shoulder patch worn by the men of the 103rd Infantry Division. He has been living in the area of the Sonoran Desert for close to forty years. After scanning many thousands of acres of the plant's natural habitat in an effort to find a solitary saguaro cactus identical in appearance to the one chosen as the division's emblem – he has yet to discover one even coming close to being similar.

...Some fifty years following the conclusion of World War II, the 103rd Infantry Division veteran returned to his home town of Strong City, Kansas for the high school reunion honoring his class, the Class of 1941. It was 1991. It was the year William Least Heat-Moon's book *PrairyErth* was published. The book has a focus only on Chase County – perhaps the last place in the United States still having a large expanse of tallgrass prairie.

While in the vicinity, the author took the opportunity to visit Cottonwood Falls where he once again stood near the old river bridge now no longer in use. A new bridge built in a different location over the Cottonwood River had replaced the weather-worn historical structure.

Once more his now aging eyes gazed up Broadway Street to relish the sight of the county courthouse building still in use as a courthouse; however, he did notice one unerring change on the courthouse lawn facing Broadway Street. The old French seventy-five millimeter artillery piece was no longer "standing guard". It had become a casualty during World War II when it was patriotically donated to the wartime scrap metal drive, presumably melted into oblivion for the war effort. In its place was a vintage *Japanese* seventy-five millimeter artillery weapon. He disliked the replacement artillery piece. Perhaps it reminded him of the war's first Holocaust – the one usually not remembered – the one carried out by the Japanese military during the rape of Nanking. The veteran longed for his long-time friend, the old French "seventy-five".

The barrel of the replacement cannon appeared to be elevated slightly more than the former old French gun. The higher muzzle elevation would be more likely to "drop" an artillery round on neighboring Strong City located on the opposite side of the Cottonwood River.

One other discrepancy noted was the grey-colored slab of granite holding the bronze plaque. Now there was an additional bronze marker recording the names of Chase County soldiers, airmen and sailors who lost their lives during World War II.

Unlike the first plaque, the names inscribed on the newest metallic marker represented young men – many of them he had known. This time he could often match a name with a face from past memory.

The names on the plaque made two columns, each containing thirteen names. 37531447 thoughtfully gazed at the alphabetized list of names until the eyes focused on two engraved names,

**Chase County-Leader News photo by Jerry Schwilling (1996)
Japanese 75 mm artillery piece on the Chase County (Kansas)
Courthouse lawn**

"Ernest L. James" and "Melvin E. Lind". His name was not inscribed between them.

On September 1995, 37531447, his wife Cindy, and daughter Kenja, met Bud and Joan in Cheyenne, Wyoming, for a two day reunion. At that gathering Joan Grove Pitts informed Bud's old army friend her husband had received a medal for valor during the campaign in Europe. Neither Bud nor Joan would elicit any details of the award that had been kept secret from the author for so many years. "Ol' R.A." still had that sly grin when he stated, "It wasn't for much of anything." His old army buddy had known him too long to give his remark the slightest hint of credibility.

Jeanne Yung (Anne's sister), wrote from Alsace on March 22, 1996, the following: "After fifty years, Bud and you have not been forgotten. We always keep a good memory of your stay in Ingwiller (Alsace, France) with our family."

37531447 spent most of his life as a science teacher (geology, astronomy and physics) much of it with the Scottsdale (Arizona) Public School District. His first teaching job in Arizona was at Kiva Elementary School (Scottsdale Public Schools). Before receiving any salary for his teaching, he was required by state law to sign a loyalty oath – promising he would not conspire to overthrow the Government of the United States of America. Among the students at the school was the future Vice-President of the United States – Dan Quayle. Senator Barry Goldwater would occasionally come to the school to speak at special assemblies. Most of the author's teaching tenure was at Scottsdale High School.

On December 26, 1997, almost 53 years to the month when 37531447 was performing FO duties in Ingwiller (Alsace, France), 1944, he received a package from Mina Yung, who still lives near Ingwiller. Mina during the war, was the youngest (about five years of age) member of the Yung family. The artilleryman would often toss the chocolate bars from K-rations to the small children of the neighborhood. Although the author never remembers Mina, she remembered him. Among the items in the parcel were two attractive containers of beautifully wrapped gourmet French chocolates. With eyes damp, the author could only think of the growing number of people in the United States who currently wish all United States veterans would fade into silent obscurity.

37531447 still wonders how long consequences stemming from World War II will last.

He currently is retired and devoting time to his family, to a computer, volunteer teaching young school children about the indigenous dwellers of the Arizona Sonoran Desert, involved in traditional medicine, playing the Native American flute, guitar, banjo and entertaining numerous other interests.

Perchance any reader questions if 37531447 ever again saw his brief war-time fiance, he would politely direct that person to the public library or a book store to obtain a copy of the delightful classic short story, *Lady or the Tiger* by Frank Stockton. It could possibly shed light on the subject for any bibliophile brimming with blazing curiosity.

The author still has a pensive feeling when ruminating over the most recent plaque fastened to the granite marker in front of the Chase County Courthouse. Perhaps this sense impression is due to the two columns – each listing *thirteen* names of men who perished while in the service of their country. Thirteen plus thirteen equals twenty-six for the total number of men loosing their lives. When adding the two and the six in the total number the sum would equal eight. The same holds true for adding the separate digits in each row; one plus three added to one plus three also equals eight. If the number "8" is turned on its side it becomes the sign for *infinity – representing a quality or condition unbound by space or time.*

#

Russell A. "Bud" Pitts; Casper, Wyoming (1945)
103rd United States Army Infantry Division
Rifle Company of the 409th Infantry WW II
March 26, 1925 – September 1, 2002

Bibliography and Suggested Reading

Army. "Yoo-Hoo!" *Time*. 21 July, 1941, pp. 30 and 31

Blackburn, Mary Ruth. Letter. *"Casper Star Tribune"*
[Casper, Wyoming] 1997
Letters to the author. 1997

Bomdan, Martin. *Spirits in the Sky.* New York: Smithmark
Publishers Inc., 1992

Bradley, John D. *The Second World War.* [West Point Military
History Series] Asia and the Pacific. Wayne, New York:
Avery Publishing Group, Inc.

Branton, Harold M. 103rd Infantry Division ("The Trail of
the Cactus"] Pacucah, Kentucky: Turner Publishing
Company, 1996

Bullock, Allan. *Hitler, a Study in Tyranny.* New York:
Konecky and Konecky, 1962

Chase Country Centennial Committee. *Chase County Historical
Centennial 1872 – 1972,* 1972

Cleary, Kristen Maree, ed. *Native American Wisdom.* New
York: Barnes & Nobel, 1996

Eastman, Charles Alexander. *The Soul of an Indian.* Novato,
CA ed. Kent Nerburn. New World Library, 1993 p. 7 & 37

Ellsworth, D.A. "A History of Chase County" [Kansas]
Compiled weekly for the *Chase County Leader-News*

Fort Bliss. *1997 Post Guide.* San Diego, California: MARCOA
Publishing Inc., 1996 pp 49 – 54

Gaer, Joseph. *What Great Religions Believe.* Bergenfield, New Jersey. New American Library, Inc. Times Mirror, 1963

Fort Bliss. *1997 Post Guide.* San Diego, California: MARCOA Publishing Inc., 1996 pp 49 – 54

Fowler, E.W.W. *Nazi Regalia.* Edison, New Jersey: Chartwell Books, Inc. and Saturn Books, Ltd., 1996

Gaer, Joseph. *What Great Religions Believe.* Bergenfield, New Jersey. New American Library, Inc. Times Mirror, 1963

Jones, James H. *Bad Blood.* New York: The Free Press, a Division of Macmillan, Inc, 1993

Langellier, John P. *War in Europe.* ["From the Kasserine Pass to Berlin, 1942-1945") Vol. 1 London: Greenhill Books, 1995. Mechanicburg, Pa.: Stackpole Bookds, 1995

Martineau, LaVan. *The Rocks Begin to Speak.* Las Vegas, Nevada: KC Publications, 1973

McMaster, Richard K. *Musket, Saber & Missile.* [a history of Fort Bliss, Texas]. Self published: seventh printing 1986

Metz, Leon C. "Camp Concordia." *Monitor* [published for the Fort Bliss/El Paso, Texas community.] 17 july, 1997 p. 14

Least-Heat-Moon, William. *PrairyErth.* Boston: Houghton Mifflin Company, 1991

Levin, Meyer. "What 'Last Day' Was Like for One American Division" [With the 103rd Division in Austria [ONA] *The Emporia Gazette,* [Emporia, Kansas], 1945

Milton. *Areopagitica.* 1644

Mozai, Torao. "Kublai Khan's Lost Fleet". *National Geographic.* Wahington, D.C. Vol. 162, No. 5. Nov. 1982 pp. 634-49

National Archives. *U.S.S. Monticello Deck Log.* [from 16 April through June 1945] Washington, D.C. *U.S.S. Monticello, AP-61.* [Confidential War Diary], Declassified.

Ogburn, Charlton. *Persons and Goods Moved in WW II Railroads.* "The Great American Adventure". Washington, D.C.: National Geographic Society, 1997

Platt, Suzy, edited by. *Respectfully Quoted.* New York: Barnes & Noble, 1993 p. 361

Polmar, Norman and Thomas B. Allen. *World War II* [The Encyclopedia of the War Years 1941-1945] New York: Random House, 1996

Pommoise, Lise M. *Les Combats Dans Le Val de Moder.* [Association Les Amis de la Liberation de Pfaffenhoffen] Bill Mauldin quote p. 63

Powers, Robert N. *Holocaust.* "The Story of the 103rd Division and Eyewitness Accounts of the Holocaust". Self Published, 1994

Sommerville, Donald. *World War II Order of Battle.* New York: Galahad Books, 1991

Stockton, Frank. *The Lady or the Tiger and Other Short Stories.* New York: A Tor Book, Tom Doherty Associates,

United States Army. *Report After Action.* [the story of the

103rd Infantry Division]. Published by Headquarters of the 103rd Infantry Division, 1945

Untermeyer, Louis, ed. *Modern American Poetry.* New York: Harcourt Brace and World, Inc, 1958
Jarrell, Randall. "The Death of the Ball Turet Gunner".
p. 647
Sandburg, Carl. "Fog" and "Grass". P. 200

About the Author

Kenneth (Ken) Lenke was born and raised in the heart of the tall grass prairie country of the Flint Hills of Chase County, Kansas. He earned both a Bachelor of Science degree and master's degree from Emporia State University.

Lenke, a physics instructor, retired from the Scottsdale (Arizona) Public School System. After relinquishing his teaching assignment, he developed a cultural interest in the indigenous dwellers of the American Southwest, including the music of these early dwellers.

His flute music has been heard by many including schoolchildren at the Desert Center Learning Facility located in Scottsdale. He served as a volunteer at the Phoenix Indian Medical Center.

The author currently resides in Phoenix.

Printed in the United States
975200003B